"Mike Stout's well-construct[ed] is about a special place and on a social insurgency that [   ] [   ] for future social progress. It is a story of skilled workers who proudly got their hands dirty—an industrial world of crane men, machinists, mechanics, millwrights, laborers, and electricians that once dominated a region; men and women who also contributed to working-class culture as writers, poets, musicians, cartoonists, and even lawyers. Today, there are new skills and different jobs, but class domination and oppression endures. Greed without end or solidarity forever? The choice remains, and the consequences for a sick earth and an imperial world order could not be greater."
—Charles McCollester, former chief steward, UE Local 610, Switch and Signal plant and former professor of Labor Relations at Indiana University of Pennsylvania (IUP)

"This book should be read by activists in workplace situations all over the United States, not just as a stirring story but as a manual that responds to the question: What is to be done? The Homestead struggle demonstrated that imaginative and aggressive use of contract language can result in substantial monetary compensation for workers who are displaced. The spirit of solidarity so abundantly displayed in Local 1397's struggle is what the rank-and-file labor movement—as well as the broader movement to change the larger society—is all about."
—Staughton Lynd, attorney, labor organizer, and author of more than a dozen books, including *Wobblies and Zapatistas: Conversations on Anarchism, Marxism and Radical History*, with Andrej Grubačić (PM Press 2008)

"I can see this book finding a privileged place on the shelves of American radicals. This is a labor history that is exciting, emotional, and thought-provoking, a splendid example of radical history at its best."
—Andrej Grubačić, professor and chair of Anthropology and Social Change, CIIS-San Francisco, author of *Wobblies and Zapatistas: Conversations on Anarchism, Marxism and Radical History*, with Staughton Lynd (PM Press 2008)

HOMESTEAD STEEL MILL THE FINAL TEN YEARS

Local 1397 and the Fight for Union Democracy

Mike Stout

Homestead Steel Mill: The Final Ten Years—Local 1397 and the Fight for Union Democracy
© Mike Stout
This edition © 2020 PM Press
Introduction © JoAnn Wypijewski

ISBN: 978–1–62963–791–4 (print)
ISBN: 978–1–62963–805–8 (ebook)
Library of Congress Control Number: 2019946097

Cover by John Yates / www.stealworks.com
© *Pittsburgh Post-Gazette*, 2019, all rights reserved. Reprinted with permission.
© *Rivers of Steel*, 2020, all rights reserved. Reprinted with permission.
All other photos and images are from the private collections of Mark Fallon, Don Rudberg, Barney Oursler, and Mike Stout. Reprinted with permission.
Interior design by briandesign

10 9 8 7 6 5 4 3 2 1

PM Press
PO Box 23912
Oakland, CA 94623
www.pmpress.org

Printed in the USA

CONTENTS

INTRODUCTION

JoAnn Wypijewski

Unfolding in these pages is the radical history of a people too commonly believed to have none. It is a history largely absent from popular records of the political tumult of the 1960s and 1970s, though its energy, militancy, and imagination grew out of that era and extended, like so many fierce but near forgotten political projects, into the 1980s. It is a story of class struggle in a society whose official scribes are mostly stupid about class when they aren't willfully deceptive. It is a story of the built world—of some of the men and women who made it, and who, in one extraordinary moment in time, strove not just to halt their own unmaking but to dream something different and beautiful.

The title tells us this is a tale of defeat. There would hardly be a history of workers under capitalism without that; violence, it must be remembered, is the nature of the beast. "Homestead"—like "Haymarket" and "Ludlow" and countless other signifiers of workers' challenge to the power of money over their bodies and their minds—was shorthand for bloody murder a century before Mike Stout appeared on the scene. The last years of the steelworks in Homestead, Pennsylvania, involved murder of another sort, more lethal than gunfire, because it happened slowly, by memoranda from Company suites, by lying language and the subterfuges of finance; when it was over, the bodies weren't lying around to count. Homestead wasn't alone in the raking. Where U.S. Steel had employed thirty thousand workers in seven mills in the Monongahela Valley in 1977, only three thousand remained ten years later. By a standard calculus, each lost industrial job sank five support jobs. Multiply that many times over, beyond the Mon Valley and the steel sector, beyond the 1980s, which set the pattern for mass layoffs and taught the country to live with insecurity, homelessness, and household debt. What was left of the land and the communities was euphemized as the Rust Belt, as if everything that had transpired there, the rise and decline of an industrial economy and every decision taken, had been a process of nature. The euphemism erases the workers' defeat, which means it also erases their victories, their craft, the product of their hours and their sweat—in a sense, their lives. It signals to children that their parents and grandparents had no power in the world, no art, no pluck, and that there are no alternatives.

Mike Stout recovers a complex experience here and reminds a new generation (and some of the old) that providing alternatives is the art of politics, that people provided some at Homestead and absorbed some lessons for the future. It is necessary to recognize the violence of the context, violence that was physical, psychological, and economic; but what Stout lived and what he tells is not a sob story nor is it romantic. The workers' effort to control their own union, to make democracy real in Steelworkers Local 1397, to practice solidarity before and after the boom came down, to advocate for eminent domain and collective ownership in a Steel Valley Authority, is a study in human creativity, by turns thrilling and messy. It is an epic of the political courage and weakness, of humor, intelligence, and sometimes guile, of flawed and brilliant people acting together, thinking together, making mistakes, discovering skills they didn't know they had, leaning on their strengths, paying for their blind spots, and changing their circumstances. This book is, first and foremost, their record.

Back in the 1970s, Studs Terkel's magnificent oral history *Working* revealed the quality of time on the job and the inner lives of workers. Mike LeFevre, a steelworker, probably from Chicago, where Studs lived and worked, told him:

> Somebody built the pyramids. Somebody's going to build something. Pyramids, Empire State Building—these things don't just happen. There's hard work behind it. I would like to see a building, say the Empire State, I would like to see on one side of it a foot-wide strip from top to bottom with the names of every bricklayer, the names of every electrician, with all the names. So

when a guy walked by, he could take his son and say, "See, that's me over there on the forty-fifth floor. I put the steel beam in." . . . Everybody should have something to point to.[1]

Homestead workers made beams for the Empire State Building. Their collective hand is embedded in the structures that millions encounter, unthinking, every day. Cross the Verrazano Narrows or the Golden Gate, that hand is there. Pose for a photograph at Rockefeller Center or the St. Louis Arch, it is there. Enter the United Nations building, curse the traffic on the Oakland Bay Bridge, depend on the Hoover Dam, it is there. Visit Carnegie Hall or the Frick Museum in New York, and the amassed wealth they represent is the surplus labor of Homestead workers, whose union Andrew Carnegie and his plant manager Henry Clay Frick decided to break by armed force in 1892, aided by the state. Of the Homestead works themselves, which had sprawled for four miles, almost nothing remains. A few brick smoke stacks tower above a grassy slope near a shopping center and some parking lots.

When Mike Stout hired in as a utility crane operator in 1977, none of the mill's seven thousand workers would have fathomed that within a few years they'd have nothing to point to. People were hired as lifers. The book brims with their names. Jimmy Cook, Ed Salaj, Bobby Pratt, Harry Brennan, Michele McMills, Ron Weisen, John Ingersoll, John Balint, Brian "Red" Durkin, Joe Stanton, Ed "King" Hamlin, George Tallon, Elmer Shaffo, Al Paisley, Rick Kornish, Norm Ostoff, Elmer DelleDonne, "Twiggy," John O'Toole, Tom Jugan, Ron Funk, Paul Glunt, Dave Horgan, Ron Mamula, Pat Halbeib, Tommy Allen, Jim Ridley, Gary Kasper, Jim Kooser, Frank Domagala, Nat King, John Pressley, Joe Nestico, Ronnie Pristas, John Deffenbaugh, Jack Bair, Joe Parkinson, Terry Bernh, "Indian" Joe Diaz . . . and that's only to page 40. Many more follow, and more are unnamed. Crane operators and welders, riggers and hookers, boilermakers, motor inspectors and other maintenance workers, people from Open Hearth and the Forge Division, from the plate and slab mills, the machine shop, and so on.

Some appear only briefly, deftly executing operations that would seem impossible with good machinery, let alone with the faulty equipment and workers who had to improvise. There is invention here, and cooperation—often required by the work itself or necessitated by corporate negligence or generated by the workers' own creative will. Pride mingles with anger over the conditions of work, mixes with bluster, with alcohol and pot, with attention. There is danger here. Men suffer or thrive, sometimes both. And there is the terrible beauty of the forge:

> When we rolled pipe, the pipe steel let off this red dust that hung in the air. It was mystical, wild, especially during daylight, when the dust was going up and the sunlight was coming through the cracks in the roof. It was like you were in a theater watching a play, and the play was industrial production.

The setting was the thing. This play had been running for a hundred years. Mike Stout first glimpsed it toward the end of a volatile period in national and world history, and that made the difference. They called him "Kentucky" in the plant, for his family roots and accent, but, like so many young people then, he had traveled what seemed lifetimes from the hidebound assumptions of his youth. He had got a social and political education as a hopeful troubadour in Greenwich Village, an antiwar activist, a yippie witness to the police riot at the 1968 Democratic convention in Chicago, a denizen of San Francisco, a fundraiser for jailed Black Panthers, a worker in a hot shop at the Grand Central Station Post Office in New York, a participant in an SDS offshoot with a brief, sour acquaintance to left sectarian politics. Those experiences changed him, forced him to confront his prejudices, and wowed him with the adventure of really seeing other people and living by his own lights. He did not go to Homestead to "organize the workers," as some leftists were doing around the country. The mill was hiring, and the pay was good. Upon discovering the place was "a hotbed of union militants," he writes, "I thought I hit the double jackpot lottery." His book is, thus, also a contribution to the record of a time.

By the late 1960s, Vietnam veterans distrustful of authority began hiring into the plant. In 1974, black Homestead workers joined Alabama steelworkers in suing U.S. Steel for discrimination, the result being a federal Consent Decree that would bring more blacks, women, and Latinos into steelmaking, with equal hiring and promotional rights, at least on paper. Not all women entering factories at this time were liberationists—just as not all veterans, minorities, or counterculture youth, also among the thousand-plus new hires at Homestead beginning in the mid-1970s, were political radicals. Their entry into the ranks, though, embodied a zeitgeist, a spirit of the time that had diffuse effects throughout society. Everyone had breathed what was blowing in the wind since the 1960s, and if it turned some people off, it also made a critical mass less inclined to shut up because union bosses told them to or to answer, "How high?" when a company foreman said, "Jump."

The Homestead democracy movement ought to be seen within this era of rebellion. Internationally, the workers revolt is famously pegged to Paris, May 1968; in the U.S., it is infamously connected to Memphis, though the sanitation strike recedes as backdrop to the assassination of Dr. King. For the corporate class, the rank-and-file revolt struck most acutely in Detroit, when, also in May 1968, four thousand auto-workers walked off the job at Dodge Main, stopping the basic assembly plant for Chrysler operations nationwide. A protest as much against an insular, co-opted United Auto Workers leadership as against brutal factory conditions, the wildcat was led by a disciplined group of black workers who had been organizing since the 1967 Detroit riots. The League of Revolutionary Black Workers would challenge company-union collusion on the shop floor, contest union elections, use walk-outs, the courts, local politics, and culture in an ambitious project until it fractured in 1972. In 1965, the United Farm Workers entered the national consciousness with the grape strike and boycott, but its real exercise of worker power came in 1970–1971, when California lettuce and vegetable workers executed and won the largest agricultural strike in U.S. history. Their power grew, and in 1978–1979, over the objection of Cesar Chavez, they orchestrated another sweeping strike victory. Chavez then purged the leaders from the union and blacklisted them with the growers.

Throughout the 1960s, miners in Appalachia had been wildcatting over safety, black lung disease, and a corrupt United Mine Workers leadership. As explosions at ROTC centers, military labs, and draft offices elsewhere in the country got the headlines, hillbilly saboteurs used the same tactic against exploitation and what miners called "environmental mayhem" by big coal and its political pawns. In the summer of 1968, four men broke into the office of a strip-mining operation in Middleboro, Kentucky, hustled away the night watchman, and destroyed a million dollars' worth of equipment with the company's own dynamite. "Appalachian guerrillas" (to their detractors but actually union men, townspeople, small farmers, and rural folk driven off their land by the devastation of strip mining) roamed the region the rest of that summer blowing up mining equipment wherever they could. In 1969, more than one-third of all miners in coal country participated in wildcats. Insurgent leader Jock Yablonski spoke of the union's duty to secure the future, meaning a livelihood and the health of their communities and environment. As the year closed, twenty thousand in West Virginia walked off the job following the assassination of Yablonski and his wife and daughter. Union president Tony Boyle was convicted of murder and conspiracy in 1974, by which point Miners for Democracy had taken over the union. In steel, Ed Sadlowski challenged the president of the United Steelworkers for leadership in 1976, riding the wave of rank-and-file insurgency; he lost the election, but reformers who'd backed him carried the democracy movement forward.

Underground newspapers, small magazines, mimeographed pamphlets—traditional media of rebellion that proliferated in the 1960s and 1970s—had their equivalent in the publications of these workers' movements. In Detroit, the League had *Inner City Voice* and the *South End*. California farm workers had *El Malcriad*, until it became the voice box of Chavez alone. The coal fields had *Miners Voice*. Homestead had *1397 Rank and File*, which "with a mill nearly four miles long and having four major entrances (including Carrie Furnace across the river in Rankin) . . . would serve to both inform and unite workers, who otherwise would never see or know each other. It was democracy in action."

Through the paper, those same welders and maintenance workers, etc. found themselves to be researchers, reporters, editors, and layout artists; they had a new "something to point to" as editorialists, cartoonists, poets, and songwriters. Workers wrote letters, debated issues, and embarrassed foremen and superintendents in a feature called "Plant Plague," exposing harassment and mismanagement. The invention and cooperation they exercised in the mill now had an additional use: expressing their own ideas, charting a course for their own organization, and taking responsibility for a collective destiny. Stout had prior experience producing anti-war flyers and newsletters and also put his love for songwriting to the service of the movement (his text here is punctuated by lyrics). After the reformers won control of the local, and he became an elected grievanceman, he surprised himself with his skill as an investigator, evidence gatherer, and de facto lawyer. At arbitration hearings before a judge, Company lawyers regularly underestimated the guy in the sleeveless shirt, jeans, and rocker boots, and almost always paid for it.

"Democracy," thus, meant more than being able to vote on your union contract and have accountable leadership, vital as those were. It meant creating the conditions in which people might be their full selves. It meant betting on the class. It signified the aspiration for a *social* movement—as the reform effort became an occasion for enjoyment as well as organizing, as the campaign to save Homestead adopted a regional cooperative vision, as the question of jobs interlaced with the question of the environment, as workers began to connect government indifference to the unraveling of U.S. communities, with its simultaneous dismemberment of Central America, as the fight against plant shutdowns implied a larger political fight in the 1980s, represented by Jesse Jackson's Rainbow Coalition, against the privatized, financialized, and militarized values of Reaganism, which were fast becoming bipartisan. (The upper photo on the book's cover depicts a 1983 protest against President Reagan in Pittsburgh by four thousand angry Mon Valley workers and unemployed.)

An obvious question at this point is: *What happened?* This book is, finally, not just an account but an accounting. Stout conveys the euphoria of militancy, when time seemed to compress and so much flourished so quickly that anything felt possible. He is astute throughout to pitfalls as well. The short answer to what happened is that capital went on strike, with the full support of the state, minus a conscious politician here or there. (In fact, before capital struck, it went on a decades-long slowdown in the form of disinvestment and disinnovation.) But Stout has written this book for today's activists, as well as for those who lived this history, so the union militants' failings matter as much as their hopes and successes. They might not have won their fight even in the best of circumstances, but it matters that they were susceptible to division, that red-baiting still had kick, that racism and sexism persisted under the scrim of camaraderie, that leadership neglected what should have been obvious priorities (aggressively enforcing the Consent Decree and fighting continuing discrimination against union members) and later stuck with a community alliance despite its ruinous tactics. It matters that flattery had force, that rumor could become a weapon. Solidarity, like democracy, is a practice. The members of Local 1397, flush with their swift victory over the union old guard, did not have enough practice time before crisis hit. But Stout's eye is on the principle; he doesn't let anyone, including himself, off the hook.

There is a contemporary import to the question *What happened?* It is writ large in current media and politics, and it affects us all. Since the late 1970s, we have been living in an extended period of backlash. The sixties dreams of peace, love, and freedom, themselves dramatic expressions of yearnings that have carried through history, have been absorbed by capitalism and sold back to us in the form of T-shirts, nostalgia, and televised anniversary specials. That is the soft attack. The hard attack came on many fronts in different guises: assassination and COINTELPRO against the black freedom movement; formation of the Christian right and demonizing of the Equal Rights Amendment against the women's movement; police repression and discriminatory legislation campaigns against the gay movement; organized hysteria over sex education and corrupting commodification against the sexual freedom movement; proxy wars and the New Cold War against the peace movement. To those should be added the regime of mass layoffs, mergers and acquisitions, anti-labor policy, deindustrialization, community disinvestment (until areas laid to waste became attractive for gentrification, corporate welfare, or both), and kneecapping the working class.

That last front of the backlash touched people in every other movement and in generations unborn. It is typically not included in rundowns of the anti-sixties backlash, in the same way that worker revolts are generally subtracted from the story of the movements for people's power and authentic life. This is partly because the New Left of the 1960s distinguished itself from the Old Left of the 1930s in identifying the battlefield for change as primarily cultural not industrial. It is partly because union radicals mostly didn't win—because institutional labor saw itself as a partner of business, was committed to war production, and held to the prejudices and parochialism that unions are paying for to this day. But there are reasons that are harder to summarize so succinctly. In the corporate media's compartmentalization of the era of upheaval, the working class was washed white, male, straight, old, conservative. White workers attracted rapt attention from reporters when they supported George Wallace in 1968 but not so much when they were wildcatting in Detroit and the hills and hollows of Appalachia the same year. Black radicals got headlines when they donned berets and posed with guns but not so much when, like General Baker of the League of Revolutionary Black Workers, they expounded on in-plant organizing, or, like the Combahee River Collective, they conceptualized identity politics as both an anti-capitalist struggle and a struggle for emancipation from sexism, racism, and homophobia—or, when, like the Black Panthers in Chicago in the late 1960s and early 1970s, they allied with the Puerto Rican Young Lords and the hillbilly Young Patriots in the first Rainbow Coalition, which one member of the group called "a code word for class struggle." Vietnam veterans were caricatured as victims of the counterculture, erasing their central role in the anti-war movement and their leadership in labor fights as late as the 1994–1995 Staley lockout in Decatur, Illinois. Women were welded to abortion and other discretely gendered issues. Environmentalists were characterized as in irreconcilable battle with workers. Homosexuals were imagined to inhabit some alternate universe that was either frightening or fabulous.

Much of this has to do with the biases of those telling the story, but it also reflects the success of the New Right project, which also emerged in the early 1970s (and is the source of the political stream that would eventually carry Donald Trump to the White House). Its goal was the same as the Old Right: to shovel as much wealth as possible to the ruling class, to crush or at least confuse opposition, and to exert U.S. economic and military power unhindered anywhere in the world. Its exponents and political candidates could hardly say they wanted to destroy communities and redistribute people's money upward to their real constituency; instead, they said, "The libbers will destroy your family, the queers will recruit your children, the blacks will steal your money, the greens will steal your job." Whether or not Ronald Reagan believed any of that is secondary to the fear-based organizing strategy of the grassroots movement that helped bring him to power by 1980. When, in August 1981, he fired 11,345 striking air traffic controllers, signaling to business that it should feel free to replace strikers permanently for discipline and profit, he revealed the primary agenda shrouded by the Culture War campaign. The result was, precisely, weakened families, hungry children, ill health, vanished jobs, embattled minority populations, with giddy wealth at the top. Succeeding Democratic administrations played around the edges of compartmentalized identity, wielding sticks or carrots to various constituencies for political advantage but sacrificing the common welfare to the goals of finance capital. The "disposable American," as Louis Uchitelle argued in his compelling book on mass layoffs, would become, like the Rust Belt, an accepted, seemingly unalterable feature of the landscape.[2]

In a full accounting, there would be responsibility enough to spread around. It can be argued that real conflicts and divisions existed—and still do. What the political and economic trajectory of this country shows, however, is that there is one fight with many fronts. What the Rainbow Coalition campaigns of the 1980s strove to demonstrate is the tactical, not simply moral or sentimental, significance of "an injury to one is an injury to all." Mike Stout does the same here. His history makes a political necessity of remembering. The cost of forgetting is too high.

FOREWORD

Charles McCollester

Mike Stout and I came to 1970s Pittsburgh by widely different paths, but we shared insights and values in common. As a new generation of activist thinkers and resisters emerges, we share a desire to pass on what we learned. The coming generation of workers faces a radically changing world of artificial intelligence, robots, drones, pervasive surveillance, genetic engineering, insidious pollution, and accelerating climate change. Mike's account of a grassroots democratic labor insurgency fighting for economic survival remains relevant, even as the nature of work changes.

A fundamental commonality underlying our collaboration has been a love and embrace of Pittsburgh—its geography, its people, and its heroic labor and industrial history. Mike recounts the story of the Mon Valley labor insurgency of the 1980s as seen from the iconic heart of union resistance—the Homestead steel mill. Homestead! Site of the best-known confrontation between labor and capital in United States; a daylong gun battle in 1892 was witnessed by thousands and reported around the nation and across the globe. Workers and the community united to preserve an organized voice in the nation's most advanced steel producer in the midst of radical technological change and the accelerating concentration of capital and power. The spirit of 1892 blossomed again in the final decade of the mill's operation (1976–1986) in the struggle of its rank-and-file union local against the phased collapse of regional industrial production. Mike Stout is the person to tell that story.

The working-class solidarity and culture intensely displayed in Homestead was essential in organizing to provide common defense

and promote general welfare. We are facing human-induced environmental degradation that poisons air and sinks down into the water and
soil, increasingly disrupting and corrupting nature itself. Our common
struggle for community survival must unite us as a species.

Unionism was changing in the 1970s. Vietnam veterans were
entering the workplace—many angry and feeling betrayed. The United
Mine Workers (UMW), godparents of the United Steelworkers (USW),
were marching under the Miners for Democracy banner fighting for
safety on the job and against corruption in their union. Illinois steelworker union leader Ed Sadlowski ran as a credible insurgent candidate
against the United Steelworkers of America (USWA) establishment's
Lloyd McBride. Teamsters were in revolt. Teachers and other public
sector workers were organizing. There was a growing restlessness from
below, as workers fought for reform and representation. That same
grassroots restlessness is intensifying today, especially among young
workers saddled with debt, stifled by inequality, and anxious about the
environment and the undermining of democracy.

Steelworkers at Homestead were experiencing changes that were
generational, as the World War II veterans retired. There were also
contractual changes brought about by legal challenges to racial discrimination inside the steel industry. A 1974 consent decree provided
plant-wide seniority to black workers and opened the door for more
women to enter the mill. These changes were long overdue but were
met with resistance, especially from high seniority white male workers.
Women, numerous in the mill during World War II, had effectively
been removed after the war by granting mill seniority to veterans for
their service. Workforce changes lent added importance to the union
grievance procedure. Mike Stout and John O'Toole's creative use of the
grievance system demonstrates how imagination and participation
invigorated a system that, because of its opacity and slowness, was
largely discredited. With the backing of Ron Weisen and the Rank and
File Caucus, their streamlining of the grievance procedure and the
direct involvement of the workers built a network of shop floor grievance filers and information gatherers that made amazingly successful
arbitration possible.

Rising labor radicalism of the 1970s was countered by corporate
repression after Reagan broke the air traffic controllers' strike in 1981.
Demands for wage and contract concessions were powerfully reinforced

by industrial plant closings. In a climate of fear, USW Local 1397 provided an example of spirited and imaginative resistance. Across the river in the militant "Old Left" United Electrical, Radio and Machine Workers of America (UE) Local 610, where I was chief steward, we were equally class conscious and anti-capitalist and internally very democratic, with an extensive steward system and fiercely contested union elections. However, given the vicious red-baiting campaigns of the McCarthy era, our union was more insular and media cautious. Ron Weisen and the Rank and File Caucus were flamboyant in your face and on your TV. Mike Stout, with many years of experience as an organizer and singer/songwriter, understood media and public speaking, providing sound bites and interviews that had insight and rang true.

The local's plant-wide newspaper, the *1397 Rank and File*, was a powerful expression of workplace democracy. Not only did the newspaper inform and educate, but ordinary workers had a voice that could be heard loud and clear. With its poetry, songs, cartoons, and well-written news articles, the newspaper unleashed the intellectual and artistic side of those who got their hands dirty. The exuberance and the humor of the *1397 Rank and File* newspaper—the sharp arrows and well-directed slings at the callous, the pompous, and the arrogant—remain relevant. People who do the work and observe from below the way things really operate can best tell the story.

Central to Local 1397's leadership role in the plant shutdown struggle was an approach to coalition-building that included a sustained search for allies among churches and community and progressive organizations. Mike and I were among the organizers of the Tri-State Conference on Steel (TSCS), which nurtured two major organizations: the Mon Valley Unemployed Committee (MVUC), focused on direct assistance to displaced workers (food banks, unemployment compensation [UC], mortgage foreclosures, job retraining, etc.) and the Steel Valley Authority (SVA), which directly fought the collapse of manufacturing, raising the threat of devastated municipalities using eminent domain against idled corporate property. The SVA was organized to provide an alternative vision of economic development that gave workers and the community a structural voice.

Perhaps the most important and enduring lesson of Homestead Local 1397 and the Mon Valley insurgency it played an important role in is that the union in its heyday deeply stirred and involved the rank and file. When democracy's power flows through an institution's lifeblood, it stimulates involvement and action. Pride in a job, mutual respect, resistance to injustice, and solidarity are powerful working-class cultural and communal values.

Mike Stout's well-constructed and splendidly illustrated memoir is about a special place and time, but it also serves as a window on a social insurgency that can provide inspiration for future social progress. It is a story of skilled workers who proudly got their hands dirty—an industrial world of crane operators, machinists, mechanics, millwrights, laborers, and electricians that once dominated a region. Today, there are new skills and different jobs, but class domination and oppression endure. Will it be greed without end or solidarity forever? The choice remains, and the consequences for a sick earth and an imperial world order could not be greater.

Our region lived through an industrial holocaust that decimated towns, destroyed families, and sent hundreds of thousands of industrial refugees all over the country and beyond. Collective suffering and governmental failure engendered a deep working-class bitterness that haunts our politics to this day. But Pittsburgh is also a story of human and regional resilience. Most of all, this book about a steelworker local union is a working-class hymn to democracy and solidarity—about a time when "the bottom rose up to the brim, when democracy from below was more than just words."

PREFACE

A number of close friends have asked me: Why write a book about a union democracy movement at a steel mill that's been closed for decades? What significance does it have in a world that in many ways has radically changed? A post-industrial world where issues such as the environment, nuclear war, terrorism, and immigration seem much more paramount? A neoliberal world where technology, globalization, privatization, and deregulation have fundamentally changed and drastically reduced our industrial and manufacturing base? In fact, there are a number of important reasons why this short-lived experiment in democracy is important, not only to historians but to millennials and future generations of working people in the United States.

First is the question of unionism: Do we still need unions, and, if so, what should they look like?

For fifty years of my life, including my entire adult working life, I was a member of a union, including a year as a clerk in the New York City Postal Union, the Teamsters Union in both New York City and Local 89 in Louisville, Kentucky, thirty-six years in the United Steelworkers Union (USWA), and twenty-three years in Pittsburgh Musicians Union Local 60-471. On and off, I've also been a proud member of the Industrial Workers of the World (IWW) and believe strongly in their concept of "one big union."[1] I take to heart the union anthems, "An Injury to One Is an Injury to All," and "Solidarity Forever." For me, these slogans are as American as apple pie and baseball.

But coming from a big family and an area of the country (Lexington, Kentucky) not known for unionism, as well as managing a printshop cooperative business for twenty-five years as a steelworker union member in Homestead, I've run across innumerable anti-union people and have spent a considerable portion of my time and life defending unions. With the disparity of wealth in this country today, which only grows worse with each passing year, and the lack of democracy or voice in nearly all workplaces of every size, I feel strongly that a union is essential, lest we all become slaves earning a minimal wage, scraping the bottom of the barrel with no voice or rights in our workplaces. As the workers in unions have steadily declined over the years, wages have stagnated, benefits have shrunk, and pensions have become a relic of the past. These are indisputable facts.

Only 10 to 11 percent of workers in the United States are now unionized, and that continues to drop with each passing year. Unions are under relentless attack from right-wing politicians and "right-to-work" proponents funded by super-predator corporations and capitalists, such as the Koch brothers. Under the current laws and regulations in just about every state, organizing a union has become extremely difficult at best, as the weight of the system always favors the employers.

Polls consistently show that a sizable portion of the American working population favors unions and would be part of one if they could. In fact, the interest in joining a union is at a four-decade high. According to a recent survey of four thousand nonunion workers conducted by the prestigious National Opinion Research Corporation and released on September 2, 2018, nearly half the respondents, 48 percent, said they would join a union if given the opportunity. This marks a sharp increase from 1977–1995 when only 30 to 33 percent said they would join a union. The scale of this change indicates that fifty-eight million American workers would join a union if they could.[2]

The majority of people now working in this country have never been in a union and have little knowledge of union history, what unions have accomplished, and how they function. On numerous occasions I've heard statements like "they've outlived their usefulness; times have changed." Many people over the years have told me unions once were good, but now they've evolved into mob-like syndicates, where union bosses just take dues money from their members and give them no protection or representation. So not only is there a question of whether or not there should be unions but also of how they should be structured. Do most unions need to be more democratic? Should they have their own independent political voice, or should they continue to rely on the Democratic Party to be their political voice?

History and my experience at the Homestead steel mill and with its union, USWA Local 1397, were both instructive and important for answering questions and addressing misconceptions about whether or not we need unions, what they should look like, and how they should function.

In the pursuit of greater profits and wealth, corporations and the 1% at the top will continue to wage class war against unions, doing everything they can to eliminate them. This is another hard, cold fact, whether or not union officials admit it. To defend the benefits of their members and the rights so many union organizers fought and died for over the past century, unions will have to become better organized and more disciplined, militant, and democratic.

In my experience, for a union to be most effective, it has to actively involve as much of the membership as possible, or, put another way, it has to be democratic. Without democracy and the direct day-to-day involvement of their members, unions will not survive the current right-wing corporate onslaught that is out to dismantle and destroy them. The current business model and structure of many unions will no longer suffice. Corruption and patronage must be rooted out and unions radically restructured to meet the challenges of the ever-changing world.

When I became a member of the USWA Local 1397 in Homestead, I eagerly joined the Rank and File Caucus, having witnessed firsthand how our local union officials took our dues money, refused to file legitimate grievances, and were nothing but yes-men lackies for management. The struggle in the Homestead local union during its final decade was a struggle by a group of dedicated activists to change the direction of our union, not only to democratize it but to make it more effective as a fighting organization on behalf of its members. We also wanted to set an example for other unions and the general public. Our successes and failures should be studied by any member of a union who is concerned about his or her job, as well as anyone who wants to form a union at their workplace.

Unions are like any other institution or organization; they are mostly staffed by good men and women who dedicate their lives to defending the members. On the other hand, some also have bad apples that not only refuse to do their jobs but spend most of their time feathering their own beds and giving unions a rotten name in the public eye. As a union activist and official at Homestead, I had a mission: to show the members that I (and the union by extension) would be their defenders, whether they liked me personally or not, and that a union didn't have to be some useless sponge, taking their dues money and giving them no representation in return. I wanted to show that solidarity and accompaniment were my guiding principles, that I was solidly in the camp of "an injury to one is an injury to all." I have tried to live this as an official, as a singer/songwriter, and as a citizen and will until the day I die.

Second, with barely 10 percent of the U.S. workforce, unions will need a broad coalition with other struggles and interests. Over the past seventy years, unions have only survived, saved decent-paying jobs, and made political gains by coalescing with other struggles and movements in society. To continue to exist, they will have to do the same today. Unions will not survive without allies!

The activists and insurgents at Local 1397 who made up the Rank and File Caucus in the decade from 1976 to 1986 always actively cooperated with other forces and movements. Whether it was around stopping plants from closing, working with environmentalists, fighting to save our manufacturing base with the creation of a federally funded jobs program, opposing unjust wars in Central America, or fighting for civil rights, we always had an "inside-outside" approach. The coalition efforts our local engaged in—the Tri-State Conference on Steel (TSCS), the Network to Save the Mon Valley/Denominational Mission Strategy (DMS), the Save Dorothy Six and South Side Electric Furnace battles, the anti-Klan Coalition, and the Thomas Merton Center—are rife with lessons and rich experience for any union and community activist.[3] While many of these efforts eventually failed, it was our pitfalls and mistakes that were the best learning experiences.

Organized labor, i.e., unions, played an important role in the progressive coalition that arose with Franklin Roosevelt's New Deal programs in the 1930s and 1940s. Throughout the years, I have found that most people are completely unaware that unions led the fight and campaigns to give us the eight-hour workday, overtime pay, unemployment compensation, safety and health protection on the job, paid vacation time, social security, and a host of other benefits we take for granted, thousands of trade unionists going to jail or dying in the process. And they always did it in coalitions with other social forces.

Now, more than ever, unions need to be part of larger coalitions to stop the rampage destroying our standard of living and our social safety net, the continued discrimination against minorities and immigrants, and especially the destruction of our environment. The Local 1397–led coalition with community activists and environmentalists during the Conneaut struggle showed the strength and overlap of the workers' fight for jobs and the environmental struggle for clean air and water. When U.S. Steel was forced by an Environmental Protection Agency (EPA) Consent Decree to install environmentally friendly technology in 1980 to clean up the mess it was making of our air and water, the Company told the public and employees at various facilities subsequently shut down that the cost of such modernization was the reason their jobs were being eliminated. "Jobs versus the environment" is a false dichotomy that still infects many union officials and members today. How our local union, through our newspaper, lawsuits, coalitions, and public activity countered this bullshit holds some valuable lessons for workers who are fighting the ravages of globalization today.

Third, this book is an attempt to set the historical record straight on the Homestead mill and its union, USWA Local 1397, in the final decade of their existence. This story has never been told by someone who was on the inside. While a number of books over the years have given excellent and detailed accounts of the town and the historic strike and lockout of 1892, I've run across only one book that delved into the final years of the Homestead mill and union Local 1397: the late William Serrin's *Homestead: The Glory and Tragedy of an American Steel Town*.[4]

I got to know Bill Serrin pretty well through those tumultuous years. We talked extensively about unions and their history. The former labor and workplace correspondent for the *New York Times*, Bill's general take was: we absolutely need unions, but many are bogged down in bureaucracy, corruption, and lack of democracy and have lost their bearings with the changing global economy. This view was the magnet that drew him to the Local 1397 rank-and-file movement and some of its key players, especially our last local union president Ron Weisen. Outside of hanging with and interviewing a small group of Structural Mill employees on May 25, 1986, the last day the mill operated, Bill spent most of his time at the union hall, especially in Ron Weisen's office, talking to him and the union officials that worked around him, including me.

Ron Weisen was certainly the focal point of the rank-and-file militancy at Homestead. His flamboyant in-your-face style, outspokenness, and militancy were amply covered in newspapers and the local media in the first half of the 1980s. On the other hand, key players in the rank-and-file movement, including those who were elected to local union positions, as well as rank-and-file activists who never ran for office, are rarely mentioned, if at all. Their names need to be in the history books, their contributions acknowledged.

From 1978 to the bitter end in 1987, I was at the epicenter of the rank-and-file movement at the Homestead steel mill—as a local union griever and later grievance chair (the Basic Steel Contracts between U.S. Steel and the USWA used the language of "grievanceman" and "grievance chairman" back in those days, so those appear within quoted text in this book), writing for and editing the union newspaper, and being a co-initiator of the many coalitions in which the local union was involved. The important story of that moment in history needs to be told from the inside.

Of course, other Local 1397 rank-and-file activists have their own experiences and achievements, many that predate my arrival on the scene. This account in no way purports to be a be-all and end-all history. It is merely my personal experience, and in telling it I had access to a treasure trove of written sources, including the 1397 *Rank and File* newspaper and internal documents I rescued and preserved. In addition, through researchers that include Professors Charles McCollester and Irwin Marcus, as well as grad students Anne Marie Draham, Jim Dougherty, and Brett Reigh at Indiana University of Pennsylvania (IUP), and former steelworker and Rainbow Kitchen cofounder Bob Anderson, I had access to extensive oral history interviews with a number of Homestead local union activists and officers, as well as conducting oral history interviews myself. All of this history, as well as the numerous grievance and arbitration records I cite in detail, are safely preserved in the Special Collections and University Archives at IUP.

The experience of the insurgency and the formation of the 1397 Rank and File Caucus at the very end of the mill's existence was an important experiment in democracy, most of which has not been repeated or heard of elsewhere. It was not something separate from 1892 but the culmination of nearly a hundred years of struggle, resistance, and the fight for democracy, economic justice, and human dignity. Though many labor activists and historians are familiar with labor history and, in particular, the steel industry and steelworkers' union at Homestead, I have included a brief history from the end of the nineteenth century up to the inception of the rank-and-file uprising in the mid-1970s, with special emphasis on the mill workers and union activists rarely mentioned in other books.

What About Socialism?

Since I was eighteen years old, I have always believed we need a different and more democratic system if the human race is to survive on this planet, and that this new system must be socialist. But if there's one thing that's been consistent in my fifty years of political activism: just about everyone I talked to on this subject has a different definition of what "socialism" is. For many, especially from the baby-boomer generation, socialism means a country like the (former) Soviet Union or the People's Republic of China, which they view as totalitarian dictatorships with one-party, top-down rule, no freedom, no democracy, etc. Whatever the justified origins and causes of these revolutions were in the first half of the twentieth century, by the time my generation came around, we were pretty well indoctrinated with the "red menace" and "yellow peril" barrage of propaganda that was non-stop in the 1950s and 1960s. At the same time, I've heard many an American in my day call a bona fide capitalist a "communist," when referring to the dictatorial, thieving ways of capitalists and their servants in our own government. The difference between communism and socialism was rarely addressed.

For me, socialism is something else altogether; it is the shared public ownership and control of those things that all of us need: education, health care, infrastructure, transportation, the energy grid, natural resources, basic industries, etc. We are all dependent on these things, and they should be owned in common. Along with equal access to these life necessities, everyone should be guaranteed a decent job at a living wage and a decent retirement. Instead of a political system ruled and dominated by big money, banks, and corporations, it would be a system run by and accountable to ordinary citizens and workers, a democratic system where every voice is heard and equal. Obviously, the Electoral College would be a thing of the past. All elections would be publicly funded, as opposed to the corrupt setup we have now, where you have to be a millionaire to even run for high office, where greed and corporate "money talks, and everything else walks." The Bill of Rights – *all* of it - would not only remain intact but be strengthened and expanded. Free and fair elections, based on "one person, one vote" would be the law, with every citizen having the right and ability to vote. All elected officials at every level would be reviewed and held accountable. A strong checks and balances system would be established. The only "dictatorship" I envision is one that doesn't let the greedy 1% and their class drive us into indebted servitude, while squandering and hoarding our wealth and natural resources, and stops them from destroying the whole planet.

My vision of socialism would allow people the right to own their own businesses, and local gardens and small-scale family farms that supply local food markets would be strongly encouraged and supported. If someone works harder, they should be allowed to earn over and above what everyone is guaranteed. "From each according to their ability, to each according to their work" seems a fair proposition to me.

Problems common to the whole of society, whether natural disasters, climate change chaos, crime, drug addiction, or poverty would be dealt with in common, with high priority placed on dealing with national emergencies, such as pervasive gun violence, the opioid crisis, and the continuous disasters we are experiencing as a result of climate change. A "Green New Deal" would only be the beginning of creating a "closed loop economy," where everything produced or manufactured is recyclable, and there is no concept of "garbage," and where the gargantuan task of cleaning up the planet, creating a viable mass transit–based infrastructure, and converting to a 100 percent renewable energy are given A-one priority.

A *progressive tax system* would be put into effect, meaning the higher the income, the higher the tax rate. The ridiculous cap on social security would be removed completely. Corporations would be taxed at the highest possible rate.

Under socialism as I define it, rather than using the bulk of our taxes for war, it would be used to meet the needs of the people. The Defense Department would be replaced by a "Peace" Department, and cooperation with other nations to help them rebuild their economies and become positive forces for saving our fragile planet from impending environmental destruction, mass starvation, and displacement. Our military would be used to save our planet, defend our country, and *prevent* wars not to engage in wars to ensure some corporation's right to plunder other nations and steal their natural resources.

The polarization of wealth in the U.S., where three individuals now own more than 50 percent of the population, a gap that only grows bigger every day, is a recipe for continuing and greater poverty and disaster. The very structure of our current system, with 4 percent of the world's population consuming 25 to 30 percent of the world's energy and resources, makes continued inequality, war, and ecocide inevitable. How can anyone in their right mind think this situation is right? As far as I've been able to tell, our current capitalist system, which is based on greed, exploitation, and privatization of our common necessities, is taking humanity to a "sixth great extinction."[5] I'm a firm believer that we need a new, completely different system. If any of this is what you mean when you call me a "socialist," then I plead guilty.

Throughout the book, when talking about the U.S. Steel Corporation, which was known as "USX" between 1986 and 2001, I will often refer to the "Company." When referring to the United Steelworkers of America International Union, which is headquartered in downtown Pittsburgh, I will often refer to the "International," or "International Union."[6] Between the International and local unions, are the district unions, which are structurally part of the International, but are located in regional offices throughout the country and Canada. Throughout its existence, Local 1397 was part of District 15, located in North Versailles, Pennsylvania. I will often refer to District 15 as the "District" or the "District Union."

The foul language used in the mill, especially the way bosses and management talked to us while I served as a griever, has been kept intact. While some readers might find this language offensive, it will give you a realistic indication of how they talked to and treated us, as well as how workers talked to each other in this dirty and dangerous industrial setting. The use of alcohol and marijuana and the roles they played in workers' daily lives are also touched on from personal experience, as is the rampant racism and sexism that prevailed while I worked at the Homestead mill.

This book is not for the ill-informed, selfish sorts, the "I got mine, screw everybody else" ilk. It is not for those who don't give a hoot about workers, the poor, or the future of the planet. This book is for workers—union and nonunion alike—and for those citizens who believe in community, who know that solidarity and democracy are our main weapons against the greed, money interests, and the system that is crushing us all.

Last, I want my friends and family—especially my children and grandchildren—to know what I was doing and why I was doing it through these difficult years. I was in the midst of a war that needed to be fought, and I felt that I ended up in Homestead for a reason. I want them to know that some of us not only believe in democracy and the common good, but we fought and worked for these ideals.

There are some out there who don't care about history, condemned to repeat its worst aspects over and over. There are others who like to study it, who are avid readers of history. Then there are those who prefer to make history, to take it in a more just, humane, and civil direction. As you will see when reading this book, I fall in the last category.

CHAPTER 1

A STRANGE BEAUTY

Homestead Steel Mill from the Pittsburgh Squirrel Hill side of the Monongahela River, c. 1910.

After growing up in a suburban southern university town like Lexington, Kentucky, and spending seven-plus years in the skyscraper jungles of New York City, I found Homestead, Pennsylvania, in 1977, to be a whole different universe. Smoke billowed everywhere. A cloud of dust hung over the town like a multicolored dome, changing hues depending on the type of steel rolled, church steeples jutting above the smoke everywhere (twenty in little Homestead alone). They were only outnumbered by bars, sometimes four on every corner of an intersection. The town was alive and lit up twenty-four hours a day, seven days a week. Its hustle and bustle rivaled my experiences in Las Vegas and Myrtle Beach—only in an industrial setting. There were ethnic social clubs everywhere—Polish, Russian, Bulgarian, Hungarian, Irish, Italian—you name it. It was like some kind of ancient giant strip mall combined with roadside stands like those that clutter the avenues in midtown Manhattan in New York City. The main avenues near the mill were lined with fruit stands, butcher shops, delis, clothing and furniture stores, five and dimes, car dealers, whorehouses, and just about anything you wanted or needed on your way into work—all of

Homestead Town and 8th Ave., with streetcar running through the center of town, 1959.

this in the colossal shadows of a giant steel mill that spanned four boroughs. I could pick up my lunch as I walked to work from up on the hill on 14th Avenue. Back in its heyday, after World War II, people from Pittsburgh and all over Allegheny County would come to Homestead on the weekends to shop; a street car ran right through the center of town.

While I had read about such places in books like *Labor's Untold Story*, by Richard O'Boyer,[1] as well as Philip Foner's ten-volume *History of the Labor Movement in the United States*,[2] seeing it before my very eyes was breathtaking, like entering a labor fairy tale. To my grandkids and future generations, all I can say is it was like nothing you've ever seen or will ever see.

Being the only Homestead steelworker from Lexington, Kentucky, from day one I was known as Mike "Kentucky" Stout. My initial experience on the job inside the 100" Plate Mill was just as amazing. As I related to Bill Serrin some years later:

> I never in my life had seen anything as big, as spread out, had never seen equipment as big. One thing I liked about it was you had all these people and it didn't matter what age, sex, color or country you were from. The mill formed the basis of a family. You went to work in the morning and the first thing you did was have coffee and a safety meeting and then went on the job. You

ate lunch together, then back to work. It was a family thing. There were differences, divisions, but generally the mill eliminated those, welded people together, and formed the basis of a lot of friendships. . .

The other thing was the strange beauty of the place. In the slab yard between the 100" and 160" mills, I'd never seen anything like that—big slabs of steel stacked up ten, fifteen, twenty feet high, pile after pile, huge cranes moving with two-hundred-pound chains picking up steel, putting it in railroad cars, moving faster than you could almost watch; that's how awesome it was. The 100" and 160" rolling mills were always kept clean, especially in the early days, when they had laborers and roll hands, whose job it was to sweep and water them down every evening. When we rolled pipe, the pipe steel let off this red dust that hung in the air. It was mystical, wild, especially during daylight, when the dust was going up and the sunlight was coming through the cracks in the roof. It was like you were in a theater watching a play, and the play was industrial production.[3]

There was nothing like it back home in Kentucky, where I was the oldest son and third oldest child, of ten. My dad had worked in his father's tobacco fields from the time he could walk, and in my early years, he worked three or four jobs at a time to put food on the table and pay the bills.

In addition to all his other jobs, he loved to play guitar and sing, landing his own prime-time kiddie-cowboy show on a local TV station and appearing in amateur stage productions. His proudest moment was when all ten of his children appeared on his Christmas show in December 1959. Some thirty-five years later at my parents' fiftieth wedding anniversary, I organized a musical celebration with my sisters Polly and Kathy and my brother Roy.

We performed a medley of dad's favorite songs, including Hank Williams's 'Jambalaya,' Sons of the Pioneers' 'Tumbling Tumbleweed,' 'Ballad of Tom Dooley,' 'Carolina in the Morning,' and others; he sobbed through the entire forty-five-minute performance.

My dad was very diligent in rounding up work for his five sons, whether it was mowing lawns, shoveling snow, or distribution for his handbill business, which he started in 1964. The handbill business was pretty lucrative for more than fifteen years. Essentially, if Woolworth's, H.L. Green, or whoever had an advertisement and the postage charge to mail each piece was, say, two cents per household, my dad would underbid the Post Office at a penny and a half, and we would go door to door delivering the advertisement throughout the city. He would get a penny, and give us (the workers) a half cent for each mailer we delivered. Outside of being allowed to play Little League and Pony League baseball for a couple of years, from the age of eleven to seventeen, I worked most every day after school and all summers for my dad, as did my four younger brothers. Other than an occasional babysitting job, my sisters were resigned to unpaid housework, which didn't sit too well with them, as I was told many years later.

Half of everything we made through the years came right off the top and was given to our mother, which she used to buy our clothes. Half of what was left was taken by our dad to save for college, and ten percent of the whole thing went to the church. Out of every twenty dollars I earned, I would end up with three dollars in my pocket. I learned about exploitation at a very young age. While at the time I hated the constant work and his taking most of what we earned, the discipline and work ethic he taught were valuable tools that pulled me through my troubled teen years and early adulthood, especially when I struck out on my own at the age of eighteen. Had he told us what was going on, I probably wouldn't have resented it so much at the time.

During my adolescent period of confinement, repression, and constant work, music became my escape, savior, and constant companion. The precursor to the Walkman, CD players, and iPhone technology was the tiny transistor radio that I glued to my ear. When confined to my room, i.e., grounded, the 45 rpm record player was always going. I can honestly say I wouldn't be here today if it wasn't for music. Where I grew up, doo-wop, falsetto singers, and black music dominated the air waves. The Everly Brothers, the Four Seasons, Del Shannon,

Frankie Lyman, Marvin Gaye, Aretha Franklin, Little Anthony and the Imperials, Pittsburgh's Moonglows and Lou Christie, the Temptations, Smokey Robinson and the Miracles, Curtis Mayfield, Martha and the Vandellas, Patti Labelle—I loved them all. Later I taught myself to play guitar. Music was the perfect antidote for the resentment, meanness, and aimless antiauthoritarianism I was feeling at this tender stage in life. In my mid-teens, the Animals' "We Gotta Get Out of this Place," the Stones' "I Can't Get No Satisfaction," Donovan's cover of Buffy St. Marie's "Universal Soldier," and Barry McGuire's "Eve of Destruction" were my anthems. The rebellious music of the 1960s took me in a whole new direction.

For me protest music, especially the rock and roll variety, was the perfect outlet to express my rage against exploitation, alienation, and injustice, without hurting myself or someone else. In the 1960s, Bob Dylan was the quintessential protest poet: anti-war, anti-racist, anti-authoritarian, and impossible to box in or pin down. His transcendence to rock and roll and the electric guitar at the Newport Folk Festival in 1965 seemed as natural as the sun rising.

After suffering through three different high schools, I went to the University of Kentucky for one year but rarely attended classes, finding them even more boring than grade school and high school. Unable to work a full-time job and afford to go to college and, quite frankly, not seeing any use in it, I took off for New York City in the summer of 1968 with a trunk full of clothes and my guitar.

Not knowing a soul there, my dream was to be a singer/songwriter in the footsteps of my musical hero, Mr. Dylan. After playing the streets and open-mic nights at Greenwich Village clubs for six months (during most of this period I was homeless), I was signed up by a manager to record ten of my own original songs for Roulette Records. The theme song and title for what would have been my first "dream come true" album was: *The President's All-American Lonely Hearts Club*, a political takeoff on the Beatles' *Sgt. Pepper* album. The cover was to be a collage of the downtrodden and forgotten—Native Americans, the rural Appalachian poor, immigrants, the homeless, prostitutes, junkies, street vagrants, etc. I still have the lyrics and music scores for all these songs.

However, after witnessing gangsterism and violence at several of my manager's clubs in Greenwich Village and having my life threatened by one of his sadistic bouncers, I fled to San Francisco to hide out until my contract expired. In November 1969, after landing a job with the U.S. Post Office and hearing my former manager had gone to jail, I moved back to the Big Apple. By this time, the anti–Vietnam War movement was in full swing, and my music career would take a back seat to politics and the youth revolution.

In the summer of 1977, I was back in Kentucky, helping on a campaign to organize the unemployed, when a former radical buddy from New York, Mickey Jarvis, called me up and told me he had heard from a friend they were hiring hundreds at the steel mills in the Pittsburgh area. He said they were paying twice what I was making at the time. On top of the better pay, I was a hard-core football fan. Watching the "immaculate reception" by Franco Harris against the Oakland Raiders in my McDougal Street apartment in New York City back in December 1972, I had become an instant Steelers fan and convert. The idea of moving to Pittsburgh was a no-brainer.

I applied at U.S. Steel's Irvin, Duquesne, and then the Homestead Works, where I got hired after bullshitting the personnel clerk Joe Jenkins about my overhead crane capabilities. With my limited knowledge of Homestead's history and production reputation at the time, I thought I had found a job for life; it was especially satisfying after the moving around and job-hopping the previous years. I'll never forget my first day on the job. This burr-headed former marine sergeant was giving us orientation. He said: "If anybody in this room has any intention of just working here for the summer, or for a year or two or five years, you ought to hit the road right now. We're looking for career people, looking for 25 to 50 year people; we want a lifetime commitment."[4]

When my son Michael was born in May 1978, I was ready to settle down and enjoy the good life. Little did I know economic whirlwinds were gathering just around the bend.

CHAPTER 2

MOVING TO HOMESTEAD—BECOMING A STEELWORKER

The first few months at my new job were a struggle. Hired as a utility crane operator, my job was to operate multiple electric overhead traveling (EOT) cranes throughout the 100" Plate Mill. I worked with maintenance crews on repair shifts when the mill was down, as well as filling in when regular crane operators were on vacation or called off sick on production shifts. It was a job that required full attention and concentration. An EOT crane had six controls: two bridge levers that took you up and down the bay, two trolley levers that racked your cables in and out, and two hook or chain cable levers that lowered and raised to pick up the steel plates for loading into railroad cars or onto trucks. On some cranes, you had a magnet instead of chains or hooks. These were usually used to load or unload scrap steel. Your only brakes were taking the bridge levers backwards.

For my first two weeks, I trained and was familiarized with an EOT crane at the abandoned 140" spare parts building at the east end of the mill (still intact) next to the pumphouse,[1] where no production took place. Over the next few months, I would be assigned to actual operating cranes with the regulator crane operator, in order to learn the various jobs.

The first crane I operated was no. 248 in the 100" mill shipping bay. The cab was thirty to forty feet off the ground, reached by a set of narrow, creaky, and wobbly metal steps. The five-foot by six-foot metal cab (lined with asbestos to supposedly keep the heat in during winter) was unbearably hot in the summer and freezing in the winter, equipped with a tiny heater that often didn't work, and most often had no fans. It was no place for claustrophobics. The old geezer (well, at least he seemed old to me at the time) who was the regular operator on this crane had a cigarette hanging out of his mouth with a two-inch ash butt. With a scruffy white-whisker beard (they weren't in style yet), he smelled like he hadn't taken a bath for a while. He was throwing the six levers so fast my eyes couldn't keep up with him. When I arrived in the cab he said, "Want a drink?" As I stared speechless, he said, "Look under the seat." Thinking he meant a soft drink or something, I opened the metal cabinet beneath his seat only to find whiskey, scotch, gin, and vodka—all in several varieties. As I stood stunned, he said, "What are you, a pussy? If you need a mixer, look in the cooler behind you." Needless to say, I turned his offer down. In a cramped metal box forty feet off the ground that was jerking back and forth, I was already doing everything I could not to crap my pants. I later discovered that numerous EOT crane operators ran their cranes accident-free for years, while fully lubricated. About once every year or two, they'd take vacation time off to dry out, and then start all over again. Alcohol seemed to be the early version of the five-hour power drink—more like fuel to this breed of industrial worker.

One afternoon during my third week on the job, I stopped by Stein's Bar at the corner of 6th and Amity on my way to work the 4:00 p.m. to midnight shift. Another 100" crane operator offered to buy me a drink. When I ordered a glass of red wine (the only thing I drink), he looked at me like I was from outer space, smirking and commenting to the bartender, "Go down to the basement and get the Reunite out of storage." While I nervously sipped the wine (hey, I was going in to operate an overhead crane), he downed five boilermakers (whiskey shot and beer) before I finished half a glass. The way some of these guys downed the booze, without missing a beat at work, smoked, and lived into their eighties—well, it almost seemed like some of these steelworkers had insides made of hot iron.

Operating an EOT crane was like operating no other piece of moving equipment, and it could be a lethal weapon. On the shipping bay cranes, each of the two cables used to lift the steel plates had two 100- to 150-pound hooks. The steel plates we lifted with the four hooks could be anywhere from eight to a hundred feet long. Sometimes the plate was so long it took two cranes and eight hooks working together to lift the steel and load it into the railroad car. The worker who attached the hooks to the steel for loading was called a "hooker." His life, not to mention his arms and fingers, were in the crane operator's hands. As if all this wasn't nerve-racking enough for a novice, the trolley on this particular crane was warped, meaning it had a bow and the hooking cables were constantly moving back and forth while you were moving them up and down; whatever other lever you were moving, you were constantly fiddling with the trolley levers. To top it all off, if an expediter, carblocker, or hooker on the ground knew you were a beginner, they screamed at you like a drill sergeant, shouting different orders seconds apart or doing whatever they could to rattle you. They especially liked to pick on young beginners and women. I truly felt like I was in boot camp the first three or four months on the job.

On the other hand, EOT crane operators were true industrial artists. Their precision and sophistication were poetry in motion. This was demonstrated while I was on a scrap bay crane with a longtime experienced operator named Jimmy "Cookie" Cook, who was showing me the ropes. His crane was equipped with a giant magnet for picking up and stacking steel scrap plates. All of a sudden, he took the crane at full speed down the bay, swinging his magnet suspended off the ground on a twenty-foot cable up and down, back and forth like a huge pendulum. He then pulled the bridge lever backwards and brought the crane to a dead stop, bringing the magnet to a dead stop at the same exact moment. Beaming, he looked at me and said, "Do that and you can call yourself a craneman."

Working in a steel mill was dangerous beyond description. You worked in extreme temperatures. Heavy equipment and machinery were flying all about you. You could be working in front of rolling red hot steel where the temperature in the front of your body was 2,300 degrees, but your back would be freezing. You worked a different time shift every week, working 8:00 a.m. to 4:00 p.m., then 4:00 p.m. to midnight the following week, then midnight to 8:00 a.m. the third week. Also, every week your two days off would change; you'd be off Sunday and Monday, then the next week Monday and Tuesday, etc. Your entire life outside of work was determined by your life in the mill. There wasn't much time or energy for anything else.

While cleaning a furnace during an outage (when the mill is down, and there's no production taking place), in 1979, a piece of cinder broke loose and nearly severed a major artery at my wrist, as well as my right thumb. In the freezing cold with thick gloves on, I didn't even feel or notice it until I saw blood dripping out of my glove. While at the 100" mill, I worked with a scrap crew of black men all with twenty-five years or more in the mill; none of them had all ten fingers. When I later transferred to the 160" mill, I saw a millwright, Bobby Pratt, lose a foot and three toes when a crane cable on the crane next to mine inexplicably slipped several inches. I saw another worker, Harry Brennan, get his face cut open diagonally from forehead to chin when he slipped in the slab yard and caught his face on the edge of a slab. Only by keeping him conscious did we keep him alive. With every crane cab lined with asbestos until the mill's closing, many of the older crane operators I worked with (including Jimmy Cook) died of asbestosis before or shortly after the doors were shut, many under the age of sixty. Getting elected grievance representative and only spending a few years steady on a crane is probably the only reason I never had a bout with Mr. Cancer or some neurological disease. Having known so many good people who died so young, my good fortune provides no consolation.

CHAPTER 3

HOMESTEAD–FORGE OF THE UNIVERSE, HEART OF INDUSTRIAL UNIONISM

Homestead, Pennsylvania, has been synonymous with steelmaking since 1880. For over one hundred years, the Homestead mill, seven miles southeast of downtown Pittsburgh on the south side of the Monongahela River, made the steel that helped shape the Industrial Revolution in America, producing armor plate during America's involvement in both world wars, as well as the Korean and

Homestead Steel Works, 1950s.

Vietnam Wars. It made structural beams for skyscrapers, including the St. Louis Arch, the Home Life Insurance Building in Chicago, the Pan Am, Empire State, Rockefeller Center, and United Nations Buildings in New York City, and the shafting for the power plant at the Hoover Dam. It made the steel for every major bridge and waterway back in the day, from the Panama Canal through the Golden Gate and Oakland Bay Bridges in San Francisco out west to the George Washington and Verrazano-Narrows Bridges back east. During World War II, it was taken over by the U.S. government under the power of eminent domain and turned into the National Defense Corporation, with the 160" Plate Mill, the 45" Slab Mill, Open Hearth no. 5 (OH5), and the Forge Division and Valley Machine Shop all built at taxpayers' expense. In 1946, it was sold back to U.S. Steel for ten cents on the dollar. The mill would eventually stretch for nearly four miles along the Monongahela River and cover more than three hundred acres making it one of the largest and most famous steelmaking facilities in the world.

The Birth of Industrial Unionism

Any reader who thinks Homestead workers didn't need a union needs a refresher course on what conditions were like in most steel mills, including Homestead:

> The monstrous crucibles of molten iron steel, the white-hot ingots, the great slabs and billets, the fast-moving cranes, the great cutting machines, the locomotives and railroad cars, the exploding furnaces, the splashing steel, the scalding water from bursting pipes, the high dark walkways—all this made the mill a natural place for injury and death.
>
> Men fell into kettles of molten steel, were knocked senseless or killed by slamming machinery, or swinging beams or moving cranes. They had their eyes put out, their arms and legs crushed or severed, and received multiple cuts and contusions. . . . At the turn of the twentieth century it was not uncommon for fifteen, perhaps twenty-five, perhaps more, to be killed in the works each year.[1]

By the time I arrived in the late 1970s, the union presence had significantly reduced the injuries and fatalities, but the mills were still extremely dangerous and life-shortening. In fact, according to the U.S.

Department of Labor at the time, the average life span of a steelworker was nine years less than the manufacturing average.

But the Homestead mill was notorious for other reasons as well. As Brett Reigh explained:

> The militant nature of its laborers is another reason the mill became so world-renowned. In its 106 years of operation, the Homestead Works witnessed some of the greatest battles ever waged between labor and capital in the United States. In 1892, the Amalgamated Association of Iron and Steelworkers (AAISW) struck at Homestead, which led to the battle that occurred on 6 July of that year between the Pinkerton agents, who were hired by Andrew Carnegie and Henry Clay Frick to break the strike, the town of Homestead and its steelworkers.[2]

In my thirteen years of schooling and history classes, the struggles of organized labor and unions were rarely mentioned. Two events that did make the cut were the Great Railroad Strike of 1877 and the Homestead strike of 1892. As my friend and fellow organizer Charlie McCollester stated in his seminal people's history *The Point of Pittsburgh: Struggle and Production at the Forks of the Ohio*: "The Amalgamated Association of Iron and Steelworkers (AAISW) was the most powerful organization of its time."[3] The home base of this union was Andrew Carnegie's giant Homestead Works. At Homestead, in the years before the great strike of 1892, every department in the mill had a union committee that represented most of the trade and craft workers around wages, working conditions, and benefits. Sunday work had been practically abolished. With strong grievance committees down to the sub-department level, it was like having an in-house lawyer on call that cost the workers pennies. In fact, this act of self-determination by the skilled craftsmen amounted to a "moral code of solidarity," which they imposed throughout the mill, including down to the lowest paid laborers.

Equally important, the whole philosophy and world outlook of the AAISW was revolutionary: "the workers and the public had earned an interest in the mill through the labor of the workers and through the tariffs that had been supported by the public."[4]

Through their hard work, ingenuity, and craftsmanship, workers believed they had acquired a piece of the pie, a voice at the table, and a

Homestead citizens and workers assail captured Pinkertons (drawing, *Harpers Weekly*).

say in the future of the mill. With owners and managers who only cared about increasing their profits at the expense of worker safety, health, and working conditions, a showdown at the O.K. "steel" Corral on the banks of the Monongahela was inevitable.

A major issue in the strike concerned not only Homestead workers, but the steel industry as a whole: "Whether rapid productivity advances which drove down the price of the product would depress wages in step with prices, or increase them in line with productivity."[5]

With the contract between the union and corporation set to expire at the end of the year, Andrew Carnegie and his plant manager Henry Clay Frick decided to break the union in order to drastically cut wages and institutionalize the twelve-hour workday.

On July 6, 1892, Pinkerton detectives escorted two barges of strike-breakers up the Mon River to the mill, where a pitched gun battle ensued between them and the workers. The entire town was mobilized in support of the union cause. Seven workers and three Pinkertons were killed and the rest of the three hundred strikebreakers captured, forced to wade through a gauntlet of thousands of angry workers and their wives who were insulting them, hurling dirt, and hitting them with sticks.

Pennsylvania State Militia troops entering Homestead, July 12, 1892 (drawing, *Harpers Weekly*).

After four days of mourning and massive funeral processions, Frick contacted the governor of Pennsylvania, who dispatched the state's entire National Guard of 8,500 men to occupy the mill. The strike leaders were completely caught off guard, thinking the state militia was coming to their aid. Instead, strike leaders were arrested and charged with murder and inciting riot, while strikebreakers were hired under the watchful eye of the troops. By November, the strike was over, its leaders and others blacklisted for life.

As Charlie McCollester told it:

> Employment at will became the foundation of American industrial relations. Workers were unprotected and wages plummeted. The twelve-hour day and the seven-day week became the norm for the bottom half of the workforce. Sunday rest, holidays and the concept of overtime all but disappeared.[6]

Though the strike and experiment in workers democracy was crushed, a spirit was born that continued for the next hundred years. With the inception of the AAISW in 1876, skilled workers exercised considerable autonomy in the workplace, maintaining an egalitarian moral code of solidarity that they imposed throughout the mill. A key element of this moral code was directed toward the bosses and owners of the mill. Worker authority on the job was in direct conflict to Frick's attempts to call the shots. It was out of this conflict with Carnegie and Frick, coupled with the solidarity necessary to perform the work safely, that this spirit was born.

A "spirit" to me is not just something inanimate. It permeates and gets passed down from generation to generation. There was a communal fighting spirit that mushroomed over the mill. I could feel it the first day I walked through the gates. For more than a month in 1892, during the Battle of Homestead, America had its own Paris Commune,[7] a workers' revolution where the entire town rose up against the foremost steel robber barons of the day, Andrew Carnegie and Henry Clay Frick. It even had its own Paul Reveres, workers who warned the town and workmen when Pinkerton strikebreakers were coming up the Mon River. The union workers controlled the entire town and its local government. The leader of the strike and the AAISW, John McLuckie, was also the town burgess. There has been nothing like it since, at least not in the United States.

The defeat of the Homestead strikers in 1892 broke the back of the AAISW and the labor movement among industrial workers in the United States for over forty years. By 1895, the membership of the AAISW had fallen to less than half of its pre-lockout strength. In 1899, three hundred Homestead workers created another Amalgamated Lodge, but their attempts to improve conditions failed, and they were all discharged.

The start of the twentieth century offered few options for steelworkers at Homestead or elsewhere, but pockets of resistance continued. Working-class residents and families of Homestead were indifferent, many outright hostile, to the paternalism displayed by Andrew Carnegie when he built the town a new library. They rejected his self-glorification and fought against the tax burden for maintenance of the facility. Rejecting the enticements of his welfare capitalism, they turned to the emerging mass entertainment, including the movies, amusement parks, and sports, for their recreation. But by 1900, the fundamental character of the town had shifted to one of total corporate dominance. Unlike the 1892 Homestead, the town was now a Republican stronghold and "company town" and would remain so until the mid-1930s.

CHAPTER 4

U.S. STEEL AND THE REBIRTH OF INDUSTRIAL UNIONISM

On April 1, 1901, the Carnegie and Frick steel and coal empires, under the leadership of Judge Elbert Gary and Charles Schwab, merged their mills, blast furnaces, and iron ore and coke holdings with banker J.P. Morgan's vast financial, oil, railroad, and transportation holdings. The result was the creation of America's largest and first billion-dollar corporation, the United States Steel Corporation. With this merger, U.S. Steel had captured 65 percent of American steel production and employed 168 thousand workers. In all, this giant entity owned 41 iron mines, 78 blast furnaces, 213 steel mills, 1,000 miles of railroad lines, 112 great lakes ore boats, and countless barges and tow boats. Instantaneously, hundreds of millionaires were created, and the power over labor and the working man was at its greatest. At the Homestead mill, the Amalgamated Association of Iron and Steelworkers (AAISW) lost strikes in 1901 and 1909, which left the skilled workers even more at the mercy of the Company. As the influence of the AAISW declined, its workers departed or fired, the Eastern European immigrants, who were the lowest paid laborers and made up the bulk of the workforce, came to the fore. During World War I, they began a new phase of the struggle to improve conditions in the mill and bring democracy to the workplace.

Homestead steelworkers were heavily involved in the unsuccessful Great Steel Strike of 1919, which attempted to win a shorter workday, union recognition, and higher wages. Unlike the 1892 battle, this effort involved the entire workforce, down to the lowest paid laborers. Once again, strikers were beaten back, literally, with clubs, guns, armed

Company thugs, and riot police. In steel towns like Homestead, basic civil liberties were outlawed, as local authorities forbade freedom of assembly and freedom of speech. During the strike, two or three workers conversing on a street corner were seen as subversive, and they would be arrested and beaten.

In another tragic turn of events, U.S. Steel brought in hundreds of poor blacks from the South to be used as strikebreakers, sowing seeds of racism and division that plagued the workforce for decades. At the end of the strike, and even later with the advent of unionism in the steel industry, black workers were pushed to the bottom of the barrel, to the dirtiest and most dangerous jobs in the mills. While black workers continued the fight for equality and justice in the workplace for the next fifty years, racism and discrimination remained to the very end.

By the early 1930s, worker militancy at Homestead rose to the surface again. Strike sentiment swelled, as the economy remained sluggish, wallowing in the effects of the great depression. Thousands of steelworkers languished on unemployment lines, with no government relief. By 1933, there were 280 thousand steelworkers jobless—56 percent of the workforce. The first active protests to spring up after the onset of the Great Depression were organized by the Communist Party USA (CPUSA), demanding relief for the unemployed. On March 26, 1930, the CPUSA organized simultaneous demonstrations in dozens of cities. In Pittsburgh, fifty thousand people turned out, as the CPUSA established "unemployed councils" throughout Allegheny County, including in McKeesport and Homestead. By July 1930, these groups had formed a National Unemployed Council and were the first to raise demands for federal unemployment compensation (UC), exemption from taxes and mortgage payments for the jobless, social security for retirees, and an end to discrimination based on race, religion, or sex when workers were rehired.

With the 1933 election of Franklin Delano Roosevelt, politics in Homestead and the Mon Valley took a radical turn for the better. Frances Perkins, Roosevelt's choice for secretary of labor and the first female cabinet member in the United States, visited Homestead in July 1933, outlining her programs for UC, public works, a minimum wage, pensions, and abolition of child labor. When the Homestead Republican burgess and strongman John Cavanaugh refused permission for her to speak in Frick Park on 10th and Amity Streets, seeing the American flag flying up the street at the post office, she moved there with a large crowd following. She gave a fiery speech befitting the spot where Mother Jones had spoken fourteen years earlier and a lightning bolt tore through the crowd and the town, signaling the major changes to come.

The 1934 elections brought the demands of labor to the fore, as the first Pennsylvania Democratic Party governor in forty-four years and the first Democratic senator in sixty years were elected. Finally, in 1936, the Committee for Industrial Organization (CIO), led by United Mine Workers (UMW) union leader John L. Lewis and his lieutenant, Pittsburgh's Philip Murray, was successful in organizing a steelworkers' union. Homestead played a major part in the organizing drive. It should be noted that open members of the CPUSA—Lester Graham, Patrick Cush, and Richard Lowry—were among the hardest working union organizers at Homestead. Their actions obviously spoke louder than the red-baiting invectives that were undoubtedly being hurled at them.

On July 5, 1936, the Steelworkers Organizing Committee (SWOC), riding Franklin Roosevelt's New Deal wave and the organizing drives in auto, mining, and other industries, staged one of the first of its many demonstrations at Homestead's 17th Street playground. The rally drew more than two thousand people and famously included a reading of the "Working Man's Declaration of Independence" by Charles Scharbo.[1] SWOC's first local union election was held in Homestead on March 26, 1937, at 410 East 8th Avenue (where the refurbished Bost Building, the original headquarters of the AAISW during the 1892 strike, now stands).

Homestead steelworkers continued to play an important role through the newly formed Local 1397 when SWOC evolved into the United Steelworkers of America (USWA) in 1942. The spirit of defiance and militancy hovered like a giant ghost throughout the mill. Following World War II, the local union would strike four times in fourteen years for higher wages and better working conditions and have a lot of influence and say on the shop floor.

In 1959, a major nationwide strike occurred, as U.S. Steel tried to take away the Section 2-B Local Working Conditions provision of the contract.[2] As a griever in the 1980s, I found out just how important this provision was for the workers and their union. In summary, if there was a past practice established either in writing, orally, or in a daily routine, such as a crew size, job description, meal breaks, the number of bathrooms and locker rooms and where they were located, important safety conditions, etc., it was protected under Section 2-B of the contract. The Company could not unilaterally do away with any of these "local working conditions," without demonstrating that their "basis" was eliminated, for example, by new equipment or technological changes. From the Company's perspective, in one way or another, this important section of the contract cost money, and it impeded their absolute authority on the shop floor. They wanted to get rid of it. Their attempt was an utter failure; the union held out for 116 days and maintained the provision in the contract.

By the end of the 1959 strike, the majority of the fifteen thousand employees of Homestead Works had settled in with a decent wage and a relatively good life compared to their pre-union days. But while many Homestead workers continued to resist on the shop floor, their union became complacent, having been run top-down from its inception. Though the USWA founders promised to bring democracy to the mills when the union was formed in 1937, democracy did not seem to be a priority for the local's early leaders following the 1959 strike.

The early USWA officials were only successful in creating a national organization capable of matching the power of the corporations by creating one that was highly centralized. During World War II, union officials became contract enforcers and opponents of wildcat strikes, as they echoed the calls of political leaders for military victory through increased production. This was especially true for steelworker activists in the CPUSA, who were concerned with the survival of the Soviet Union, which, as our ally, took the brunt of the Nazi onslaught from mid-1941 to 1944.

The development of the dues check-off system, which sent union dues directly to union headquarters, and the increasing complexity of collective bargaining caused an expansion of union administration and centralization. Labor leaders increasingly saw contract administration as their main concern, while workers continued to see the shop floor as their main battleground.

Through its first three decades, this lack of union democracy carried down to the local union level. There were always workers, especially the more radical elements, who challenged this setup. These radicals had a different conception of democracy and how a union should be organized and run, but they were far outnumbered by those who favored "labor peace" at any cost. Following World War II, the Taft-Hartley Act was passed in 1947. The act restrained strikes, encouraged management control over all aspects of production, and increased the control of union leaders over their members. Throwing the "baby out with the bathwater," hundreds of the union's most militant and best organizers were labeled "communists," blackballed, ostracized, isolated by the union leadership, and often driven out of the mills and workplaces.

One of the most famous organizers and dedicated activists in the late 1940s and early 1950s and the leader of the 1946 strike at the Homestead mill was Elmer Kish. Elmer and his wife Ruth were open members of the CPUSA. Not only was Elmer well-known and well liked in the mill, they were both very popular and active in numerous community organizations. Following the strike, Elmer was removed from his trustee union position at a local union meeting, when the USWA inserted a clause in its constitution making it illegal for "communists and fellow travelers" to hold any office in the union. Throughout the 1950s, any worker who disagreed with the top-down control by union officials or the tendency to bargain only for bread-and-butter issues could easily be ignored or suffocated with a charge of being "communist," whether they were or not.

Though dissidence and militancy subsided in the 1950s and 1960s, it never entirely died, especially at Homestead. In just one of many examples, a black assistant griever, Al Everett, actively fought discrimination and filed grievances on behalf of African American workers. When he was fired by the Company, black workers poured into a local union meeting demanding his reinstatement. An official complaint was lodged with the International Union executive board but later dropped by the local's white leadership, further incensing black workers, who were already dissatisfied with their lack of representation.

In another example, local union leaders from Homestead and the Monongahela Valley were at the center of the dues protest movement in the mid-1950s, challenging the top leadership's implementation of a dues increase, and then running against them for office.

Black rank-and-file Homestead steelworkers again took the lead in 1974–1975, when they joined in a class action discrimination lawsuit with steelworkers in Alabama to win a major federal Consent Decree, giving blacks, other minorities, and women equal hiring and promotional rights.

While the United States steel industry entered the 1950s as the unchallenged world leader, it left the decade under increasing pressure from foreign competitors, especially Germany and Japan. The International Union had won the union shop and wage increases and benefits, but it experienced continued resistance from the rank and file, especially around the issues of democracy and lack of real representation on the shop floor.

The USWA International and many local officers concentrated on improving relations with management and actively joined their campaign to restrict foreign imports, which began flooding into the U.S. with the 116-day strike in 1959. On March 29, 1973, Company officials and local union presidents agreed to sign an Experimental Negotiating Agreement (ENA), prohibiting nationwide strikes or lockouts. Union members had no say and no vote in the decision. In exchange for giving up their most potent weapon, 350 thousand steelworkers were guaranteed a 3 percent annual wage increase, and a one-time bonus payment of 150 dollars each. Some called this agreement a bribe. I call it the last supper before our execution. Both the Company and union leaders claimed the ENA would drastically reduce foreign imports, which they claimed had eliminated 150 thousand jobs since the 1959 strike. By the time the 1980 contract was signed seven years later, the ENA had been discontinued, having proved to be a complete disaster. Imports continued to flood the domestic steel market. Neither the Company nor the International Union recognized the looming crisis that was about to hit workers like a "slow-motion holocaust."

After the 1959 strike, and especially with the signing of the ENA, many local union officials became complacent, including successive administrations at Homestead. Instead of fighting for the workers, they spent more time feathering their own nests and doing the bidding of the Company by keeping the workers down and subservient. This is clearly borne out by the number of grievances filed by rank-and-file Homestead workers in the mill from 1958 through the mid-1970s that reached the third step of the grievance procedure versus the number appealed to arbitration by International Union officials.[3] This was the labor relations reality I encountered when I arrived at the Homestead mill.

CHAPTER 5

ORIGINS OF THE LOCAL 1397 RANK AND FILE CAUCUS—UNION DEMOCRACY COMES ALIVE

After I was hired at Homestead, having learned from a previous union experience, I lay low during my probation period, which lasted several months. While initially unaware, in a matter of weeks I realized I'd landed smack dab in the middle of a militant rank-and-file steelworker union rebellion, one poised to take control of the local union in a year. After attending my first union meeting, it was apparent there was a radical element in the local union completely dissatisfied with the current administration.

As I went into work through the Amity Gate one day in early 1978, there was a table set up in front of the Gateway Restaurant with newspapers scattered on it. A group of workers were getting petitions signed, demanding the right for steelworkers to vote on their contracts. These guys included John Balint and Brian "Red" Durkin from Open Hearth no. 5 (OH5),[1] as well as Joe Stanton, a motor inspector in the 100" Maintenance Department where I worked. As the 100" Plate Mill was at the extreme west end of the mill complex, this was my first contact with the 1397 Rank and File Caucus, which at that time was based in the Central Maintenance Department two miles upriver. After I signed the petition, Joe asked me to get involved and said he'd tell me more about the group when we got together at work. An invitation was all I needed. Their demands for greater union democracy, along with their energy and enthusiasm, were infectious. As a longtime activist, organizer, and born rabble-rouser, the insurgency movement they were part

Demonstrations at the Amity Street Gate entrance to the mill were a common occurrence in the late 1970s. (Joe Stanton is on my far left, with Joe Szuch, 100" motor inspector, on my right).

of was like a high-powered magnet that drew me in. Wow—a job for life *and* a hotbed of union militants—I thought I hit the double jackpot lottery that day!

Becoming a Political Activist

It wasn't my Kentucky home but my stay in New York City that introduced me to political activism and the value of militant unionism. One bright sunny day in late July 1968, wanting to explore Times Square, I got off the 7th Avenue IRT Subway at 42nd and Broadway and found myself in the middle of tens of thousands of anti-war protesters. Having just smoked a joint, I was swept up in the exuberance of the crowd and the wild spirit of protest. This is where I heard Phil Ochs for the first time, singing *I Ain't Marchin' Anymore*, and then heard folk singer and activist Barbara Dane, who was selling tickets to the Democratic National Convention that would take place in Chicago the following month. After marching with thousands to an armory at 34th Street and Park Avenue and getting kicked by a police horse, I bought a bus ticket for Chicago that set the spark to the fires of radical politics that are still burning inside me. Witnessing what a congressional committee later termed a "police riot" in Grant Park and watching hundreds of demonstrators get the shit beat out of them with night sticks, I was ready to join the counterculture anti-war resistance. In a short period of time, I went from Catholic to hippie to yippie to revolutionary.[2]

For six years, I honed my skills as an organizer, public speaker, political singer, and all-round rabble-rouser. From 1970–1975, I worked with a group called the Indochina Solidarity Committee (ISC). This organization did not accept the official version of the war, that it was a battle between communism and free enterprise capitalism but, instead, believed the Vietnamese were fighting for the liberation of their country from outsiders in a war of independence similar to ours in 1776. During this time, I also met and got involved with Vietnam Veterans Against the War (VVAW), a group of mostly working-class veterans that gave me an inside look at a dirty, unjust war. In the anti-war circles I ran in, if anyone would have spit on a veteran or blamed them for the war, we'd have been right up in their face spitting and kicking back. These veterans taught me the defining and lifelong delineation I still adhere to: "You can love the warrior but hate the war." I learned to separate the soldiers sent to fight the dirty wars (usually out of a patriotic desire to defend their country) from the instigators and orchestrators of war—Wall Street empire zealots who think we have the right to rule the world, and the military-industrial complex profiteers making millions off the death and destruction.

Through these two organizations and voracious reading, I learned what our government and military were doing with our tax money in Southeast Asia and around the world, and it wasn't promoting freedom and democracy or fighting "communism." For the most part, it was interfering in other country's affairs, overthrowing governments, plundering resources, and preserving and extending the U.S. corporate empire. After reading several books by the Australian journalist Wilfred Burchett, who had been embedded with the resistance fighters in Vietnam, I came to see the "Viet Cong" and "gooks" as human beings fighting for their country's independence. The release of the Pentagon Papers in 1971 merely confirmed what I had already learned: the American military could not win the war. In addition to the anti-war and youth movements, after reading *The Autobiography of Malcolm X* when I was nineteen,[3] I began to understand the racism I was force-fed and grew up with as a youngster, which seemed to be just as prevalent up North as down South. I began to understand the need for the Black Panther Party and helped raise funds for its 21 New York members who had been framed and unjustly imprisoned (charges were subsequently dropped against all of them).[4] At the time, the Panthers were number one on J. Edgar Hoover's COINTELPRO hit list.[5] By the time I turned twenty-one, my whole worldview had been turned upside down.

During my short stay in San Francisco for several months in 1969, I applied for and landed a job with the Post Office (about the only place that would hire "long hairs" at the time.) My introduction to unions and the labor movement occurred when I transferred in December 1969 to the Grand Central Station Post Office facility in New York City. With more than five thousand workers of every age and nationality, and the recent hiring of hundreds of young blacks, women, and long-haired counterculture types like myself, Grand Central Post Office was a city within a city. I saw arrests almost daily, and you could buy any illegal drug there, usually in the bathroom. With a photographic memory for numbers and memorizing zip codes, I rapidly advanced in the clerk ranks. Working a 2:00 p.m. to 10:30 p.m. shift sorting mail was monotonous and ruined your whole day. By the time you woke up and ate something, it was time to head to work. By the time you got off work, everyone else had plans for the night or was already home in bed. When I started there, the wages were poverty-level, working conditions horrendous, and the workforce disgruntled. There was no grievance system, no benefits, and no collective bargaining rights. I was making $2.95 an hour.

In March 1970, the local union centered in the Bronx called a walkout that exploded into an illegal national wildcat strike. Grand Central workers led the walkout. After the Nixon administration's futile and failed attempt to get twenty-two thousand National Guard troops to sort and deliver the mail, the strike was settled, with wages substantially raised and better benefits. The Vietnam War and expanding invasions into Cambodia and Laos had become a ball and chain around Nixon's neck. He was in no position to alienate the U.S. working class any further, so he caved in to most union demands. Fearful of our militancy at the Grand Central Post Office, management dispersed dozens of us to other locations. I ended up at the Rockefeller Center Post Office, where I worked through the summer of 1970. After the shootings at Kent State on May 4 of that year, I was in full rebellion.

After leaving the Post Office, I got a job at a picture framing factory on Greene Street in the SoHo (south of Houston Street) district below Greenwich Village. We framed art for all the big museums and shows uptown. I started out on a big saw cutting wooden and metal frames to size, ending up as a matte cutter, which was a real art. I was the only white English-speaking person of more than a hundred workers, many lacking green cards. On at least one occasion, the Immigration Naturalization Service (INS) did a surprise raid, scattering workers in all directions.

One day a sharp-dressed man in a dark suit, along with the three picture frame factory owners, called all the workers to the center of the shop and announced, "You're all in the Teamsters Union." When I raised my hand and asked, "So what's this all about?" the Teamster official told my boss, "Al, he's your shop steward; we like a guy that opens his mouth." Afterwards, I was told the Teamsters had alerted the owners that if they didn't sign us up, no supplies would be moving in or out of the factory. Sometimes I think that those "good old days" were better than what we have now, with many unions seemingly totally powerless!

Later, I again landed in the Teamsters—and got another taste of undemocratic unionism—after moving to Louisville to help organize the unemployed. I worked for a short stint at the American Standard Plant on 7th Street. This plant produced bathtubs and brass fixtures. With a huge foundry, cleaning house (where the sand was blasted off the hot molten iron), and enamel shop, the work was dirty, hot, and dangerous. Hundreds of workers contracted silicosis from the sand and unsafe chemicals they absorbed all around them. I started out as a janitor but quickly bid on and got a position as a utility equipment driver.

Management tried to illegally fire me on the last day of my probation period, not realizing I had already worked for two weeks in another department. I filed a grievance with a union official from one of the craft unions (there were thirteen different unions in this one plant) and kept my job. Needless to say, I was pegged as a "radical" and relegated to the worst outdoor forklift and bulldozer jobs on the graveyard shift, sloshing around in either the heat, cold, rain, snow, or mud, depending on the time of year. When our union shop steward quit and I was elected unanimously as the new shop steward for the janitors and drivers by a vote of 16–0, the Teamsters completely ignored our election and appointed someone they wanted in the position, claiming our election was illegal, because it wasn't held at the union hall. When we asked for a date to rent the union hall, they said it was "booked for the indefinite future." Apparently, democracy was on vacation in Local 89 at that time. (More than forty years later, my stepson would become a shop steward with Local 89 at the UPS airport hub in Louisville; in a complete reversal, Local 89 became one of the most militant rank-and-file UPS locals in the country.)

CHAPTER 6

LOCAL UNION DEMOCRACY AT HOMESTEAD

What were the conditions at the Homestead mill that gave rise to a local union insurgency?

After the settlement of the 1959 strike, the steel industry in the U.S. began to steadily decline. Profits were shrinking and foreign imports increased substantially. New nonunion mini-mills were penetrating the domestic market for the first time.[1] Foreign mills, especially in places like Japan, Korea, and Germany, utilized the latest technology, including basic oxygen and electric furnaces, as well as continuous casters, which greatly reduced the cost of producing quality steel by cutting out entire steps in the steelmaking process. At the same time, U.S. Steel refused to modernize or upgrade their equipment and mills. At the only new mill they built after World War II, the Fairless Works in Eastern Pennsylvania, in 1956, they installed outmoded openhearth furnaces. No new equipment or technology was introduced at the Homestead mill during the 1960s and 1970s. When something broke, workers were told to just "patch it up" and get it back in operation. Management would literally cannibalize other mills for spare parts, instead of spending money on new ones. Nobody told it better than Central Maintenance welder Ed Salaj:

> You'd have a broken shaft and you'd weld it, then weld it a second, third, fourth and fifth time. We did this routinely. They didn't buy a lot of good spare parts. I saw shafts run without bearings or grease. They just kept them going and let the next turn worry about them.

I did a lot of buildup work, like putting teeth on gears that had worn away. You sat there for hours building up little pads of weld higher and higher till you formed a tooth. It wasn't a real tooth; it was just a pile of weld, and it met the next pile of weld in the tooth, tooth touching tooth, until the shaft rotated and allowed the table roll to move. I did much of that, on top of cranes, in gag presses, in mill sections—things that should not have been done, but we did them. As things got worse, nobody could get money. If you needed something bad, you stole it from different parts of the mill.[2]

Multiply Ed's experience by those of all the other craftsmen and maintenance workers in the mill, and you begin to understand what we were up against. When I arrived in the mid- to late 1970s, major and minor accidents and injuries inside the mill seemed to happen almost weekly.

In addition, the safety program enacted by the Company was a complete joke, a disguised disciplinary procedure that was constantly used to harass workers. When the Occupational Safety and Health Act (OSHA) was passed in 1973, the Company was forced to take safety on the job a bit more seriously. However, foremen would use real or very often imagined safety violations to write up—give disciplinary slips to—workers who had gotten on their wrong side. With the second or

1397 Rank and File newspaper, April 1978.

third slip, you were suspended without pay. Each foreman was given a quota of so many slips a week (I was told by a foreman that it was three). If a foreman didn't like you, you could be up to a four-day slip—a four-day suspension—in no time, waiting to get fired with the next infraction. I personally witnessed an assistant general foreman in the 100" Maintenance Mill office ask a millwright if he could give him a slip to make his quota. The whole system made a mockery of safety on the job.

Labor management relations on the shop floor were archaic, with every department resembling feudal fiefdoms. Workers were treated and talked to like serfs, with the foremen being the overseers, general foremen the barons, and superintendents the overlords. While workers received decent wages and benefits, working conditions on the shop floor were horrible. Basic democratic and human rights were nonexistent inside the mill. As management became lackadaisical and complacent, so did the union, including the local union officers and grievers at Homestead.

Portrait of a Grievanceman

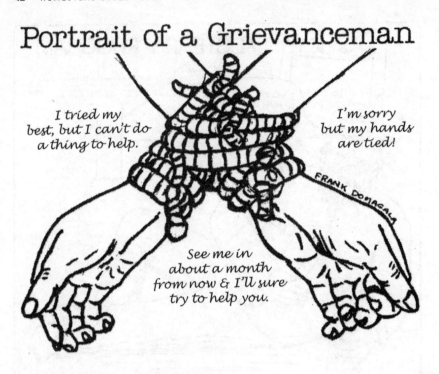

1397 *Rank and File* newspaper, August 1978.

While workers filed hundreds of grievances and complaints, mainly around local working conditions and management's archaic disciplinary program, most grievances would make it to third step into the hands of the grievance chair, and then would just disappear. By the mid-1970s, many grievances were also dropped at the first and second steps. In some departments, grievers and their assistants refused to even file grievances. Most employees basically had no real representation. When I attempted to file my first grievance in 1978, after being given a disciplinary slip for an alleged safety violation (I took my goggles off for a few minutes to clean them), my grievance representative, who they called "Scotty," looked at the slip, handed it back to me and said, "If I was you, I'd keep my mouth shut and mind my own business," and walked away.

For all you non–steel union laypeople out there, I should explain the archaic grievance procedure that evolved under various labor agreements between U.S. Steel and the United Steelworkers of America (USWA) and how I experienced it at Homestead:

First step: this was handled by the assistant union griever (appointed by and beholden to the elected zone griever) and mill foreman who issued the infraction or discipline—kind of like letting a perpetrator be his own judge.

Second step: handled by the elected union zone griever and the Company general foreman (who was usually the one who had ordered the foreman to issue the reprimand or discipline in the first place). Every zone (or division) also had its own labor contract administrator (LCA), i.e., lawyer, who advised management on all contractual or grievance matters.

Third step: handled by the plant superintendent and grievance chair, who recommended arbitration, a settlement, or the withdrawal of the complaint. The worker who filed the grievance and his grievance representative were not usually present by this stage. A plant-wide LCA would usually advise management on the merits of the grievance and decide whether or not to settle or let the case go to the next step.

Fourth step: if appealed by the grievance chair, the grievance was reviewed by a union staff representative working out of the District Union office and a Company lawyer from corporate headquarters in downtown Pittsburgh. Again, neither the grievant nor his or her grievance representative were present. By this stage, both the union and Company representatives were more often than not completely divorced from the case.

Fifth step: arbitration/court. The same union staff representative and Company lawyer who reviewed the case at the fourth step present the case before an "arbitrator." The board of arbitration is a group of judges selected and paid for by the Company and union, fifty-fifty.[3]

To say the least, the system was cumbersome and repetitive; it took months, sometimes years, to get a case through the procedure. The Company strategy was to discourage the union from pursuing the grievance at the early steps. If that wasn't successful, the Company would stretch it out for so long that evidence would be lost, witnesses scared off, or the grievant would simply give up. When I arrived on the scene at Homestead, the Company was winning four out of five cases that made it to arbitration. The Company had access to paperwork

1397 Rank and File newspaper, Special Contract issue, 1977.

and paid management witnesses, not to mention going up against a union staff representative who usually didn't know the grievant(s). The grievance procedure seemed clearly stacked in the Company's favor. The outdated structure and lack of any real protection in the grievance procedure became a major bone of contention for rank-and-file workers at Homestead.

While I can't directly speak for the experiences of steelworkers at other U.S. Steel facilities and elsewhere, at Homestead steelworkers were complaining about the grievance procedure from my first day in the mill, especially the new steelworkers entering the workforce, who were not prone to acquiescence. During the mid- to late 1970s, more than a thousand workers were hired at the Homestead Works, and thanks to the Consent Decree of 1974, U.S. Steel was forced to hire more women, African Americans, and other minorities. As I said in an interview with Brett Reigh:

> These 70s hires were a lot more open to change, more open to militancy, and more prone to not take shit off of anybody. Many were veterans of the Vietnam War, or had participated in the

social movements and political struggles of the 1960s. This new breed of steelworker was not afraid to speak up against bosses who they felt were not treating them fairly, or to question union procedures that seemed to them undemocratic. When combined with the older generation of steelworkers who had their roots in the organizing drives of the 1930s and the strikes of the 1940s and 1950s, the combination proved to be a powerful one.[4]

In 1976, Ed Sadlowski, USWA director of District 31 in Chicago, became the champion of a new coalition of reform-minded steelworkers by announcing he would be running for the presidency of the USWA International in the 1977 election. Running as a reform candidate, he promised to give power back to the rank-and-file steelworker by reinstating the right to strike in the contract, giving the membership the right to ratify their own contract, and a multitude of other reforms, including revamping the grievance procedure. When he lost the election to Lloyd McBride in February 1977, the union reform movement at the international level petered out. However, it did inspire many local union activists to organize rank-and-file movements of their own.

CHAPTER 7

BIRTH OF THE *1397 RANK AND FILE* NEWSPAPER

The 1397 Rank and File Caucus was started by three employees at Homestead: Ron Weisen, a welder, John Ingersoll, a rigger—both out of the Central Maintenance Department, and a woman, Michele McMills, who was a motor inspector apprentice in the Forge Division. The unique and complementary combination of these three was the kindling that provided the fuel that lit the fires of insurgency at Homestead.

Ron Weisen was a former Golden Gloves boxing champion, barroom brawler, and local tough guy. Born and raised in Homestead, by 1958, he was an amateur Golden Gloves champion of Pennsylvania. He looked like a fighter: short, stocky, muscular, with a pug nose, and curly black hair. His early boxing style was indicative of his approach to life, and certainly his approach to his union job later on:

> He did not dance around the ring, jabbing at his opponent; that was for sissies he thought. He bored in. He could hit and take a punch, but he never developed the discipline to stay with his plan for a match. He never was knocked out, but when his opponent started hitting him he would often fly into a rage and begin punching as hard and furiously as he could, and continue until he was exhausted.[1]

In his younger days, Ron and his brother Jake were known to go bar to bar in town looking for anyone to fight. They especially liked to go to black bars—in a way a tribute to the toughness of black steelworkers. Some years later, I was talking to Ed "King" Hamlin, an African

American steelworker and native Homesteader who was elected as a local union trustee on the rank-and-file ticket in 1982. I asked Ed, "So how do you know Ronnie, and how come he likes you so much?" Ed responded, "Because whenever we fought in a bar, we both were still standing at the end." For the average Joe out there, Ronnie was no one to mess with.

"King" Hamlin (left) with 100" mill lampman, Jim "Cuts" Cannon (right) and me at the 1397 Union Hall, 1982.

Instead of going pro, Ron married a beautiful Homestead girl, Jean Stevens, and entered the mill the summer after finishing high school. By the late 1970s, he already had over twenty years in the mill. His father before him had forty-three years in the mill. His attitude in the mill was the same as in the ring: he didn't take shit from anybody. If a boss suspended him and took money out of his pocket, the boss's car was key-scraped or sugar was put in his gas tank—and that's if he was lucky. An "eye for an eye" to this guy was putting it lightly. When he filed a grievance in early 1976 and got screwed by his union grievance representative, he decided to run for griever himself. Though he lost by only nine votes, his baptism into local union politics was a done deal. In a short time, he would become the epicenter of the rank-and-file insurgency at Homestead and eventually nationwide.

John Ingersoll traveled a different path to the Homestead Works. He was born and raised in McKeesport, ten miles up the Monongahela River from Homestead. As far back as high school he worked in U.S. Steel's National Tube Works in McKeesport on weekends and during the summer. After enlisting in the army for three years right out of high school, he attended Slippery Rock University for three years, eventually earning his teaching degree at the University of Pittsburgh. Back in the mill at National Tube in 1951, he entered the riggers apprentice program and eventually became a certified craftsman. The job of rigger was to construct any new buildings, to reline blast furnaces, and to handle overall building structure repairs.

In 1966, he transferred to the Homestead mill and was in charge of setting up training programs for riggers, boilermakers, and other crafts at the mill. Before being transferred from the National Tube mill in McKeesport, where he had sixteen years of service, he was involved with the union as a grievance representative. He was an avid reader and knew the contract inside and out. Fellow rigger George Tallon described him as "one of the most enjoyable and outgoing people you'd ever want to meet." What I liked most about John back in the early days, when I first met him, was the fact that not only did he use his brain and think things through, he was able to put it in mill jargon that was easy to understand. Plus, he had a wry sense of humor, which seemed to be a staple of every work gang in the mill. For example, management or union officials who did stupid things were called "yum-yums." In many ways he provided both a complement and a contrast to Weisen's shoot from the hip, brash, tough-guy persona: he was mild mannered and soft-spoken, a meticulous organizer with a college degree. As he described his first encounter with Weisen:

> I'm working on this job and all at once this guy comes up to me and he says, "Hey, are you John Ingersoll?" I says, "Yeah," and he says, "Well, I'm Ronnie Weisen," and he says, "I'm gonna run for grievanceman." He said, "I heard all the guys like you and you were a grievanceman over at National Tube," which I was, and he says, "Would you be my assistant?" I says, "Yeah, I'll be your assistant, I'll help you," because I liked him, he was a good guy.[2]

Michele McMills was the actual initiator of the plant-wide caucus idea. She was considered the chief strategist and communications whiz of the trio. By far the youngest of the three, only twenty-four years old in 1976 (Weisen and Ingersoll were in their forties), she had entered the mill straight out of college in 1973. After graduation from Upper Saint Clair High School, just south of Pittsburgh, she received her degree from Denison University and began law school at the University of Pittsburgh. With a father in the corporate boardrooms downtown, in 1973, she got a summer job at Homestead in the labor gang. She liked it so much she decided to stay. She was the first female maintenance craft apprentice at Homestead. With journalist and activist skills honed in college, she was the originator of the 1397 *Rank and File* newspaper

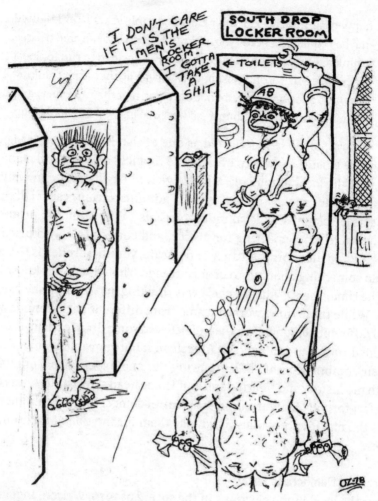

1397 Rank and File newspaper, January 1980.

idea. Her transition from mill worker to union activist is best told in
her own words:

> I loved the mill. I loved the mill as a job. I mean it was just huge
> and wonderful, and I just had to be a part of it. But I had to walk
> three miles to the ladies' room from my workplace, and it got to
> be a drag. So I went to the union to see if I couldn't get some-
> thing done about it. But they weren't really interested in fighting
> my case, so I started going to union meetings to see what was

happening, and, heck, I don't know, a couple years later I figured maybe I could do a better job, so I ran for and I got elected trustee. I think it was at the union meeting when I decided to run for local office that I met Ron Weisen, and he was at that time thinking of running for grievanceman. So we got together and met, and Ingersoll worked with Ronnie, so we three just kind of hooked up.

In 1976, Michele was elected as one of the three trustees at Local 1397. The trustee job was to oversee the finances and physical management of the local union hall. Michele viewed firsthand the incredible waste of dues money by the current administration, especially the "lost time" claimed by local union officials.[3] When you are prone to activism, have a hankering for justice, and come into a workplace so archaic and dictatorial, so dirty and unsafe, your first reflex is to want to do something about it, to change things. Though I didn't know her at the time, I sense what Michele was thinking and feeling: she cared!

While these three workers came from different backgrounds and had different personalities, they all believed some drastic changes were needed in the union and the American labor movement in general. Their combination of skills, upbringing, and experience, combined with the history and fighting spirit of Homestead steelworkers, was the perfect formula for igniting an outbreak of democracy and militancy; it was the magic carpet that would take them for the ride of their union lives.

Forging a Democratic Local

After the local union elections in the spring of 1976, Weisen, Ingersoll, and McMills decided to run to represent Local 1397 as delegates at the August 1976 United Steelworkers of America (USWA) constitutional convention in Las Vegas, Nevada. International conventions were held every two years, theoretically at least, to provide the membership of the USWA with a chance to come together to propose resolutions concerning union policy, as well as to discuss upcoming labor contracts. In reality, most all decisions were made by the International executive board (made up of the five top officers and the district directors) at their meeting just before the convention gathering. For the most part, convention delegates merely rubber-stamped these decisions. While I don't know how conventions are conducted of late, back in the 1970s and 1980s when I was in the union, I witnessed first-hand that the convention process itself was hardly democratic. Hundreds of small locals could not afford to send delegates, so their staff representative (whose job was beholden to the district director) carried their credentials to the convention. Some staff representatives could carry the votes for as many as ten or fifteen locals. They voted the way the district director told them to, because their jobs depended on it.

While locals were allowed to

1397 Rank and File newspaper, August 1980.

draw up and submit resolutions to be discussed and voted on at conventions, many were ferreted out by the time the delegates arrived or had been squashed at the executive committee meeting. There were always comment periods when resolutions were introduced at conventions. But if they didn't like you or thought you were a dissident or a radical or were in opposition to whatever it was they were proposing, they simply cut off your mic when it was your turn to speak. The International president would then direct you to another mic—which by that time had fourteen or fifteen staff lined up at it to speak. As an elected delegate, I was an eyewitness to this over and over again at the 1982 and 1984 conventions. On several occasions, by the time Ron Weisen got to the mic, he was speaking to an empty room, as everyone had filed out for lunch or dinner. This didn't fit my definition of democracy.

Conventions were usually held in cities where there were numerous entertainment opportunities for the delegates, such as Las Vegas or Atlantic City. This was because these cities had enough hotels that were unionized. Steelworker delegates had always been notorious for drinking, gambling, and partying at conventions, and who wouldn't in such a setting. Back in the mills and locker rooms, ordinary workers really resented what they considered a waste of their union dues and hard-earned money. Having a convention every two years seemed an even bigger waste of money. (This policy was later changed to holding conventions every three years after our local was long gone.) Unlike most workers or union people, my experience with international steel-worker conventions was many-sided: three times as an elected local union delegate at Local 1397, as a small business (Steel Valley Printers) that printed convention material for over a decade, and as an entertainer; my band performed at the 1998 and 2000 conventions in Las Vegas. I took part in and can attest to the waste of dues-payers' money. I've seen it from both the inside and the outside. I'm not saying there don't need to be conventions and international gatherings; they obviously are important and necessary. I'm saying they need to be more streamlined, serious, and democratic. Convention proceedings need to be more directly connected with the average rank-and-file worker; they need to go beyond empty speeches by politicians and economists to something where delegates can plan, strategize, and discuss actual shop floor problems. While I was associated with the union, convention reports and resolutions were printed in a thick book never seen by most shop floor workers. Conventions should be occasions to share experiences, for workers from different areas to learn from each other, occasions for action planning and discussion about *how to more involve the members*.

The slate of the 1397 Rank and File Caucus for the 1976 USWA convention included Ingersoll, McMills, Weisen, and Elmer Shaffo, a welder coworker of Weisen's. They pledged to concentrate on business and bring back their own convention report. Besides the Rank and File Caucus Slate, ten other members of Local 1397 from the current regime were elected to join them in Las Vegas. For every five hundred members of a local union, one delegate could be elected to the convention. At that time, Homestead employed around seven thousand people, so fourteen delegates attended the convention, with the Rank and File Caucus representing almost one-third of the group. In a few short months, its influence would increase dramatically.

While at the 1976 USWA convention, the Rank and File Caucus slate remained serious. As McMills said, "I'm not going to Las Vegas for fun and sun. I'm going to see how this union is run."[4] They campaigned against any dues increase and supported the right for the membership to vote on their contract. Under the setup at the time, only local union presidents in Basic Steel voted on contracts; the rank-and-file steelworker had no direct say. For the 1397 Rank and File Caucus delegates, this was a glaring example of the lack of democracy that permeated the union.

While in Las Vegas, the 1397 Rank and File Caucus met another group of insurgents, Steelworkers Fight Back. Led by Edward Sadlowski, these insurgents were fighting for the same causes at the International level. As mentioned previously, Sadlowski ran for International president in the 1977 election. The rank and filers from Local 1397 were very impressed by the Chicagoan. They attended all his rallies and pledged their support to his campaign. When they arrived back home, McMills dove into the campaign, becoming the face of Local 1397 at the Sadlowski headquarters for the three USWA Districts in the Pittsburgh region on 8th Avenue in Homestead. She also kept her promise to the members of Local 1397 by publishing an eight-page convention report, the precursor to the *1397 Rank and File* newspaper. The report urged the members of Local 1397 to vote for Sadlowski in the upcoming nomination election on February 8, 1977, stating: "Vote for a change—you might not get another chance." If elected, Sadlowski even promised to take his oath of office in Homestead on June 1, 1977.[5]

Despite all of their efforts, including winning at Homestead and many Basic Steel locals, Sadlowski was defeated by Lloyd McBride for the presidency of the USWA by a vote of 328,861 to 249,281. McBride was the International's hand-picked candidate, chosen by the sitting president I.W. Abel. After the election, Steelworkers Fight Back eventually dissolved, and Sadlowski withdrew from the national labor scene.[6] For the insurgents at Local 1397, the fight was only just beginning.

Birth of the *1397 Rank and File* Newspaper

The "Convention Report" issue of the *1397 Rank and File* newspaper was received favorably by the millworkers.[7] Michele McMills then published the first issue of the *1397 Rank and File* newspaper, a "Special Election" issue, just before the Sadlowski election.[8] The newspaper gained national attention for its no-holds-barred comments on life inside and outside the Homestead Steelworks. Formatted and edited by McMills, it included articles concerning upcoming elections, plant conditions, the lack of union representation, and many other issues related to the Homestead Works and the steel industry. *National Lampoon*–like cartoons were a staple from the beginning. The first installment of

"Plant Plague," which would become the centerpiece of the paper, was also in this first edition. Written by Ron Weisen and edited by McMills, it pulled no punches when dealing with mismanagement or harassment in the mill. Weisen was well-known and very popular in the mill. As a welder out of Central Maintenance, he had to travel throughout the plant to perform his various welding jobs. While on the job or in the bar after work, fellow workers would come up to him and tell him about a foreman who was "jacking them off" or harassing them. Weisen would collect these complaints and "whenever Ronnie had enough stuff, we'd put out a paper." The "Plant Plague" named names and publicly ridiculed any boss guilty of aggravating workers or violating their rights. The goal of the "Plant Plague" section was to allow any worker who had a complaint or grievance to air it in the paper for all to see. In a mill nearly four miles long with four major entrances (including Carrie Furnace across the river in Rankin), the paper would serve to both inform and unite workers who otherwise would never see or know each other. It was democracy in action. As fellow worker, George Tallon said, commenting about the "Plant Plague" section:

> Every foreman or superintendent is at the mercy of this column. No boss is safe. He [Ronnie] gathers information throughout the mill and is absolutely fearless in printing it. This is an image that anybody can readily identify with—especially those who feel powerless and under the thumb of a domineering boss. Ronnie is what a lot of men would like to be. They admire his style and trust him. They feel he understands their problems and frustrations. This image of strength is woven into the fabric of the rank-and-file movement at Homestead.[9]

One of the unique aspects of the *1397 Rank and File* newspaper was the style of the writing. Most union-related publications were dull and boring, with the same committee reports, financial updates, and rah-rah news stories from the International appearing month after month. The problems the average worker was confronted within the mill were never addressed. The *1397 Rank and File* newspaper was written in millworker prose, with all its Pittsburghese jargon—e.g., "jackoffs" were transformed into "jagoffs." It was anything but boring. There were cartoons lambasting foremen and managers, with four different worker artists from the mill serving as cartoonists. Three of the

1397 RANK & FILE

P.O. BOX 417, HOMESTEAD PA. 15120   INTERNATIONAL ELECTION   "SPECIAL EDITION"

FEB. 77

Statement of Purpose

This paper is dedicated to members who can't find their grievance men, who can't be heard at union meetings because they are "out of order," who have things to say about local mill conditions, union activities or just plain old "mill talk." This paper is for all of us – the rank and file of 1397. We hope you think of this paper as <u>yours</u>.

If we want safe and secure jobs, we need rank and file involvement in our union. We know what our gripes are – let's share them. We can teach each other what our rights are and how to fight for them. We ask that you join us to build a strong and democratic union that represents all of us and not just a few.

Our next meeting will be at Steelworkers Fight Back Headquarters, 119 E. 8th Ave. (461-1700) at 7:00 PM on Thursday, February 3. Everyone is welcome to help prepare for the election.

By this newspaper is financed exclusively by the sale of $1 raffle tickets for a 25" RCA Color Console TV (or $500) to be drawn on March 1. If you would like to buy or sell some tickets, they are available from Ron Weisen or John Ingersoll (644-9255).

Editors and contributors for this newspaper include:

Ray Gerst Jr.	John Pressley
Elmer DelleDonne	Ed Schutzman
John Ingersoll	Bill Shirk
Michele McMills	Ron Weisen

Special thanks to Alvin Paisley for his art work and to all the people buying raffle tickets and distributing the papers.

If you would like to contribute ideas,

"HARASSMENT" PLANT PLAGUE

Harassment and ridicule, this is what we receive when we are seen by the so-called doctors at our plant hospital. How long do we have to endure their type of treatment!

It's hard to understand how they established a practice outside the plant (if they have one). Their qualifications are questionable when they repeatedly give the wrong diagnosis.

Clairton Works dismissed a certain doctor and we had the misfortune of acquiring him. This doctor has a habit of calling people "obese" yet he is over 250 pounds himself.

Recently he was seen throughout the plant checking on an employee who just returned to work after a disabling injury. The doctor was checking to see if the man could do his job "properly".

This is an example of just a few of the many incidents that continue to plague us! Our union and management know this persecution is going on, but they continue to drag their feet concerning this harassment.

by Ron Weisen

"Some wise guy for his unsafe condition report, wrote—the whole plant."

Union Newspaper Fails to Report Sadlowski Victory

Maybe it wasn't important to the <u>Sentinel</u> Journal Agent Andy Poklemba,

Contracting Out

In November of 1976 we had Iron Workers doing work in Homestead Works that our people normally can perform.

---

worker cartoonists, Al Paisley, Rick Kornish, and Norm Ostoff, stayed on until the very end, even after being laid off. R.J. Gibson and Ray Gerst Jr. out of the weld shop, Bill Shirk, and rigger George Tallon were among the earliest and most prolific writers and supporters. Articles sometimes used "colorful" language to get the point across. Their submitters were told that as long as their accusations could be backed up by witnesses, anything could be said, especially in the context of satire and comedy. Workers were also invited to submit their own articles, as well as poems and songs, of which there were many. In short, the paper both entertained and informed. As welder Ed Salaj, the incentive chair on the plant union committee, said, "It [the newspaper] was funny, and the men were willing to read it, and it wasn't so damn serious or dogmatic; they liked that. Everybody did."[10] By the time later editions came out, rumor had it that some management personnel would pay five or ten dollars for a copy. Another rumor had it that any foreman or superintendent who made the paper often enough would get a promotion and hefty raise.

The "Special Contract" issue of the paper included a "Statement of Purpose" that explained what the newspaper and the 1397 Rank and File Caucus movement were all about:

The first demonstration organized by the Rank and File Caucus, 1976.

1397 Rank and File is dedicated to members who can't find their grievanceman, who can't be heard at union meetings because they are out of order, who have things to say about local mill conditions, union activities or just shop talk. This paper is for all of us—the rank and file of 1397. We hope you think of this paper as yours. If we want safe and secure jobs, we need rank-and-file involvement in our Union. We know what our gripes are—let's share them. We can teach each other what our rights are and how to fight for them. We ask that you join us to build a strong and democratic union that represents all of us and not just a few.

We all feel that we are taken advantage of every day with harassment, intimidation and contract violations. We feel that conditions of health and safety, incentives, forced overtime, job infringements and others are lousy and need to be changed. Our local leadership does not tell us what is really going on. Too often all they have to say is "We'll look into it." 1397 Rank and File does not believe in secrets.

We have to build a communication network so that we all know what is really coming down in every area of the plant, to find out what the Company is doing, to find out what the Union is doing, and to find out what other people are doing. We have to organize and really stick together. It takes a long time to build unity and active involvement among groups of people and we see 1397 Rank and File as a first step.[11]

City Farm Lane mill entrance.

Structural, 48" mill entrance.

Amity Street mill entrance.

As noted earlier, the Homestead mill was nearly four miles long, with four major entrances. Workers going through one entrance could go a lifetime without meeting or knowing the workers going through another entrance. McMills had surmised that only a plant-wide newspaper could put these workers in touch with each other. The newspaper was a giant success, serving as a catalyst that ignited the insurgency at Homestead. In subsequent issues, the paper would step up its attacks on the local union administration, with its policies of excessive "lost time" and its ineffective use of the grievance procedure. It would expose poor plant working conditions and excessive management waste. It would give voice to democracy and birth to a powerful workers' movement in the mill.

Elmer DelleDonne and Michele McMills preparing food at a beer blast, 1978.

There were 1,500 copies printed for each of the first two issues. By the September 1977 edition, the newspaper had grown to eight pages and 3,000 copies. Within a few months, dozens flocked to support the 1397 Rank and File Caucus, as it began meeting regularly in the back rooms of local watering holes.

One of the earliest activists was Elmer DelleDonne, a progressive Italian with more than thirty years in the mill and Michele's closest friend and advisor. Elmer was a rank-and-file thinker who bridged the generation gap between the older steelworkers in the mill and the new rebellious younger generation. No doubt much of Michele's strategy and many of her ideas were developed with Elmer. I loved Elmer, and I miss him deeply. He died on February 8, 2018, at the ripe old age of ninety-eight. Workers like him were truly among the many unknown "heroes of history" whom I memorialized in song a decade later:

Heroes of History
Here's to all the people who do all the work and never get recognized.
You never grab any headlines; your name is never memorized.
I'll remember you, put you in my heart, keep you close to me.
I'll sing this song for you, tell the world the part that you played in
our history.

Here's to all the thinkers, whose thoughts we get from someone else,
The ghost-writers and singers, whose songs are sung for somebody
else's wealth.
Though you're behind the scenes, faceless in the dark, lost inside
insanity,
I'll use every means to show the world the mark that you made in our
history.

Here's to all the people who stand up and fight for what is right.
In the face of fear and intimidation, shine like a beacon light.
I'll drink a toast to you; celebrate the love and life you gave to me.
I'll brag the boast for you and tell the stories of the heroes of our
   history.

Along with new supporters and the increase in readership came increases in the amount of money being contributed to the 1397 Rank and File Caucus for the paper. A who's who of the early rank-and-file nucleus was evident by who wrote for, had their picture in, or contributed to the paper. The early newspapers listed the many contributors by name. These contributions were only a small portion compared to another fundraising endeavor: selling strip tickets. Strip tickets were lottery tickets that had ten numbers on them. For every hundred tickets sold, there would be a thousand numbers. A winning number would then be drawn from the thousand strip ticket numbers. Each strip ticket with ten numbers would cost a dollar. After paying the winning number fifty dollars and the printer five dollars for making the tickets, the Rank and File Caucus would make a profit of forty-five dollars for every one hundred tickets sold. While this might not sound like much in today's dollars, in the 1970s it was a stable and steady source of funding, not to mention the constant interaction between the ticket sellers and the membership. The tickets were extremely popular in the mill, and eventually several thousand were sold every week, providing the rank and filers with more than enough money to finance their newspaper.[12]

By 1978, six thousand copies of each issue of the *1397 Rank and File* were printed, with a mailing list well over six hundred (the paper was extremely popular with workers at other mills around the country). Distribution was now mill-wide, from the 100" Plate Mill in the west to the Structural Division and 48" Plate Mill to the east. As Central Maintenance rigger George Tallon noted, "The opposition simply has nothing like it. The *Sentinel* [the local union administration's newspaper] is about as controversial as the Betty Crocker Cookbook compared to the rank-and-file newspaper. It just doesn't pack a punch . . . it simply does not address the problems as directly or forcefully."[13] The *1397 Rank and File* newspaper also blew away the false divisions between intellectual and manual work; it showed that industrial workers, many with no college education—some even high school dropouts—could be writers, poets, cartoonists, and songwriters, while also working with their hands and being masters of their trade, craft, or job at the machine. One of the most incredible poets and earliest Rank and File Caucus members was a pipefitter who went by the moniker "Twiggy." His political poetry was some of the best I've ever run across:

An Epitaph for McBride's Inauguration
Who is this man who can't think for himself
Who knows everything he is, he owes to somebody else

He came on the scene with no idea of his own
He was given the key the crown the throne

Yes, who is this man, this man so meek
Who stands with his master, his tongue in his cheek

Who is this man who seldom speaks
Who dines with the butcher, and laughs at his sheep

Yes, who is this man, this man so small
Are we to believe he's a man at all

And who was the man he came to defeat
Whose only concern was for you and me

Yes, who was this man, this man so tall
And how did he lose to one so small?
—Twiggy, the pipe shop[14]

Another activity the Rank and File Caucus organized early on that allowed workers from different areas of the mill to interact in a social setting were the "beer blasts," usually at the West Mifflin Social Club, just up the hill from the mill. The first beer blast took place in June 1977, attended by two hundred or so workers. By the third beer blast, in December at the Polish Club, over four hundred attended. By the fourth, on March 10, 1978, back at the West Mifflin Social Club, over five hundred workers attended. Usually occurring twice a year, these giant parties included all types of grilled foods prepared by the workers; the

INCENTIVE RIP-OFF
Eye Witness Report

1397 Rank and File **newspaper, September 1977.**

Rank and File Caucus usually bought the booze. In general, the older workers would drink boilermakers (a shot and a beer) and play cards; the younger workers would drink beer, smoke marijuana, and play softball and volleyball; both would congregate to battle at the horseshoe grounds. It was like a mini–worker Woodstock that crossed generational lines; an effectively brilliant strategy for workers to socialize, get to know each other, and become friends!

Within a year of its formation, the 1397 Rank and File Caucus had established itself as a force to be reckoned with at the Homestead Works. It had its own newspaper, its own funding, its own social activities, and an ever-growing number of supporters. In late August 1977, an event took place that would attract hundreds, and eventually thousands, to this movement.

The Central Maintenance Payback

During the first year of its existence, most of the activists who joined the 1397 Rank and File Caucus came from the Central Maintenance Department, which performed all the major maintenance work at Homestead. It was a large department housed in the center of the mill, containing between twelve and fifteen hundred men and women of various crafts, including welders, boilermakers, riggers, bricklayers, pipefitters, and carpenters. Central Maintenance was also where most of the militancy in the Homestead Works was initially centered. This was because they had the worst and most dangerous working conditions and the least routine jobs in the mill. Central Maintenance people also received less "incentive pay" than other workers at Homestead.[15] Production workers generally had a routine and good bonuses compared to maintenance employees, who were on an indirect bonus, which oftentimes was at the discretion of management. In August 1977, there was a huge controversy around these maintenance incentives, which would serve as a rallying point for the militant activists in Central Maintenance and spread the Rank and File Caucus influence throughout Homestead Works.

On August 27, 1977, Central Maintenance employees received letters from Personnel Superintendent Harry Dolan claiming that they owed U.S. Steel money. Management claimed there was a clerical error in the calculation of the Central Maintenance incentive plan. The error amounted to 385 thousand dollars and was to be paid back to the Company by the employees at the rate of twenty dollars a pay, with some employees "owing" as much as five hundred to seven hundred dollars (big money back then, folks). It had taken the Company over eight months to notice its mistake. For Central Maintenance workers and the 1397 Rank and File Caucus activists, this was unacceptable. They were not about to let the Company take away their pay without a full accounting of the error, who was at fault, and a list of the exact amount allegedly owed by each employee before any payments were deducted.[16]

Two days later, on August 29, a mass meeting was held at the Local 1397 union hall, attended by over two hundred angry Central Maintenance employees. The Rank and File Caucus decided to demand that the District and the International assist in this fight. Surprisingly, a delegation sent to the office of USWA District 15 got an assurance from District Director Paul Lewis that the District would help with the case. An outside attorney, Frank Lucchino, was retained, and an injunction was served to U.S. Steel that prevented them from taking money out of the paychecks of the affected Central Maintenance employees. At the request of 1397 Rank and File Caucus members, Dick Sears, a top troubleshooter from another USWA District, was also brought in to help with the arbitration hearing. Director Lewis agreed to pay for the services of both these men.[17]

Meanwhile, the administration at Local 1397, led by President "Mike" Bekich (a crane operator out of the Structural Division) was less than enthusiastic about fighting the case. Members of the Rank and File Caucus were informed by Bekich that Local 1397 had a "one-tenth of one-percent chance of winning this case." Bekich also stated that the International Union's top attorney downtown had advised him that the case was unwinnable. As reported in the September 1977 issue of the *1397 Rank and File*: "This is the way the Executive Board [of the local union] thinks all the time: The company is always right and the membership is always wrong." In fact, just prior to the controversy surrounding the alleged Central Maintenance incentive overpayment, the Forge Division was forced to pay back money due to a clerical error made by U.S. Steel. Nothing was done by the local union administration at that time to fight the Company, even though the chair of the grievance committee Tom Copeland worked in the forge department.[18] Fortunately, the Rank and File Caucus took the bull by the horns and fought the Central Maintenance case when the local union officials refused. To his credit, in spite of opposition from local union officials, Director Lewis followed through with his legal support and immediately sent the case to court.

By the end of 1977, the arbitration case had been heard and the Central Maintenance employees were not forced to pay back U.S. Steel for its error. It was a big victory for hundreds of Central Maintenance employees. At this juncture, most of the workers in Central Maintenance began to align themselves with the 1397 Rank and File Caucus, whose influence also began to seep into other departments. The current administration of the local was viewed by many of the workers as do-nothings, since it was the Rank and File Caucus that had stood up and fought for the rights of the workers. This episode would be the beginning of the end for local union president Milan "Mike" Bekich and his administration.

Expanding throughout the mill, the Rank and File Caucus now included activists such as boilermaker John O'Toole, Tom Jugan from Open Hearth 4 (OH4) car shop, Ron Funk, Paul Glunt, and Dave Horgan from Power and Fuel, Ron Mamula and Pat Halbeib from the 48" mill, John Balint and Brian "Red" Durkin from Open Hearth 5 (OH5), Tommy Allen, Jim Ridley, Gary Kasper, and Jim Kooser from the 45" Slab Mill, Frank Domagala and Nat King from the 160" Plate Mill, Joe Stanton from the 100" Plate Mill, John Pressley, Joe Nestico, Ronnie Pristas, and John Deffenbaugh from the Forge Division, and Jack Bair, Joe Parkinson, Terry Bernh, and "Indian" Joe Diaz from structural. Besides this core group, there were many others who joined in our activities.

After the Central Maintenance victory, the 1397 Rank and File Caucus began to focus on the upcoming 1978 USWA convention and the local union elections that would take place in April 1979. Together, they hoped to unseat what they saw as a "corrupt" administration and bring some democracy to Local 1397. At a raucous Caucus meeting in late 1978 in the backroom of Lapco's Bar and Grill, an 8th Avenue bar, the slate for the upcoming local union elections was hammered out: Ron Weisen would run for president and John Ingersoll for vice president. While the majority at the meeting urged Michele McMills to run for the full-time financial secretary position, she opted to stay as journal agent, an unpaid and unofficial union position. Michele said she never had any intention of seeking power herself and was only intent on empowering the workers. In my opinion, this was a big mistake. It took Michele out of the official loop when the Rank and File Caucus took power later. Her watchdog skills and integrity were unquestionable. Instead, after a heated argument, it was decided Joe Stanton would run for financial secretary. One of the earliest and brightest rank-and-file activists and one of the hardest workers, Tom Jugan, would run for recording secretary. Power and fuel's Ron Funk, with his number crunching expertise and attention to detail, would run for treasurer.

CHAPTER 8

1978-1979, END OF THE HEYDAY

For the Homestead mill and *1397 Rank and File*, 1978 was a very good year. The mill and the town were in the middle of their respective last hurrahs. Homestead had hired over one thousand people from 1976 to 1979, and the plant was booming. After the Rank and File Caucus helped to win the Central Maintenance payback case, its popularity soared. With the increased notoriety, the writers for the *1397 Rank and File* newspaper became even bolder, unmercifully slamming not only the Company but the local union Bekich administration. More donations poured in. The number of workers contributing articles, poems, and cartoons quadrupled. The official union newspaper for the local, the *Sentinel*, was no match for the Rank and File Caucus paper. As described in an article by early Caucus activist Tom Jugan titled "The Lost-Time Gazette: 'The Voice of Management,'" the *Sentinel* was "a waste of union dues . . . a union paper that is censored by union officers, officers that only want the membership to read what they, the officers, want them to read."[1] I can personally attest that hardly anyone I knew or worked with in the mill read the *Sentinel*; everyone read the *1397 Rank and File*!

In April 1978, the National Labor Relations Board (NLRB) found Bekich guilty of harassing fellow Structural Mill workers Joe Parkinson and "Indian" Joe Diaz by making public statements that "tended to restrain and coerce employees in the exercise of their rights." Specifically, Bekich threatened to turn in both employees to management for allegedly stealing an order slip, stating in front of numerous witnesses: "if you ever get a slip, [i.e., disciplinary infraction] of any kind or need the union in any way, nobody on my staff will represent you." Copies of the NLRB ruling circulated throughout the mill. The Bekich administration was also accused of holding undemocratic union meetings, where nothing substantial was discussed, and whenever the rank and filers attempted to speak they were ignored or gaveled out of order. If rank-and-file activists refused to sit down and stop talking, the meeting was adjourned, sometimes five or ten minutes after starting. Occasionally fights broke out between the two factions and had to be broken up by the cops. A Homestead police officer, paid fifty dollars by the local, was now posted guard outside the union hall.

By the time I started going to meetings in 1978, you couldn't cut through the tension with a chainsaw. At the first local union meeting I attended, I got up and

NLRB Sentences STOOL PIGEON BEKICH to 60 days for Unfair Labor Practices

According to a NLRB Order, Local 1397 President Mike Bekich must cease and desist from committing unfair labor practices. Mr. Bekich must also sign and post this "Notice to Members" for 60 days. If you don't see this notice where union notices are normally hung, please call the NLRB at 644-2973.

1397 Rank and File newspaper, April 1979.

complained about the unresponsiveness of my grievance representative "Scotty." After the meeting, Joe Ruder, a Bekich assistant griever from Structural, took me over to Lapko's Bar across the street, bought me a drink (red wine, of course), and warned me of the dire consequences of getting involved with the group around Ron Wiesen. He called them troublemakers, strike-happy, and said they would end up getting the mill shut down. The fear in his eyes was palpable. He looked like he was an officer in General Custer's army watching the Sioux warriors bearing down on him.

Back in the late 1970s and early 1980s, all you had to do was open your ears and listen to workers in the locker room or on your work

crew to know they were dissatisfied with the union and looking
for change. While they had won
some battles, the 1397 Rank and
File Caucus knew they had not
won the war. In the Caucus's eyes,
there was still much to accomplish. Their biggest and most
important test would come in the
August 1978 election for delegates
to the next International Union
convention to be held in Atlantic
City, September 18–22.

1397 Rank and File newspaper, August 1980.

USWA Constitutional Convention

The election of delegates to the
1978 convention was 1397 Rank
and File Caucus's test of strength,
the result of two years of solid
organizing. The Rank and File Caucus ran eleven delegates on their
slate, including Tom Allen, John Balint, Elmer DelleDonne, Ron Funk,
John Ingersoll, Tom Jugan, Ron Mamula, Michele McMills, Joe Stanton,
Bob Stevenson, and Ron Weisen. All eleven were elected. Ron Weisen
led the way garnering 1,459 votes, with a record turnout of 2,097
members of Local 1397 voting. With over 6,000 dues-paying members
in the local, this meant that roughly a third of the workers came out
to vote, a clear demonstration of the disenchantment and apathy most
workers felt toward the local union at that time. Nevertheless, the
writing was on the wall. . . . The Bekich regime was on its way out for
good.

While in Atlantic City, the delegates from Local 1397 led the fight
for contract ratification by rank-and-file steelworkers. They held informal rank-and-file meetings every night of the week at the Mardi Gras
Hotel where they were staying, using these gatherings to discuss strategy for the following day's issues. CBS TV taped their first meeting
on Sunday, with over 250 delegates present. The biggest turnouts
came from the Chicago-Gary area, the Iron Range in Minnesota, and
the Monongahela Valley in Pennsylvania, all hotbeds of rank-and-file

activity. But along with this positive activity, John Ingersoll and other 1397 Rank and File Caucus delegates also saw some negative aspects to the events that occurred in Atlantic City. It seems that when they arrived, they discovered that some delegates were interested in things other than union affairs. According to Ingersoll:

> We went down there and we were pretty well organized, and then the local [1010] from out in the Chicago area was supposed to be with us, and something happened with their credentials, they got held up or something. So they never got there til' late, so we were there by ourselves, you know, and then these guys, they got crazy down there. Some of the 1397 delegates went their own way. You had something that nobody wanted, it was like a big party to them, you know, they didn't take it serious.[2]

While basking in the glory of their convention electoral victory in their test of strength with the Bekich administration, cracks in the armor of 1397 Rank and File Caucus began to appear. It was becoming apparent that some of the activists in the Caucus weren't involved for altruistic purposes.

CHAPTER 9

1397 RANK AND FILE CAUCUS TAKES OVER THE LOCAL

B y the summer of 1978, I was immersed in the rank-and-file movement, getting petitions signed in the mill for the Right to Ratify Our Contract issue, distributing the newspaper at the Amity Street gate and inside the mill, and pumping up coworkers for the upcoming local union election. At Michele's invitation, I helped put the newspaper together. Back in the pre-computer days, everything was typed on an IBM Selectric-Two electric typewriter and laid out manually. Headlines and subtitles were press-typed letter by letter; different sections were glued in place with rubber cement or a spray adhesive. When money became available after the Rank and File Caucus took over the local, pages were professionally typeset by a union printer, H.B. South in McKeesport, whose owner Jim South had grown up with Ingersoll. By this time the newspaper had grown to sixteen pages. Having been honed by ten years of writing and designing newsletters in the 1960s and 1970s movements, my skills were a perfect fit.

Meanwhile, the Rank and File Caucus continued to get its point across loud and clear. In an extensive two-page interview in the August 1978 edition of the paper, Weisen and Ingersoll laid out the basic agenda and goal: make the union better for the membership and the pensioners. They pulled no punches in condemning the unsafe conditions in the workplace and the ineffectiveness of the grievance procedure. They both expressed their disgust with the leadership of the local, and announced their plans to run for office during the forthcoming April 1979 local elections. They also addressed the slanderous charges that the Rank and File Caucus were a bunch of "communists." Both men stated clearly that they weren't, and that they and the organization were simply being "red-baited,"[1] an age-old divide and conquer tactic employed by Company and union officials alike.

There were certainly some individuals involved in the rank-and-file movement whose ideologies were radical and to the left of center, including mine. As I said earlier when explaining why I am a socialist, I believed then, and still do, that working people have been totally disenfranchised. I believe unions need to be radically restructured to provide a greater voice for the rank and file, both on and off the job. I also believe that the interests of workers in a fair wage and decent benefits are in fundamental conflict with most corporations and their never-ending drive for greater profits. I also believe that the fate of organized labor lies in uniting with other progressive movements, foremost the environmental and health care movements, and not with global predator corporations that will cut their throats in a heartbeat (like Bill Clinton did with NAFTA). If this is being "red," then, once again, I plead guilty!

1397 RANK & FILE

P.O. Box 417, Homestead, PA 15120   ☛   JANUARY, 197

New Rank and File headquarters open. Local membership finds a temporary home.

By January 1979, the Rank and File Caucus had, to all intents and purposes, taken control of the Homestead local union. Denied access to the union hall by the Bekich regime, they opened up a storefront headquarters at 605-1/2 Amity Street, just outside the Amity Street entrance to the mill, right next to the Steins Hotel Bar on the corner of 6th and Amity Streets. In a front-page article in the January 1979 issue, I explained:

> 1397 Rank and File has been denied any use of our local hall for membership meetings, beer blasts or anything else. With nowhere to hang our hat or relax before and after [work] turns, we have opened up a storefront for all union brothers and sisters, several hours before and after each shift. There is coffee, toast and doughnuts. Union members are welcome to come hang out, relax and just shoot the bull.
>
> Also available is a large assortment of free educational material on our contract and grievance procedure, information on other steel struggles in the Valley, as well as past Rank and File newspapers and literature. Please note: supervisors or vicing-foremen not allowed.[2]

At the new storefront, informal classes led by future grievance chair John O'Toole and outside attorney friend Bob Eddins were set up to help members learn about their rights under the contract and how to properly file grievances. Union literature, including Staughton Lynd's *Labor Law for the Rank and Filer*,[3] was available free of charge. The place was always stocked with coffee and doughnuts from the local bakeries. Pensioners even started gathering there.

Meanwhile, the Bekich administration did everything they could to slander the Rank and File Caucus. They put out undocumented, unsigned flyers accusing the Rank and File Caucus of being "strike-happy, communists, radicals, and radical liberals," as well as accusing them of being controlled by "outside forces" that funded the newspaper and their organization. In another portent of things to come, a notable event took place at the storefront just prior to the April 1979 local union elections.

After the March local union meeting, a bunch of us—Michele, Greg Klink, John Pressley, "Karate" Joe Nestico, and me—drove together to the storefront, smoking a "doobie" on the way. Giddy and happy when we entered the storefront, Elmer DelleDonne rushed over to us all sweaty and nervous, warning that John Balint was on the warpath "looking for communists." Apparently, some days earlier, Balint had been invited to a "study group" by an Open Hearth no. 5

(OH5) coworker who was a member of the Communist Workers Party, a small group based in New York City, with a dozen or so members in the Pittsburgh area (by 1985, they had disbanded.) According to Balint, he was not told who or what the meeting was about, claiming he was blindsided. The secretive nature of the meeting really freaked him out. As if it was 1962, he was seeing reds everywhere.

When Balint approached Greg, Michele, and me and asked if we were "members of the Communist Party," I said with a "You've gotta be kidding me—look: No." Michele and Greg, stoned to the bone, just burst out laughing and walked away. Unfortunately, it was no laughing matter. The division and suspicion that ensued was destructive and unnecessary. Both Balint (as his numerous articles in the local union newspaper at the time attest) and the activists being red-baited—me, Greg, Michele, and, later, even Weisen himself—were all good union members who opposed the Company and the do-nothing local union. When on the same team and singing out of the same union hymnbook, we had a powerful voice. As the unity started coming unglued, our voice started to crack.

After the witch-hunting had subsided and the room cleared, Ron Weisen and Red Durkin sat me down and asked to know the truth. I told them about my history as a yippie and anti-war activist and about my brief association with some far-left groups. I then asked if they wanted me to leave the Rank and File Caucus, and they both said no. Red Durkin thanked me for the little bio, saying, "Better to find out the truth now than later." I thought this was the end of the red-baiting nonsense; I was sadly mistaken. As I found out later, red-baiting is one of those viruses that never go away.

My Introduction to Communism and Socialism

While I was active with the Indochina Solidarity Committee (ISC) and Vietnam Veterans Against War (VVAW) in New York City in the early and mid-1970s, literally dozens of socialist and communist sects were vying to be the "vanguard" of the working class. Most of these groups consisted of college students who had been radicalized with the draft and the Vietnam War and the black rebellion and race riots of the 1960s. Dozens of these groups attempted at one time or another to recruit me and the ISC and VVAW friends I worked with. The only one that appeared even remotely real to many of us at the time was the Revolutionary Union (RU), which was a spin-off from Students for a Democratic Society (SDS). The RU championed and appealed to working-class radicals like me; they seemed to have genuine workers in their ranks who were really concerned and fighting for economic and social justice and a new democratic socialist system. Also, at that time, the RU was in the midst of negotiations with radical black, Asian, and Puerto Rican organizations, so they appeared to be serious about a new multinational revolutionary party, with an equal say for minorities. Unfortunately, this effort was undermined by a suspected high-level FBI informant in the RU's top leadership, hell-bent on making sure the merger never happened.[4] Meanwhile, a "busing plan" was forced on public schools nationwide by a Boston judge. The headline on the next issue of the RU's national newspaper blared in bold letters: "Smash the Boston Busing Plan," defending white working-class students being forced to attend inner-city schools miles from home but for the most part leaving out what was happening to black students. With black children being harassed and attacked and white supremacists (some in confederate uniforms, as I saw firsthand in Louisville) taking to the streets in numerous major cities against the plan, the RU position was labeled "racist," and they were quickly isolated from most other organizations and individuals on the left.

The RU sped full steam ahead and declared itself the new Revolutionary Communist Party (RCP) in the summer of 1975, in an effort to beat out other sects and win the Communist Party of China (CPC) franchise. This infantile and completely ridiculous move was made especially pointless with the death of Mao Zedong less than a year later. China would completely reverse course and adopt a capitalist economic system with a totalitarian government, leaving the RCP "franchise" in shambles.

Most people in this country have never experienced or known a real communist or socialist up close and personal; I have. As with adherents of any other philosophy or belief system, one of my guiding principles in life has been to look at *what people do* and *how they act* with others, not what they call themselves. This applies to religion as well as politics. During the tumultuous 1960s and 1970s, I met many activists who professed to be communists or socialists who really cared about the poor and oppressed, who dedicated their lives to the service of others. Most people in the U.S. don't know that it was communists who spearheaded the campaigns for unemployment compensation (UC), social security, and union organizing. They were the most ardent fighters against fascism and our staunchest allies during World War II.

Then there were others I met or worked around who were simply dogmatic, rigid, infantile, and verging on delusional. I experienced more than a few self-professed communists who resembled petty tyrants and dictators, only interested in building their own little sectarian fiefdoms, satisfied with a small cult of people around them. Their only template for a modern-day U.S. revolution was modeled on some foreign government from some other century.

During my brief experience with the RU/RCP, I met a lot of really dedicated rank-and-file activists who genuinely wanted to fight for a more just and non-exploitative society and world—good, decent, caring people. On the other hand, some of the RCP leadership, mainly centered on the west coast, was another story. Their slavish adherence to the Communist Party of China, their hierarchy, dogmatism, and authoritarian internal policies were everything they said they were fighting against externally. They tried to tell me what to wear, how short to cut my hair, who to marry, where to live, and what music I should listen to. (The last straw was when they started critiquing and editing the songs I wrote, and one of their "leaders" ordered me not to shake my hips while performing at a New York City show.) These bankrupt policies ensured that the RCP would follow dozens of other communist and socialist sects into factional oblivion. They weren't the revolutionary change I was looking for; I wanted to get as far away from them as I could. My flirtation with a U.S. communist organization was to be short and sour. But my belief that we need a new system that provides for everyone's needs, instead of a political system ruled and dominated by big money, banks, and corporations, remained intact.

Despite all the red-baiting both inside and outside the group, the Rank and File Caucus's momentum could not be stopped. When the April edition of *1397 Rank and File* came out, more than 6,500 copies were mailed and dispersed throughout out the mill. Its front-page article, written by rigger George Tallon, made a bold prediction:

> This year's union election will feature the "political steamroller effect" or "how a well-organized, highly-talented group of individuals dominates an election." It won't even be close. The Rank

1397 Rank and File newspaper, April 1979.

and File candidates should carry 65–75 percent of the vote. . . .
Unless the world should end on April 18, Ronnie Weisen and the
rest of the Rank and File Team will make political mince-meat
out of their opponents. So sit back and enjoy it. The show is about
to begin.[5]

The rest of this issue was replete with similar predictions, as well
as appeals to get out and vote. It had the most bombastic "Plant" and
"Union Plague" columns ever (including a cartoon where the Rank and
File Caucus wields a can of insecticide spray to get rid of the union
hall roaches. There were pictures and short bios for each Rank and
File Caucus candidate. This issue also contained a two-page center-
fold spread of the "greatest hits" of all the cartoons in previous issues.
There were prose, poetry, and articles by sixteen different workers, as
well as the lyrics to my newly composed acoustic rocker, "We Are the
1397 Rank and File":

> I was walking down the mill when I heard someone yell,
> This foreman walks up and starts giving me hell.
> He says, "You're out of your workplace, I think I'm gonna give you a
>   slip." Well,
> I stood there like a fist, like a bump on a log;
> We were all pissed at bein' treated like a dog.

I spoke for the others when I said: "We ain't lettin' you harass,
Take your discipline and slips and shove 'em up your ass."

Down in Central Maintenance just the other day,
The Company said they're gonna cut their pay.
They said they gave them too much incentive, now they're gonna take
   it away.
But the workers got together and they stood their ground;
Not a penny was missing when their checks came around.
Messing with their pay was taking things a bit too far;
We let 'em know just who the hell we are. . .

[Chorus] We are the 1397 Rank and File;
We're putting Mr. Bekich and his flunkies on trial.
We're gonna make our union safe for democracy,
So we can be strong to fight for what we need;
We got to unite, to fight this company—

We hit the union meeting, it was early last week;
The officers' reports they almost put me to sleep.
Bekich pounds his gavel down every time we get up to speak.
He says, "Listen to me, boys, I know what's best for you;
Just shut your mouths and kindly give me your dues.
I promised Lloyd McBride I'd keep you under the gun;
I promised leader Lloyd I'd keep you under my thumb."

Well the union hall was shakin' as the going got rough;
The rank and file stood up and said "enough is enough,
With your stool-pigeon, ass-kissing, Company-union stuff."
So turn in your keys, Milan, you're gonna fall;
The rank and file are taking back our union hall.
Open the doors and let the membership through;
We have the wheels, we're rolling over you. Because. . .
We are the 1397 Rank and File;
We're putting Mr. Bekich and all his flunkies on trial.
Gonna make our union safe for democracy,
We got to be strong to fight for what we need;

We got to unite, to fight this company.

[Bridge Finale] And like a hurricane, the rank and file will rise,
We'll throw off our chains, and like a tumbling tide,
Crush all the bosses, push their union flunkies aside—
We're taking back our union, taking back our union!

In the end, there was nothing the Bekich team or the District and International Union could do or say to stop the 1397 Rank and File Caucus. The local election was held on April 18. A record 4,325 of the 6,300 Local 1397 union members turned out to cast their ballots. All of the top twelve union positions were captured by the Rank and File Caucus. Weisen once again was the top vote-getter; the insurgents won by greater than a two to one margin.

At the same time, the Rank and File Caucus only took five of the eight grievance positions. The incumbent griever in Structural, Dan Barbarino, beat the Rank and File Caucus candidate Jack Bair, and the incumbent griever from the Forge Division, Tom Copeland, beat Rank and File Caucus candidate John Pressley; both of these leftovers from the Bekich regime retained their positions for another three-year term. Wendell Brucker was reelected by the zone 1 inspectors. At the Irish Club next door to the union hall, Wendell was the best bartender by far. Everybody loved him. Politically, he bent with the wind. In addition, over two thousand workers did not vote, indicating there was still a high degree of apathy. Obviously, for the Rank and File Caucus, the job was not done, victory not complete.

In another interesting turn of events in the Slab and Plate Division where I worked, two Rank and File Caucus candidates ran against each other: Tom Allen from the 45" Slab Mill and Nat King, an African American from the 160" mill plate treating line (a department within the 160" Plate Mill much smaller than the 45" mill). Nat King won handily, besting both Allen and the incumbent. As I experienced directly, racism and discrimination were still

Nat King with John Ingersoll at Local 1397 beer blast, 1979.

prevalent inside the mill, especially among some of the older white male workers. But unlike the racism I had encountered and been part of in the South, it was more a whisper behind the scenes. With the ascendancy of the civil rights and youth movements of the 1960s, racism retreated to dark corners behind the backs and out of earshot of blacks. Nat King's overwhelming win was proof that for the hundreds of newcomers who had entered the mill in the 1970s, race was not the defining factor in their vote.

1397 RANK & FILE
P.O. Box 417, Homestead, PA 15120 ◄▶   APRIL, 1979

1397 Rank and File newspaper, April 1979.

The April 1979 local union election was truly a landslide victory. A movement that had started with only three people in early 1976 now had control of the nation's third largest steelworkers' local union. By late election day afternoon, the Rank and File Caucus storefront was jammed shoulder to shoulder with some two hundred workers, with many more hanging outside on the sidewalk and in the street. The hotdogs, kielbasa, and beer flowed aplenty; the jubilancy in the air was exhilarating. Ronnie and Michele asked me to sing "We Are the 1397 Rank and File"; I gave my best Springsteen acoustic rocker rendition, replete with jumps in the air. At the insistence of Bobby Stevenson and others, I had to perform it three times in a row. However short-lived, the solidarity I felt that day was beyond euphoric; it was a dream come true for any working-class organizer, for any lover of justice and democracy. I felt like I was on a wave of something bigger than myself and the Rank and File Caucus. I wanted to freeze-frame that feeling and moment for all time.

CHAPTER 10

LEARNING THE ROPES AND HOW TO HANDLE POWER

After the new officers were sworn in at the May 1979 union meeting, a number of immediate changes were made: e.g., a women's committee was officially formed and the safety committee was rejuvenated and strengthened. John Pressley, a militant African American and one of the original Rank and File Caucus members, was appointed to head up the civil rights committee. His induction and speech at the May local union meeting reminded me of Fred Hampton of the Black Panther Party; it was as though Fred had been transposed to

a steel mill. The grievance committee was revamped. At my suggestion, workers who filed grievances would be encouraged to be present at every step. A plant-wide grievance forum that met twice a month was established to give members input, and a twenty-four-hour-a-day hotline was set up for those who needed immediate help. The union hall was declared open to *all* members and pensioners for education and recreation. Membership participation in all phases of decision-making was promised. The secretaries hired by the previous

Civil rights committee chairman John Pressley, May 1979.

administration, Cheryl Bacco and Darlene McIntosh (with their hard work ethic, honesty, and outgoing personalities) were kept on board and a third secretary, Linda Lapko, was added. A number of committee people from the previous administration who were doing an effective job were also retained, including Ed Salaj, chair of the plant incentive committee. Ed and I would stay good friends long after the mill closed.

Immediately after the election, I was told by the newly elected Slab and Plate grievance representative Nat King that I was to be the assistant griever for the 100" Mill Maintenance Department (which included crane operators, laborers, and all of the craftspeople.) When I half-ass protested because of my lack of seniority and time in the mill, I was told, "You got a brain. You're a fighter. Take the job." Having never held such a position, I was at first a little intimidated, but it didn't take long to settle in and get the hang of it.

Some higher education might have helped me learn the intricacies of grievance handling, but I had barely made it through high school. Learning by doing was always my preferred school. After being kicked out of two Catholic high schools, I graduated from a public school, Henry Clay, in Lexington, Kentucky. For the most part, I hated school and spent most days staring out the window daydreaming about the day I'd get out for good. Outside of geography and history and memorizing numbers in math class, I found it boring and useless. Most of it was rote; critical thinking was not encouraged. As far back as I can remember, I questioned everything, whereas schools back then wanted to teach you obedience and to question nothing. Even my favorite subject, history, would just skim over dates and events, without explaining anything, never making it come alive.

My freshman high school year at Lexington Catholic was a complete disaster. I got busted numerous times for skipping, cheating on tests, pitching nickels on the playground (gambling), and other offenses, which by today's standards would be considered relatively minor. My brother Steve and I were sent to St. Bede Academy, an authoritarian boarding reform school in Lasalle-Peru, Illinois (120 miles southwest of Chicago, right off Interstate 80.) Benedictine priests routinely whopped you with open hand and fist. I was on the receiving end at least three times, constantly on the bad side of the clergy establishment. I was kicked out of there twice in one year. The first time was for drinking (along with my brother Steve and a dozen others). My dad had to drive five hundred miles and beg them to take us back. The second time was for breaking into the canteen. Without my little transistor radio, WLS out of Chicago, and listening to the top ten countdown every night, I'd have never made it through these years at St. Bede, which I viewed as a prison at the time. Being outsiders, my brother Steve and I had each other's back. It was my first taste of real brotherhood and solidarity.

Solidarity and resistance were the main things I learned in school, and after my organizing years in New York and Louisville, fighting a big corporation that bullied its workers was right up my alley.

The first case I handled was on a morning after the midnight shift ended in late May. As I was coming off my crane in the 110" shipping bay, a young African American woman, Tinsie Brooks, came running up to me in tears, claiming she had been docked seven hours of pay. Apparently, the shift foreman couldn't locate her all night. I told her to give me her time card and go to the locker room, that I would handle it. The first thing I did was line up Carol Belluci as a witness. Carol was another new hire, a young and wild rocker who was operating the crane next to me. She lived right around the corner from me on Louise Street in Munhall. We both would claim we saw Tinsie working throughout the night. I then headed for the 100" mill general foreman Lloyd Fenstermaker's office. Halfway there, the shift foreman who had disciplined Tinsie came up, put his arm around me, and said, "Let's go teach this nigger bitch a lesson." I couldn't believe my ears. I thought I was in Lexington, Kentucky, back in the 1950s or 1960s.

When we got to the office, I slapped the time card down in front of the general foreman Lloyd Fenstermaker and told him if he didn't punch it and give her eight hours pay, on top of filing a grievance, I was also going straight downtown Pittsburgh to the EEOC (Equal Employment Opportunity Commission) office with Tinsie to file a discrimination and intimidation complaint against the foreman for calling her a "nigger bitch." Both the foreman and Fenstermaker's faces got beet-red; I thought their heads were going to explode. With an angry sneer on his face, Fenstermaker punched her time card for eight hours and said, "Get out of my office."

Word spread quickly among both the workers and management that they were dealing with a new breed of griever. From that day forward, I was marked as a target for removal by Jim Brown, the slick-talking

1397 Rank and File newspaper, July 1980.

and shrewd Company labor contract administrator (LCA)—the real authority and legal power in the Slab and Plate Division. When it came to anything to do with the contract or discipline in Slab and Plate, Jim Brown had the final word; he ruled the roost.

Most of the grievances I fought during this period were disciplinary in nature, usually involving absenteeism and safety infractions. With management's chickenshit "slip quota" system, I was kept pretty busy at my first official union position. In addition, with so many women entering the mill over the previous couple of years, the discrimination was rampant. Not only did management give them a hard time, but a cabal of male workers also preyed on them. Once when I remarked to an older worker about the amount of cavorting going on inside the mill, he reminisced, "Shit, this ain't nothing; back during World War II, sex was goin' on everywhere—down on the tracks, in the railroad cars, in the maintenance shanties and foreman's offices." Women working in the mill needed more than a "union committee," they needed an armed patrol!

Cracks in the Rank and File Widen

A few months after the election, the contradictions in the union—both locally and at the District and International levels—came bubbling to the surface. The Rank and File Caucus, with a good portion of its most vocal leaders now officials in union positions, quickly unraveled. Several factions formed. There were major disagreements about which direction to go in. Some of the new officers buckled down, getting acclimated to their new positions; others started acting like big shots, like it was the first time they put on a suit. They didn't know how to act. They started taking needless "lost time" and adopting other bad habits of the former local union officials. They called for the cessation of the 1397 *Rank and File* newspaper, saying it was no longer needed. Worst of all, they started sucking Ronnie's butt, treating him like he was some kind of Jimmy Hoffa or Huey Long–type political boss, encouraging a cult of personality that I had experienced all too often in previous movements and organizations. Inexperienced in his new position of power and feeling his political oats, Ronnie ate up all the attention. Put on a pedestal by some of the officers around him, he developed a whole political persona, replete with one-line zingers he would throw out everywhere he went. His favorite was: "The Company and union have been in bed together for so long, they both should file for maternity benefits." My absolute favorite, and the one that I agreed with the most was: "I'm not anti-union; I just want to remove the many stains from the union flag."

The seeming inability of some of our newly elected officers to deal with power was something I had already experienced many times. Whether in government, community organizations, a church council, or even a local union, people elected to or put in a position of power have a strong tendency to surround themselves with those who ensure and strengthen this power. Their power, no matter how limited, becomes intoxicating. Without a strong institutionalized checks and balances mechanism to control this negative human trait, corruption almost always ensues. With the next election three years down the road, Ronnie, Michele, and a number of us recognized that some of these officers had quickly forgotten why they had run and why they were elected.

A group of us, including Michele, Greg Klink, Jack Bair, John Ingersoll, Joe Diaz, Elmer DelleDonne, Mark Kenezovich, me, and a few others, held a meeting at my house. After a heated discussion, we all agreed that the Rank and File Caucus should continue as the conscience and watch guard of the new administration. Most importantly, we wanted to make sure the newspaper continued. As Ronnie was stuck in the middle of the various factions forming, he wasn't invited. When he found out about the meeting, he just about hit the roof. He demanded to know why he was excluded, wanting to know "who the hell we thought we were." He was right; he should have been there, dealt with face-to-face, not behind his back. His anger and opposition nixed the formation of an "independent" caucus. Though he eventually cooled down, this meeting fueled the red-baiting charges of secrecy and hidden agendas.

Yet another faction formed, including John Balint and newly elected grievance chair Bob Stevenson, that was intent on rooting out the so-called "communists" and "leftists" from the new administration. They even whispered behind the scenes that Ronnie was a "commie sympathizer." The red-baiting and slander machine was cranked up, blanketing the union hall like a cloud of smog, choking democracy and sowing division. At the same time, many of the new grievance representatives such as John O'Toole went about the business of trying to learn the ropes of a complicated and cumbersome system, so they could undo the damage of past administrations. The political hairsplitting going on didn't interest them at all.

For those of us concerned with the issue of union democracy, some in the new administration started to resemble the former local union officials of the old administration. Strip tickets were still being sold, but no one knew where the money was going. While a women's committee was formed and institutionalized and the civil rights committee reactivated, with John Pressley as its chair, blacks and women were still cut out of any decision-making role in the new administration. In addition, racism manifested itself in numerous instances, both on the shop floor and in the union. In a matter of months, John would not only be pushed out of the local union and civil rights committee but out of the Homestead plant altogether.

In one of his first acts as local union civil rights chair, John asked the Company for information on their implementation of the Consent Decree and for employee lists, starting with his home department, the Forge Division. According to the April 12, 1974, federal court mandate, 50 percent of all new hires for production and maintenance operations were to be minorities and women.[1] As a machinist apprentice in the forge, John was very familiar with the employees and lines of promotion in this area.

When he reviewed the Company documents, he noticed that three white male machinist apprentices were listed under the racial/sexual code as minorities. He multiplied that by the many other departments throughout the mill, as well as the other steel mills that might have made the same "mistake," which he suspected was intentional.

At the July 17, 1979, plant-wide civil rights committee meeting, he presented these discrepancies to management and asked for lists from other departments. Plant superintendent Harry Dolan stood by the accuracy of their lists and refused to provide additional lists. John then took his complaint and evidence to Ronnie Weisen, as well as our District staff representative at the time, Ernie Clifford, who was African American. According to John, "The more I pressed the local, the less I became a 1397 rank and filer." This would have been an excellent moment for the local to take the lead in fighting against the rampant discrimination in the mill and for the implementation of the Consent Decree. The chair of the grievance committee at that time was still Bobby Stevenson. (O'Toole would not be elected until December 1979 in a special election; see details below.) The Forge grievance representative was Tom Copeland, a leftover from the Bekich administration. Neither filed a grievance on John's behalf. The District Union and Ernie Clifford, embroiled in an internal union war with Ronnie by this time, did nothing.

Within a month, John was laid off from his machinist apprentice job in the Forge; under the I-Job provisions of the contract he took a temporary transfer to American Bridge, in Ambridge, Pennsylvania.[2] At the same time, he was removed as chair of the civil rights committee and replaced by Piper Newland, an African American woman from the 100" mill where I worked at the time. When his department picked back up in early 1981 and John attempted to transfer back to the Homestead mill, he was told his transfer to Ambridge was "permanent." When he demanded to see the paperwork he allegedly signed designating his transfer permanent, the Company refused to provide it. With no allies in the union, John bitterly accepted his fate and remained in Ambridge.

The duplicity of some white workers on the race issue always perplexed me. It showed just how ingrained racism is. When on the job or eating lunch together, white workers would treat black workers like genuine brothers. They would even go on picnics or drinking after work together. As soon as the black worker's back was turned and out of earshot, the "N-word" came flying out like they were at a Klan rally.

My own education on race started during my two years at Saint Bede. I arrived there in 1964, the same year as the one black student, who had the shit beaten out of him every day until he left several months later. It sickened me. Also, I met and became friends with two Latinos, Gallo Arends, from Aruba, and Miguel Guajardo, from Mexico—about the only two boarding students who didn't treat me like an out-of-state alien hillbilly. They taught me how to cuss in Spanish, how to fight, how to smoke in the men's room without getting caught, and how to become brothers with people who weren't white. Thirty years later I penned a song for them and my experience at St. Bede:

Gallo and Miguel

Sent away to a boarding school academy of pain,
Under the Benedictine order of guilt, fear, and shame;
Me and my brother Steve in a far-away move,
With the Illinois rough boys who had something to prove;
Where corn was king, and the sting of the prefects ruled.
They shaved my head, swore they'd straighten me out,
Cage the wild spirit that was raging all about.
It didn't take long to step on some toes;
Land me in the doghouse where involuntary solitary grows and eats
    your soul.

Gallo was from Aruba, Miguel from old Mexico.
Third Worlders in the land of the snow-white show.
Unphased by the gringos, so cool and multilingual,
No one touched their space even when they had to mingle;
Two Latin brothers apart from the others in that jungle.
Like a godsend they took me under their wing;
Made me a friend, helped me be a human being.
Speaking dirty Spanish, blowing smoke rings,
Taught me common sense, how to fence from the heart—

[*Chorus*] Gallo and Miguel, you broke the choke hold of the jingo man's
    spell.
Gallo and Miguel, fellow mates at the gates tempting fates to rebel—
Gallo and Miguel.

At mid-term when less than half of my sentence remained,
War broke out between the border rats and day dog gangs.*
This day dog, Beckerini, way bigger than me,
Called me out to battle in a bathroom arena meet.
The sell-out crowd was loud predicting my defeat.
But on the night before the fight Gallo taught me self-defense;
The element of surprise, how to shake his confidence.
The fight was won before it begun, and Father Hugh Crowe came and
    took me to my penance—[Chorus]

Decades later when I think about the places I've been,
The locations and relations that made me who I am.
When character is formed, fears overcome;
The spirit is born, the soul unstrung.
Back to the time when the mind first awakes and finds freedom.
There they were, those two amigos of mine;
Human bridges on the ridges of a troubled time.
Lights in the nights of an early circle of hell,
I'd have never made it with this story to tell without—Gallo and
    Miguel
[Chorus]

*["Boarder rats" were those of us from out of town who lived at the
school. "Day dogs" were the students from town, who went home
every day.]

While these two amigos put a serious crack in my "jingoist spell,"
it was only after several bad bouts with LSD at age eighteen that I
was forced to come full face with myself and begin the slow, difficult
process of discarding my mean, racist, selfish side.

At the Homestead mill, it was the same thing with women: rampant
verbal (and sometimes even) physical abuse. While some male workers
would be respectful to their faces, they were disrespectful behind their
backs. I'll never forget the day when I was in the 100" Maintenance
Department lunchroom. There was a female crane operator named
Sue Kwiatkowski in our crew. Every time she turned her back, went up
to the sink to wash her hands or whatever, several of the guys would
start making weird sexual gestures, wagging their tongues or making

Women of steel (left to right) Beth Destler, Steffi Domike, Linny Stovall, and Allyn Stewart.

crotch-groping motions with their hands. After several of these imma-
ture teenage displays, I called them out on it, asking them in front of
her why they were wagging their tongue and groping like that, especially while her back was turned? Both of the workers involved glared at
me. After she left the room, they asked, "Why did you do that, embar-
rass us like that?" No matter how hard I tried to explain, they couldn't
see the hypocrisy much less the inappropriateness of their behavior.
Penthouse and *Hustler* magazines were strewn across benches in just
about every lunchroom, decorations declaring the mill was "a man's
world." When someone would gather them up and throw them away,
four or five more would be back the very next day. Racism and sexism
were alive and pervasive, both in the mill and the local union. No election was going to erase this reality.

As a dozen former women steelworkers, including Homestead 45"
Slab Mill woman steelworker Carolyn Grinage (now Carolyn Grinage
Pressley), stated in interviews thirty-five years later:

> Ask any woman if she'd return to her job as a steelworker during
> the 1970s and 1980s, and she'd say yes in a nanosecond. . . .
> Women felt empowered doing men's work, earned better money

than pink-collar wage earners and even loved the steel plants for
their hypnotic dangers. . . . Stories are legion about holes drilled
into women's locker rooms for easy spying, as most showers were
without curtains or stalls. . . . Men exposing themselves in the
shadows were part of the scenery. On the production floor, grop-
ings were so swift, they felt almost innocent. Sexual profani-
ties were background noise and more creative than even Falstaff
could make up.[3]

Despite the inhumanities these pioneer women endured, their
fight for dignity found institutional expression in the numerous and
strong women's committees that sprang up in nearly every mill. Not
only in the locals, but several districts organized conferences, meetings, and in some cases district committees that took up the struggle
for equality and dignity on the job, not to mention having their own
bathrooms. There were two such groups in United Steelworkers of
America (USWA) District 15 in the Mon Valley. At USWA Local 1219,
women at U.S. Steel's Edgar Thomson Works published *Hear Here*, a
newsletter addressing specific issues in that mill. *Women of Steel*, an
organization and quarterly newsletter that existed in 1979–1980 and
included women from various U.S. Steel plants at Homestead, Clairton,
and Duquesne, "opened the door for the USWA to discuss maternity
coverage, safety, job training and full disclosure of hiring and firing of
women."[4] Three of these women steelworkers, Steffi Domike from the
Clairton Works and Beth Destler and Linny Stovall from the Duquesne
Works, worked with artist Allyn Stewart to produce the *Women of Steel*
documentary in 1984,[5] highlighting the plight, hardships, and struggles of these early women pioneers. While their struggle is far from
over, women have made great strides. For Jaimee Grinage, Carolyn's
daughter and the safety representative for the galvanizing department
at U.S. Steel's Irvin Works, where she's worked since 2005:

> I don't know where we'd be without women of [her mother
> Carolyn's] generation—how they spoke up to bring about change.
> I don't know if any of us would have the guts to be one of them.[6]

Women like Michele McMills, Lynn Morton, Sheri Farris, Candice
Wargo, Carolyn Grinage Pressley, Mary Hirko, LuJuana Deanda, Kathy
Kozachenko, Moureen Trout, Kathy Martin, Kay Bolton, Barb Weibelt,

THE SENTINEL

"On July 6, 1892 armed guards and 300 Pinkerton Agents hired by the Carnegie Steel Company, brutally engaged into combat with the workers at the Homestead Plant of Carnegie Steel Company. The death and despair of that day appeared totally fruitless just six days later when 8000 National Guardsmen marched into Homestead and placed the town under martial law. The plants were reopened with strikebreakers.
   On September 1, 1941 the Steel Workers Organizing Committee dedicated a Monument in Homestead, Pennsylvania to those who had struggled and died that infamous day in search of dignity in their work place.

Thirty-eight years have passed since the dedication of the Homestead Monument. Tremendous gains through labor unions have been achieved and the United Steelworkers of America is recognized as the collective bargaining agent for more than a million members insistant upon dignity in the work place, and the communities in which they live."
   Thus District 15 Director Paul Lewis called for the rededication of the Homestead Monument on Labor Day, Monday, September 3, 1979. We stand united with Director Lewis in remembrance of the people who died to make our Union strong.

STOP CONNEAUT
Save The Steel Valley

Kathy Bodnar, B.J. Buchannon, Carol Belluci, and a host of others at Homestead whose names are forgotten, along with those at other U.S. Steel facilities, including the Women of Steel activists mentioned above and many more too numerous to list—they should all be prime candidates for the "Heroines of History" club.

1397 Rank and File Newspaper Continues

Immediately after the election of the Rank and File Caucus slate, controversy arose as to what to call the *1397 Rank and File* newspaper. Should it keep its name, or should it be dissolved? Should the official organ of past administrations, the *Sentinel*, become our paper, which was the position Michele initially took? It was decided to let the membership have their say. After the Rank and File Caucus took office in May 1979, the first issue of the paper in June was called the *Sentinel*, and included an article by Michele addressing the issue:

> Many of you assumed that we would change the name of the "Sentinel" to "The 1397 Rank and File" and continue on as we always have. We hope that we can be as hard hitting and representative of the rank-and-file members of this local as always. But, the name "Rank and File" has been associated with one

PLANT PLAGUE

Slab and Plate

THE PHANTOM
SHITTER
STRIKES AGAIN!

While New York City had their "Son of Sam" and San Francisco had their "Zebra" killer, the 100" Mill has someone just as deadly: the PHANTOM SHITTER. Over the past several years, this Phantom Shitter has dropped his smelly turds in 2 locker rooms, a shower stall, Angelo Arilotta's works shoes, a sink and the top of a toilet seat. In the last few months, this "shit-ass" has struck again, hitting the cab on #13 Crane, and the outside tunnel leading to the 100" Mill.

Because of Management's ongoing policy of eliminating as many jobs as possible, we highly suspect that this is a plot by the white hats to "stink out" some of our union brothers and sisters. But as one Millwright said recently, "It's no big deal. We work in shit and the Company shits on us everyday anyway!"

Despite the number of times the Phantom Shitter has struck, no clues have been found. A 5-years' supply of Pepto-Bismol is being offered for any information leading to his capture.

And while on the subject, what was the real reason 100" Maintenance turn foreman, Don (Vaseline) Seigworth, was seen cleaning up the human excretion in the 100" Tunnel on Friday, October 12? Speaking of Mr. Vaseline, the maintenance crew on Don Seigworth's turn will be at the Amity St. Gate this month to solicit funds for a 6-month's winter supply of barf bags and some good ol' petroleum jelly.

1397 Rank and File newspaper, December 1979.

group, and as large and popular as that group may be, it is part of a larger local union. We must represent all of our members, not just a faction.

To this end we are asking you, the members, to suggest a new name for your paper. And by dropping us a line with your suggestion, you'll be telling us not just what you want *your* paper called, but *what you want it to be*.[7]

While suggestions flew in every direction, in the end there was no vote and Ronnie decided it would remain the *1397 Rank and File*. Despite the arbitrariness of his decision, it turned out to be the right one: *1397 Rank and File* represented the future; the *Sentinel* represented the past.

After the local came out with its December 1979 edition—renamed *1397 Rank and File*—it received a letter from the International's United Steelworkers Press Association (USPA), dated February 14, which stated:

If the "Rank and File" wished to continue its membership in USPA for the year 1980, and participate as a member in good standing, the Executive Board of the USPA is in unanimous concurrence that appropriate retractions be made about the following items in the undated publication issued in December, 1979.[8]

The list of "retractions" included the entire "Plant Plague" section, with my comic spoof of the "phantom shitter" (a worker in the 100" mill was going around shitting in the locker rooms, in shoes, and even in the roadway tunnel leading down to the mill), Ronnie's "President's Report," the grievance reports, and, of course, the cartoons. Ronnie and Michele led a giant chorus of "shove it," sending a letter back to the USPA asserting that neither the Company nor the International would ever dictate what went into our newspaper. Needless to say, we were kicked out of the USPA. Between December 1979 and the end of 1980, five issues of *1397 Rank and File* were published, including a "Special Convention Report" in August; each issue more hard-hitting, raunchier, more defiant, and more informative. With the mounting attacks on the local by the District and the International, the "Union Plague" section became even more prominent.

The backbiting, red-baiting character assassination and internal squabbles continued unabated inside the local, and, by early 1980, Michele and Greg decided they'd had enough. Battle fatigue had set in. On April 25, they resigned from the newspaper and withdrew from any active involvement with the union. Losing both a friend and a valuable asset with Michele's departure was not only disheartening; it put some of us in a panic. It was like the head had been cut off the horse. As Ronnie noted later, "She was a good union person. I should have leaned against them, the people attacking her; but I didn't."[9]

While losing Michele was a major blow, a number of us didn't want to see the paper fall apart, change format, lose its character and look, or, worst of all, go down the drain. It was the strongest voice of and

1397 RANK & FILE

Official Newspaper of Local 1397
UNITED STEELWORKERS OF AMERICA
615 McCLURE STREET • HOMESTEAD, PA 15120
PHONE: 462-2522

Editor .... DON McKINNEY
Assistant Editor .... MIKE STOUT

CARTOONISTS:
Rick Konish
Norm Ostoff
Al Paisley

This newspaper is printed and published by Local 1397 U.S.W.A. Contents herein are solely the opinion and responsibility of the contributor and are not the responsibility of the local. Any inaccuracies and liability for such inaccuracies is hereby denied.

for democracy that we had in the local union. Ronnie appointed Don McKinney out of Power and Fuel as the new editor; he declared he wanted the paper to remain as it was. Aware of my writing, editing, and formatting contributions in past issues, I was made assistant editor to ensure that it did. For at least a few more years, the members would retain their democratic voice.

CHAPTER 11

LOCAL UNION 1397– INTERNATIONAL DIVIDE

A long with the internal differences in the local, the District and the International Union made a number of blunders that sharpened the schism with the new Rank and File Caucus local at 1397. In the first issue of the newspaper after the Rank and File Caucus took office, attacks on the District and on the International Union had abated. That now changed.

In the summer of 1979, District Director Lewis responded positively to our invitation to join Local 1397 in refurbishing and rededicating the steelworker monument erected in 1941, which sat in disrepair at the corner of 8th Avenue and the Homestead High Level Bridge (later renamed the Homestead Grays Bridge). In the ceremony held on Labor Day at the Local 1397 union hall with hundreds in attendance, Lewis presided over the program and refused to recognize Ronnie, much less allow him to speak. From that point on, Lewis was enemy number one on Ronnie's shit list. His earlier support around the Central Maintenance incentive payback arbitration case was all but forgotten and buried. This wedge would remain until Lewis died on November 2, 1981.

Another ploy the International used was to get their supporters who lost their grievance positions to file charges declaring illegalities during the recent local union elections. They thought this tactic would make the Rank and File Caucus look inept and would cost the local a lot of money. In November 1979, elections had to be rerun for all eight grievance positions and the grievance chair job. This boondoggle totally backfired on the International. Not only were the outcomes exactly the same, showing it was a waste of money, but it gave the Rank and File Caucus a golden opportunity to right a mistake made concerning the grievance chair position.

Bobby Stevenson, one of the earliest and most outspoken members of the Rank and File Caucus, had been elected chair of the grievance committee in May 1979. While on the campaign trail for the zone 3 griever position in Central Maintenance, he had stated in the newspaper: "If 1397 Rank and File is elected, the Company will not control the officials in our local. I have decided to run for zone grievanceman because in the past we have been sold out. . . . There will be no deals made under the table. . . . I would like to put honesty back in our union."[1] Within a few months, it was discovered by the local that he had cut a deal with the plant-wide labor contract administrator (LCA) for the Company, to "weed out" the majority of grievances

Monument erected by the Steelworkers Organizing Committee in 1941, on 8th Ave. and High Level Bridge, in front of Chiodo's Tavern.

when they reached the third step—the exact same thing the past administration had been doing. As Ronnie angrily stated in the "President's Message" of the December 1979 issue of *1397 Rank and File*:

> I would like to call to the attention of the membership that there are many grievances that are being dropped and deals being made by our own rank-and-file grievancemen. I am very disappointed in that, and I have called it to their attention. It seems to me we were a united group when the membership voted us in;

but as soon as some of our rank and filers were elected, instead of worrying about the membership, all they worry about was their own personal gain.[2]

In the reelection for grievance chair on December 11, 1979, Ronnie's handpicked candidate John O'Toole beat Stevenson 323 to 254. With O'Toole's victory, in a flash the direction of the grievance system took a 180-degree turn; the wheeling and dealing at the third step stopped. A high school graduate with no college education like me, O'Toole was smart, aggressive, organized, and a quick learner. No more would grievances be routinely discarded. He pledged open reports on the status of all grievances.

At the January 1980 third step grievance review meeting, Ronnie announced to the Company LCAs, "O'Toole will be handling our grievances at fourth step and arbitration, not the International staff." Thinking O'Toole was some uneducated, dumb mill hunky they could walk all over,[3] the Company representatives said, "Whatever, we don't care." Looking at the workload he would be relieved of, the District Union staff representative, Ernie Clifford said, "Fine with me too; less work for me."

At fourth step, Clifford was doing the same thing Stevenson was at third step: vetting grievances. In fact, while on a bus ride heading to

Picketing the District Union office, May 1981.

an anti-Klan rally on October 25, 1979, in Uniontown, Pennsylvania, an hour or so south of Pittsburgh, I heard Clifford in the seat in front of me mention Homestead and grievances. I tapped him on the shoulder and asked him what he said. Not knowing who I was, he replied that the District had "a six-ten policy" for Homestead grievances, explaining that "for every ten grievances that reached fourth step, six would be dismissed outright," without

Grievance chairman John O'Toole's sign says it all.

even being examined or reviewed—simply because they were from Homestead.

When I told Ronnie and John O'Toole what he had said, Ronnie pressured the International to have Clifford removed, which was finally done by the summer of 1981. Shortly thereafter, O'Toole began doing the staff representative's job, handling all of Homestead's arbitration cases. The following year, our third staff representative in two years, George Meyers (Clifford had been replaced by Steve Cray, who died of a heart attack shortly thereafter), echoed Clifford and Cray's response, "Fine with me," with that same "hey, less work for me" look on his face.

With O'Toole now in charge and Ronnie's backing, newly elected grievers were given a crash course on contract rights and labor law; newly elected Rank and File Caucus grievers became more accessible to the members. Within a few months O'Toole would completely reverse the local union's win/lose ratio at arbitration. With O'Toole at the helm, the local was now winning more than half of the grievances. Not only could workers who labored with their hands be artists, writers, songwriters, and poets, now they could also be lawyers.

CHAPTER 12

CONNEAUT, YOUNGSTOWN, AND THE BEGINNING OF THE END

At the same time as the militant caucus at Local 1397 was completely changing the direction of the local union, U.S. Steel and the entire steel industry were also making a major shift in direction. On April 24, 1979, David M. Roderick took over the helm as chairman.

Born in Pittsburgh and the son of a postal employee, Roderick served as a platoon sergeant in the Marine Corps. He joined Gulf Oil at the end of World War II, starting as an accountant, and then went to work for Union Railroad Company, a subsidiary of U.S. Steel, working his way up to assistant comptroller in 1973 and becoming chairman of the finance committee in 1977. Clearly, his work history was finance—not steelmaking.

While 1978 had been a banner year with $242 million in profit, by the time Roderick took over the Company's strength and market share was plummeting, losing $363 million in his first year as chair, its market share down to 23 percent. In the words of one International official, the Company had become "big and fat and stupid," having failed to anticipate or prepare for the onslaught of foreign competition from countries like Germany, Japan, and South Korea, with their state-subsidized companies and modern plants. Domestically, "mini-mills" had sprung up everywhere in the U.S., utilizing the more cost-effective process of electric arc furnaces, which used scrap steel, as opposed to the costlier open-hearth process used by U.S. Steel at most of its facilities. Dating back to the post–World War II period, the Company had failed to invest in any new technology for its aging facilities. In the fourth quarter of 1980, U.S. Steel lost $561 million, the largest quarterly loss in American corporate history.

Wall Street analysts began advising steel companies to take a different path, one that emphasized profits over all other considerations. As Prudential-Bache researcher David Fleischer argued, "The proper strategy for running a steel mill in this country was to invest nothing in it, to strip as much cash out of it as you could and just walk away from the goddamn thing."[1] That this advice failed to take into account the tens of thousands of steel industry employees who would soon lose their livelihoods did not deter U.S. Steel, with Roderick now at the helm, from following it to the letter. As he stated in the December 6, 1981, issue of *Fortune* magazine: "There are no more sacred cows."

A massive downsizing of the steel industry was accelerated, coupled with a divestment into other lines of business, including chemicals, gas, oil, and real estate. This set a trend for other industries in the following decades. U.S. Steel scoured the globe looking for ways to increase its rate of profit through joint ventures, buying foreign companies, and just flat out purchasing foreign-made steel, all at the expense of their own American workers.

In specifically dealing with their aging steel facilities in the Monongahela and Mahoning Valley in Western Pennsylvania and Ohio, U.S. Steel revived an idea that had been talked about since the days of Andrew Carnegie and Henry Clay Frick: a proposal to build a brand new "super-mill" at Conneaut, Ohio, on the shores of Lake Erie, just west of the Pennsylvania/Ohio border. The new plant would be completely integrated, meaning all phases of the steelmaking process would be at this one site. In terms of geography, it was a very sensible idea. Iron ore could be brought in from Minnesota by barge and dropped off in Conneaut, instead of traveling overland by train to the steel mills around Pittsburgh or other steel centers in Ohio and Western Pennsylvania. Finished steel could also be shipped out by way of the Great Lakes and the St. Lawrence Seaway. Another advantage of the proposed mill would be its modern facilities. It would be a steel plant that would be built with new technologically advanced steelmaking equipment. While to U.S. Steel this sounded like a great idea, to steelworkers in Ohio and Pennsylvania, it sounded like a death sentence for their mills and jobs. To environmentalists around Lake Conneaut, it sounded like poison.

As noted earlier, mills like the Ohio-McDonald Works in Youngstown, Ohio, and the Homestead Works were old and decaying, running on machinery that should have been upgraded or replaced years earlier. Rank and File Caucus activists surmised at the time that if Conneaut was built, U.S. Steel would have no need for its older facilities and would most likely close them. Already, in the Youngstown region, the Campbell Works of Youngstown Sheet and Tube had shut down in September 1977, putting over 5,000 people out of work. By the end of 1979, two more mills in the Youngstown area would be closed, including the LTV Corporation's Brier Hill Works, shut down in December 1979, throwing 1,200 more people out of work. Then U.S. Steel's Ohio-McDonald Works were closed in January 1980, putting another 3,500 workers out on the streets. In three short years, over 10,000 workers in steel and related industries lost their jobs in the Youngstown region.

Many of us began to recognize that "the shutdown winds were blowing in our direction." Like an incoming rain storm, you could smell it in the air. At Michele's urging, in July 1979, Ronnie and Local 1397 joined others in retaining the services of Staughton Lynd to file a lawsuit against the U.S. Army Corps of Engineers to rescind U.S. Steel's permits for construction at Conneaut.[2]

Attorney and activist Staughton Lynd.

Along with Local 1397, the suit included two local unions from the Youngstown area, five Conneaut residents, two unemployed Youngstown steelworkers, and a number of regional groups and coalitions, including the Tri-State Conference on the Impact of Steel, an ecumenical coalition based in Youngstown that was formed to help fight the closing of Youngstown's steel mills, along with others in Ohio, Pennsylvania, and West Virginia. The coalition and lawsuit not only spanned two states, it was an excellent example of an organizational form that united workers, unions, communities, and environmentalists.

The plaintiffs asked for a new study to consider the impact of job losses in the tri-state area and the effect of the new mill on Lake Erie

Michele McMills and me at Youngstown demonstration, May 1979.

and the surrounding wilderness. In opposition to U.S. Steel's plan, they proposed what would become known as "brownfield moderniza- tion:" instead of building a new plant from scratch on what was called a "greenfield site," at great expense, the Company should invest in updating their older mills at so-called "brownfield sites." The financial savings would be substantial. It would also save miles of lakefront prop- erty from pollution, as well as take advantage of the skilled workers and infrastructure already in place at the brownfield sites. The court battle would carry on through 1979 and continue into 1980. Eventually, with opposition mounting and U.S. Steel's massive downsizing underway, the Company decided against building their Conneaut "super-mill," and the court case was dropped. A small victory and short reprieve had been won, but it only masked the carnage to come.

By late 1979, the fears of the "shutdown winds" heading toward the Mon Valley became reality. On November 27, U.S. Steel announced the entire or partial closing of over a dozen of its facilities, including the Ohio-McDonald Works in Youngstown and the 48" Plate Mill at Homestead. More than 13,500 workers would be thrown into the unem- ployment lines. For the Youngstown workers, this was the last straw. On November 30, seven chartered buses filled with four hundred dis- placed steelworkers and their families left Youngstown for Pittsburgh,

1397 Rank and File newspaper, September 1980.

to protest in front of the headquarters of U.S. Steel at 600 Grant Street. They were joined by 150 to 200 workers from Pittsburgh-area mills, including Ronnie, Joe Stanton, me, and a sizable contingent from Local 1397. Unbeknownst at the time, there was a small group of workers from the United Steelworkers of America (USWA) International headquarters who snuck up at lunch time and joined the rally, including my future wife Stephanie.

Youngstown steelworkers had already been waging a valiant struggle against insurmountable odds to keep their mills open. They were led by two union leaders out of the Brier Hill Local 1462, President Ed Mann and Vice President and Grievance Chair John Barbero. Avowed socialists, anti-war activists, and outspoken and militant advocates for the IWW's "one big union" concept, they both epitomized everything I thought a union official should be. They were the first living industrial worker heroes I had experienced in the flesh. I first met them in May 1979, when Michele took Greg Klink and me up to a big rally in downtown Youngstown.

The resentment the Youngstown movement felt for the USWA International Union was not without merit. On numerous occasions, Lloyd McBride and the International told Youngstown steelworkers "they were on their own." Not only did he refuse to help those trying to save the mills, he accused them of being "Phonies . . . people who put other people's blood and money on the line."[3]

Ed Mann and John Barbero.

During this Youngstown rally, a technician from the International Union was informing displaced workers about their severance and pension rights (at the time, we called them "funeral benefits"). All of a sudden, I heard this guy shout, "Bullshit, bullshit, we want our jobs not bullshit." When I asked Michele who that was, she said, "Oh, that's Ed Mann. Wanna meet him?" Later at a local restaurant, I met Ed Mann, John Barbero, and attorney Staughton Lynd for the first time. They were men of action, my kind of people. At the lunch table, for the first of many times, I heard John Barbero compare the carnage in Youngstown to what he had witnessed at Hiroshima after the atomic bomb was dropped, asserting the steel owners were just using a different kind of bomb. Several years later, I composed a ballad in honor of these two forgotten heroes.

Flowers of the Working Class
John Barbero and Ed Mann were from Youngstown, Ohio.
Steel warriors of the rainbow, they were kind and gentle souls.
Native sons, two of the ones who would speak for the community.
Union misters, human resisters to every kind of slavery.

Barbero and Mann were a force pushing forward our history.
And, you know, they were never afraid when confronted with the
   enemy.
Prophesizers, organizers of the people in the mills and factories.
Future molders, courageous foot soldiers in the fight to be free.

Then raise your heads, let your conscience arise;
The rain and wind are swirling outside.
Seize the time, grab hold of the day;
Pick up your sword, we have dragons to slay.
Hear what they said, remember their names;
They may be dead but their spirit remains
In the hearts of you and me!

Barbero and Mann have come and gone, like the sand in the hourglass.
Their spirit will live on. They were flowers of the working class,
Of the working mass, of the working class.

At the November 30 demonstration at U.S. Steel's downtown headquarters at 600 Grant Street, I got to see these three in action. When Ed Mann got up to speak with a megaphone on the sidewalk outside, he said, "It's really cold out here, let's go inside." As he burst through the glass doors of the Ivory Tower, John Barbero, Staughton, and the entire crowd followed him. We marched around the first-floor corridor in circular fashion three or four times shouting and chanting slogans. As Staughton Lynd spoke through a handheld megaphone at the foot of the escalators that led to the second-floor mezzanine, followed by Local 1330 president Bob Vasquez, Eric Stovall, a steelworker from Duquesne Local 1256, and I edged closer to the security guard at the bottom of the escalator, who put his arm out to block us. Eric looked at me, shrugged his shoulders, and said, "Let's go," knocking the guard's arm out of the way with me right behind him. As office workers stared in disbelief, the six hundred demonstrators marched up the escalator and around the second-floor mezzanine chanting, "The threat is real from U.S. Steel" and "We want Ayatollah Roderick," the CEO of U.S. Steel, whose office was on the top floor. (The *Ayatollah* reference was to the Iranian hostage crisis occurring at the same time.)[4]

After four or five circuits around the second floor, a few of us said, "Let's go for the elevators." But the electricity had been shut off, preventing demonstrators from going up or executives from coming down. As nervous union officials tried to coax us back outside, the crowd erupted in chants of "Hell no, we won't go." While a handful of us were determined to stay, by 4:00 p.m., the leaders had decided that the point had been made, filing out of the building and back onto the

November 30, 1979 demonstration at 600 Grant Street.

Local 1397 demonstration to extend UC, 1983.

Local 1397, Network to Save the Mon Valley, MVUC, Tri-State mass demonstration, downtown Pittsburgh, December 1983.

buses. As a consequence of this action, U.S. Steel subsequently spent tens of thousands of dollars revamping the security system for the entire building.

Two months later, on January 28, 1980, Youngstown steelworkers and supporters from Homestead and Pittsburgh—after a militant speech by Ed Mann at the Local 1330 union hall—followed him down a steep hill and stormed into the U.S. Steel headquarters in Youngstown, holding the building for an entire day. Of course, hindsight is always 20/20, but we should have never left; in each of these instances, we should have made them drag us out of there kicking and screaming.

Takeover of the U.S. Steel headquarters in Youngstown, Ohio, January 1980.

This was a mistake repeated at nearly every critical juncture in our struggle.

With the U.S. Steel Building occupation on November 30, a handful of us began to sound the alarm for workers at Homestead, as well as other steel mills in the Monongahela Valley—and not usually to receptive ears. At a local union meeting in June 1980, after seven of us had attended an unemployed conference in Youngstown (while I was on layoff myself), I reported that Homestead and other Mon Valley facilities could soon suffer the same fate as the Youngstown mills, that many of the conditions were the same. When I was finished speaking, this Central Maintenance worker cornered me against the back wall. He shoved his finger in my face claiming, "I don't know where you came from or who you think you are, but you don't know shit. They can shut every plant in the country down, but Homestead will still be here." The disbelief that Homestead would ever close was as solid as concrete, not just for this brother but for hundreds of other Homestead steelworkers. Because of Homestead's consistent production history—government and military contracts, etc.—many of its workers thought the mill was invincible, that it would be there forever. Some of us knew better. Five or six of us, including top officers Ron Weisen, Michele McMills, and Joe Stanton, became active participants in the Tri-State Conference on the Impact of Steel, a coalition of academics, priests, community activists, and steelworkers mainly from the Youngstown, Ohio, area who were committed to fighting layoffs and the plant shutdowns. This coalition was the precursor to the Pittsburgh-based Tri-State Conference on Steel (TSCS) that Charlie McCollester and I reconstituted when we were laid off in 1980 and the shutdown winds shifted to Pittsburgh and the Mon Valley.

CHAPTER 13

MY LAST HURRAH INSIDE THE MILL

From 1978 until early 1980, I worked hard and partied hard. With my utility crane job, I would be on a different crane practically every week, sometimes every night; I fell in love with operating the electric overhead traveling (EOT) cranes. To see the steel mill operations from thirty or forty feet in the air was to see a whole different world. Operating a crane, picking up steel and driving it the length of a bay without swinging or dropping it, placing long sheets of plate steel in railroad cars or on trucks that could barely hold it and picking up huge scrap

Mike Stout in his mill garb, 1982.

buckets thirty feet below the ground and dumping the contents in railroad cars was more than simple mechanical rote; it was an art. I loved every minute of it.

With my new assistant griever position in May 1979, I not only got to go toe to toe with the bosses and fight for real justice, I also made lots of new friends and relished the familial mill comradery. The 4:00 p.m. to midnight shift was the wildest; there were fewer bosses and a lot of card playing in between jobs. Maintenance crews were like firemen: always on call but not always putting out fires. At lunch, sometimes thirty or forty workers would gather at the smoke stack behind the 100"/160" slab yard along the Mon River, where the joints were passed around like a ritual before the sandwiches broke out. Unlike anywhere else I had lived or worked, in this area back in the late 1970s, marijuana was openly smoked—in the mill *and* in the bars around town. I even saw guys light up right in front of certain foremen. The Company didn't seem to care. Unlike other drugs, such as heroin and cocaine, when new hires or recalled employees were given their physicals, I was told directly by management that marijuana detection was overlooked. Marijuana can stay in your system up to thirty days after its use. One Company labor contract administrator (LCA) even told me in 1983 that they knew I had marijuana in my system and didn't care. U.S. Steel seemed to be way ahead of their time on this issue. While I didn't condone using marijuana inside the mill (I could have never done my crane job high), what people do after hours is their own business.

One thing I learned about marijuana in my youth was that it affected different people in different ways. For the majority of users, it's akin to an after-work martini or beer—it simply relaxes you. Having used marijuana myself for twenty-five years, as well as watching hundreds if not thousands around me for three decades smoke or eat it, it was obvious that it did not impair people the way alcohol does. It might make some people drowsy and lethargic, but for me—being extremely hyper and overly energetic—it calmed me down; made me more discerning, levelheaded, and focused. Placing marijuana in the same crime category as heroin and cocaine is beyond ridiculous. Claiming it's a "gateway to harder drugs" is even more ridiculous, as 99 percent of its users know full well. If someone is looking for harder drugs or escape, it won't be because they smoked marijuana. It should have been legalized back in the 1970s, as is now being done state by state. Anyone who has a beer, glass of wine, shot of whiskey, or takes prescription drugs and condemns someone who uses marijuana has either never tried it or is an unadulterated hypocrite.

Outside the mill and union life, hardly a day off went by that I didn't go to a concert, frequenting the Stanley Theater, the Civic Arena in downtown Pittsburgh, and clubs like Mancini's in McKees Rocks and the Decade in Oakland. Ritchie Blackmore, the Police, Heart, Blue

Öyster Cult, Foreigner, John Mellencamp, Pat Benatar, Greg Lake, Styx, Bob Marley, the Clash, Springsteen, AC/DC—I caught all the major acts, not to mention a host of local talent, including Joe Grushecky and the Iron City Houserockers, who were about as working-class rock as you can get. While working in the mill and being active in the union gave me little time and energy for writing and playing, music was still my constant companion. Inside the mill and out, I was having a good time. After Reagan's election, deregulation, disinvestment, and Roderick's announced shutdowns, the party would soon be over.

The Job Slaughter at Homestead Begins

Homestead's 48" Plate Mill was closed at the end of 1979. Chaos ensued. An obscure and unknown Slab and Plate local seniority agreement from 1966 allowed close to two hundred displaced 48" mill workers to bump into the 100" and 160" Plate Mills and the 45" Slab Mill at similar jobs, carrying all their seniority and leapfrogging over employees who had been at their jobs for years in these facilities. Fights broke out everywhere; resentment and hostility were the order of the day. Solidarity was almost completely absent. Slab and Plate management and the elected Slab and Plate grievance representative treated these 48" displaced workers like pariahs—superintendents ignored their rights, and the union refused to pursue grievances on their behalf. It was bloody, and it was a taste of things to come.

By the end of April 1980, the cutbacks caught up to me, and I was laid off. With the fifteen or so grievances I had filed that were still pending, Slab and Plate contract administrator Jim "Country Bumpkin" Brown accused me of stacking the grievance procedure. He put the word out through the grapevine that I'd never be coming back. Of course, I had been through this movie before at American Standard in Louisville. I was not about to fade into the night without a fight.

While laid off and collecting unemployment compensation (UC), I immersed myself in a host of activities, including writing for and assembling the union newspaper, constructing and organizing the Pittsburgh-based Tri-State Conference on Steel (TSCS) with Charlie McCollester, and working with the newly formed unemployed committee. The local union unemployed committee was first proposed by a female coworker, Lynn Morton, and endorsed by Ron Weisen at the April 1980 local union meeting. Some of her male coworkers referred

to Lynn as the "Amazon woman," which she considered a compliment. She took no crap from anyone—management or fellow workers. She always went to bat for her sister workers. Close to two dozen laid-off workers at Homestead got involved with the committee; it's where I first met my close friends Jay Weinberg, Artie Leibowitz, and Jerry Laychak from the Forge Division, as well as young furloughed workers from other parts of the mill.

Working with several dozen political activists from other mills, including Steffi Domike from Clairton, Linny and Eric Stovall, Beth Destler and Jim Benn from Duquesne, Barney Oursler, Jim Cottone, Tim Sessions, Sheryl Johnson, and Lois Brown from Irvin Works, as well as a host whose names I've forgotten, a "postcard campaign" was launched to get a bill passed through Congress extending UC benefits, which at the time could only be collected for six months.

We also pushed for another bill that would open up Trade Readjustment Allowance (TRA) benefits to thousands of laid-off steel-workers.[1] After getting eleven thousand postcards signed, a trip was planned to Washington, DC, in September 1980, to meet U.S. Senator John Heinz (R-PA) and congressional representatives to present our petitions and demands. With the bad blood between Ron Weisen and the District getting worse, the District Union was wary of any independent activity. Director Lewis reneged on his promise to pay for

Above: Inside the White House.

Left: Steelworkers argue with Senator Heinz in support of TRA and UC extensions.

the printing of the postcards, and United Steelworkers of America (USWA) legislative director in DC, Jack Sheehan, unilaterally cancelled our meeting at Heinz's office with the press and congressional representatives. Instead, we were stuck in an obscure wing of the White House, with fourth-level administrators of the Carter administration and some International Union officials present. As I explained in the newspaper:

> Realizing we were being used, we all started yelling and reminding Sheehan, Lewis and company that we were there to try to get the TRA and UC extension bills passed, and no other reason. We walked out of the meeting, re-phoned the press, and demanded to see our representatives. While outside talking to the press, Senator Heinz pulled up in his shiny limousine and informed us that though the UC extension passed the House, it wouldn't

make it through the Senate. Faced with an increasingly hostile crowd, he looked at his watch, said I have another appointment, and sped off in his limo.

After returning to Pittsburgh, District Union officials told Irvin Mill unemployed members that the District would only help them further if they did things through "proper channels" (the District Legislative committee) and disband the unemployed committee. Needless to say, that wasn't going to happen.[2]

A few years later, Sheehan and assistant John Powderly quietly told Barney Oursler and me that we had taught them the power of confronting congressmen by bringing real workers to speak and fight for themselves.

CHAPTER 14

LOCAL 1397 ACTIVITY GROWS

With more layoffs looming in the wings, the Weisen administration continued its fight to make the union more effective and Homestead a better place to work by initiating a number of new programs for the membership. Along with establishing the Local 1397 unemployed committee, many of the committees that had been dormant under previous Local 1397 administrations were revitalized: the community services committee, headed by John Sinchak, the legislative committee, headed by Ron Mamula and later Ed Wuenschell, the job classification committee, headed by Jack Bair, the education committee, and especially the grievance committee, headed by John O'Toole. Through 1980, the women's and civil rights committees remained active and continued to grow, attending conferences and off and on involving dozens of women and African Americans, including Piper Newland, Carolyn Grinage, LuJuana Deanda, Kathy Kozachenko, Mary Hirko, Carol Belluci, and Lynn Morton, among many others. Also, under the direction of 45" mill crane operator and sports enthusiast Gary Kasper, the sports programs and activities were revved up: bowling and basketball leagues were established, and the golf league was expanded to five teams. Alcoholic Anonymous meetings were held every week at the Local 1397 union hall for people who needed counseling to help them beat the disease. Scholarships were also awarded to dependents of members of Local 1397 on a yearly basis. Coupled with the dramatic increase in grievances, the union hall was a beehive of activity. While Ronnie always made sure everybody knew who was in

charge and where the buck stopped, he was very adept at giving committees leeway in their activities.

On Labor Day, September 1, 1980, Local 1397 marched in a major
parade through town, celebrating the borough of Homestead's cen-
tennial. Our local union banner was carried by Ronnie, 160" laborer
Kathy Kozachenko, Central Maintenance apprentice B.J. Buchannon,
my stepkids Richie and Shannon, and longtime activist and friend Paul
Piccurilli from Local 1211, up in Aliquippa. Behind our contingent were
Charlie McCollester and a half dozen Capuchin friars, including Father
Rich Zelik, representing the Tri-State Conference on Steel (TSCS). They
carried a banner that read: "People United to Defend Steelworkers
and Steelmaking." Most observers on the parade route were baffled by
the idea that steelmaking in Homestead needed defending, but with
our experience in Youngstown, some of us were more than a little bit
worried.

The "beer blasts" continued in 1980 and 1981 in the form of
huge picnics held at the Kennywood Amusement Park, a few miles
down Route 837 from Homestead in West Mifflin. Back in the day,
Kennywood was known for one of the fastest and wildest wooden roller
coasters in the country, the "Thunderbolt," which I rode over and over
every time I visited the park. Raffles were held with prizes such as

televisions, microwave ovens, Pittsburgh Pirates baseball tickets, and gift certificates. Health-O-Ramas, which provided free health tests to the local's members, were also held at the Homestead Works. To help strengthen the local financially, eleven investment bonds were purchased, each valued at ten thousand dollars. With the publication of five issues in 1980, the newspaper continued to grow, expanding to twenty pages.

CHAPTER 15

RANK-AND-FILE ATTEMPTS TO GO DISTRICT-WIDE

I n addition to the increased activity at Local 1397, Weisen ran twice for the office of District 15 director, attempting to build a district-wide rank-and-file movement. His first bid came in 1981, when he lost to incumbent Paul Lewis by a very close margin. According to local union vice president John Ingersoll:

> Weisen beat Lewis, but the voting and final count was controlled by the District office and its staffmen; they did not want Weisen in office, and he wound up losing by five hundred votes. Running for higher union offices in the USWA was like "playing cards against someone that has four aces; you can't beat 'em."[1]

On November 2, 1981, Paul Lewis passed away. Some of his staff, including Jack Coates, accused us of contributing to his death with our relentless bombast against him in the local union paper. In fact, Lewis weighed over three hundred pounds, and his heart simply gave out. Outside of his political infighting with Ronnie and his often blind loyalty to the bureaucracy downtown, Lewis was a decent guy and good union man who did some progressive things, like supporting and helping to organize a rally in Uniontown to oppose the KKK. As noted earlier, he assisted the Central Maintenance employees in their fight against the $385,000 payback. He was also instrumental in establishing a serious veterans' program, helping Vietnam vets experiencing PTSD (post-traumatic stress disorder). Homestead Vietnam veteran Joe Nestico was its chair and most active advocate and voice.

With the death of Paul Lewis, a special election was held on July 29, 1982, to choose the District director for the remainder of his incomplete term. Weisen again ran for the post but was defeated in a four-man race by the International's handpicked candidate Andrew "Lefty" Palm, a mill clerk who garnered 6,528 votes to Weisen's 4,984. As to the two other candidates, Ernest Wadsworth collected 2,975 votes, and Russell E. Bergsted received a total of 2,059 votes. While Ronnie thought his militancy, outspokenness, and anti-corporate rhetoric would carry the day, his unrelenting attacks on the District staff ensured his defeat.

A Final Tribute

PAUL E. LEWIS

1929-1981

A Tribute
PAUL E. LEWIS
1929 - 1981

Local 1397 and Paul Lewis did have their differences, but that doesn't detract from the fact that Mr. Lewis was a labor leader. In these Anti-Labor times, Labor needs all the friends it can get.

1397 Rank and File newspaper, December 1981.

In speech after speech, he urged all the staff representatives to "buy Winnebagos," telling them they would soon be hitting the road. It was a mistake he would repeat over and over again, grouping the District staff into one big lump. Some of these staff were disgruntled with the District and the International, as witnessed by the fact that two of them were running against the International's chosen candidate. Ronnie could have formed an alliance with at least one of them, which would have easily put him over the top. Gingerly, I tried to get Ronnie to stop painting all District staff with the same corruption brush but to no avail. Because of my short time in the union, before I became Slab and Plate zone griever I didn't have much political influence with Ronnie.

Though he did not win the District directorship, Weisen and the 1397 Rank and File Caucus were making strides not only in changing Local 1397 but also the direction of the union at other locals in the area. Rank-and-file groups were sprouting up in other mills. New contacts and friends were established, from Steubenville, Ohio, to Johnstown, Pennsylvania. Our staunchest allies were at the Irvin Works, with Local 2227 president Mike Bond and grievance chair Ross McClellan.

★

From May 1980 through the end of the year, I immersed myself in the Tri-State Conference on Steel (TSCS) formation effort, the unemployed committee postcard campaign, and putting out the 1397 *Rank and File* newspapers. In my estimation, the newspaper achieved the height of its democratic expression that year, with dozens of workers contributing. In addition to the "Plant" and "Union Plague" sections, committee reports, pictures, and cartoons, the twenty-page July issue gave a detailed breakdown of the new Basic Steel Contract point by point, including its complete neglect of the major issues confronting steelworkers at Homestead: job eliminations, contracting work out to nonunion shops, the antiquated grievance procedure, and, of course, the plant shutdowns and job loss. With its promise to keep the local's financials transparent, the newspaper gave the yearly totals of "lost time" (payments for time off the job to do union business) taken by every officer, griever, and their assistants. Transparency and democracy were the name of the game.

The September and December issues were increasingly hard-hitting, with even more outlandish cartoons, including a picture of

"Dumbest Foreman of the Year"

All year we've been running a contest to find the "dumbest foreman in the mill". From the beginning, we stressed 3 criteria: low levels of intelligence, incompetence, with harassment and mental torture abilities important to take into account.

As you all know, picking *one* winner was difficult with so many prime candidates. While several dozen contestants ran neck and neck, they all were a distant second behind the truly dumbest foreman alive: Dave Maravich, the ex-cry baby from the Open Hearth - turned Gestapo "Safety Man".

In the space of a few months last winter, as a safety man, this clockwork orange looney tune pissed more people off and made more enemies than Atila the Hun did in a lifetime. Ignorant, inhuman, incompetent, infantile — Cry Baby Dave has it all.

Every employee who worked in OH5 and didn't have wax in their ears knew that Cry Baby Dave was a heavy gambler. After falling thousands of dollars in debt, and building an army of mill workers that wanted to wring his neck, this Pinkerton clone decides to kill 2 birds with one stone: burn his own house down to collect the insurance money to pay off his gambling debts, and then blame it on the union or any one of a dozen employees who threatened to punch him out the week before.

Being the incompetent jerk he is, he left a trail of clues a detective on quaaludes could follow.

Maravich claimed that after a fellow foreman received an 'anonymous tip' that a 'hit was going down on him,' he sent his wife and children to stay with his in-laws. Around midnight that same evening, February 19, he was allegedly awaken by two masked men who put a gun to his head, tied him to a bedpost, doused the house with gasoline, and set the hallway on fire. Somehow, he miraculously wasn't shot, knocked out, hit, overcome by smoke, and escaped out a bedroom window.

But according to an Allegheny Police Report, there was absolutely no sign of forced entry, the fire started in the bedroom, not the hallway, a used book of matches were found on the patio awning Maravich had jumped over during his 'escape.' The belt he said his hands were tied with was soaked with gasoline, and a gas-wet towel

was found on the front seat of his flashy Lincoln Mark VI parked in the garage.

Was he trying to get caught? Is there anyone really *that* dumb?

After he was officially arrested in March, Maravich quietly dropped out of sight, and crawled back into the hole from whence he came. But just like the retired Steelers of Super Bowl fame, his legend will live on at Homestead, and his record-breaking feats will stand in the books for quite some time: personal responsibility for more than 10 discharges, most disciplinary slips issued, ten times as many enemies as any other member of management, one of the truly sick people in the world.

On more than one occasion local union members tried to tell upper-level management that all of Maravich's brain was not there; that he was dangerous, vindictive, and belligerent. Of course, management never listens to us.

Congratulations, Dave, you are living proof that you are what you eat, everyone catches their lunch sooner or later, and the chickens DO come home to roost.

1397 Rank and File **newspaper, March 1983.**

Director Lewis at the convention in Los Angeles reading our paper. We also began a "Dumbest Foreman in the Mill" contest, including a form to fill out coupled with a Howdy Doody drawing with a bolt going through his hard hat.

With the layoffs of some five hundred workers through the year, I wrote an article detailing the various methods the Company was using to cut their man-hours per ton: crew size reductions, forced overtime, job combinations, and using foremen to do our work. The article strongly urged workers to file grievances against these contract violations. Privately and off the record, both Ronnie and I urged workers to slow down and refuse to do the added workload. I also urged those on layoff to get involved with the unemployed committee. In December, I wrote a full two pages devoted to the work and campaigns of the unemployed committee. Also in this issue, a couple of us helped Ronnie craft a letter to Roderick, with specific proposals on how "we can work together to try to save the Homestead Works." This letter is worth reprinting:

Mr. David Roderick Chairman of the Board
United States Steel Corporation 600 Grant Street
Pittsburgh, PA 15219

Dear Mr. Roderick:
On this first anniversary of United States Steel's announce-ment of the closing of its Youngstown Works and other mills around the country, I am writing to you about the future of the Homestead Works.

. . .

I am aware that labor is often accused of opposing neces-sary technical progress. Because modernization often means loss of jobs in the short run, trade unions have sometimes opposed modernization.

Let me assure you that this is not my attitude. All of us in the Monongahela Valley have learned from the example of Youngstown. As I understand it, every mill which closed in Youngstown made steel by the open-hearth method. Those mills closed because of their failure to replace open-hearth steelmak-ing with a less costly process. We must not let that happen here.

At the same time, as I am sure you can understand, I am deeply concerned that modernization occurs in such a way that the existing workforce is not hurt. I believe this is possible. Can we not, working together, devise a plan and timetable for modernization such that jobs are permanently lost only by normal attrition as workers retire? In the case of Homestead, this might mean that even if BOFs or electric furnaces require 300 fewer men or women than the open-hearths, this reduction of force would come about through the retirement of the next 300 workers.[2]

The above would be a humane way to modernize. It would accommodate capital's need to modernize with-out sacrificing labor's concern for job security. It would be a plan worthy of the city of Pittsburgh, the community which stands for steelmaking in the history of this country.

Therefore, my second request is that *United States Steel and Local 1397 create a joint committee to explore the modernization of the Homestead Works.*

This committee would be advisory, as I see it. It would consider information available either to the company or the local union concerning possible modernization of the Homestead Works, and seek solutions beneficial to both. It would make recommendations to the corporation, the United Steelworkers of America, and the membership of Local 1397. By separate letter to the International Union, I am inviting the International Union to appoint a representative to the committee, to be present at its meetings, and to take part fully in its deliberation.

As of today, I am naming three members of Local 1397 as a committee of modernization. In the event that the company sees fit to do likewise, these three persons would then be the local union's representatives on the joint committee.

I look forward to hearing from you, as soon as possible, about the matters dealt with in this letter. I want to reemphasize the urgency with which I write. In this day and age, it cannot be expected that a local union will passively stand by and permit its membership, its income, and the source of livelihood for its members, to be destroyed. We believe we can play a creative part in determining the future of the Homestead Works. We insist that this local union, with its proud historic tradition, be treated as a partner in those decisions.

Sincerely, RONALD WEISEN
President, Local 1397
United Steelworkers of America[3]

Since the Rank and File Caucus was formed and took office, we—and Ronnie in particular—had been labeled troublemakers, anti-union, and a destructive force with nothing positive to say or offer. The above letter proved otherwise. It was only one of many attempts to get management to sit down with us and find some sensible solutions to the impending production and job loss. Of course, neither Roderick nor anyone else at U.S. Steel ever responded to these proactive proposals. As far as they were concerned, workers had no say in the decision-making process. Things hadn't really changed that much since 1892.

CHAPTER 16

UNEMPLOYED AND LIVING ON THE EDGE

B y the end of 1980, I was in dire straits financially. I had lost my cute little middle-class house at 4647 West Run Road, my family had moved back to Kentucky, and I had run out of unemployment compensation (UC). I was living on the first floor of an old ramshackle two-room wooden house across from Mesta Machine on Route 837, the main drag running through Homestead and other boroughs. My bedroom window was by a road that had potholes so big that every time a truck drove by it shook the windows and sounded like mini-bombs were going off. It was not a good residence for a chronic insomniac.

Once my UC ran out, the only thing that kept me alive through the winter months was a part-time job cleaning up the old St. Mary Magdalene grade school on 10th Avenue. I was given the job by its pastor, whom I had met during the Tri-State Conference on Steel (TSCS) organizing drive. Food-wise, I was down to cereal and maybe one square meal a week, usually as a guest at some friend's family dinner table. Holidays were dismal and lonely. When I wasn't at the union hall or working on TSCS's program with Charlie McCollester, I was running six miles a day, going from 140 pounds down to 120 pounds by the end of the year. Physically, financially, and emotionally, I was teetering on the edge. Listening to music was my only comfort and solace during this downward spiral in my life. Any sane person would have packed up and moved on.

Luckily, in late February and early March 1981, the plate mills started adding more work shifts, at least temporarily. Laid-off workers were getting called back in the 45″ mill and the 100″ shear

160" Plate Mill on a rolling turn, June 1982. This is where Mike Stout worked from April 3, 1981, to November 22, 1985.

bay, including some with less seniority than me. I had been going to the union hall checking work schedules and seniority rosters at least twice a week. Around the third week of March, I busted them when a friend with less time in the mill, Doug Coggin, was called back as a job class 3 laborer and let me know about it. I filed a grievance, and by the time it got to the third step, they had to put me back to work—on April 3, with back pay.

Things seemed to just fall in place when I returned to work. First, I immediately won a bid to be a utility crane operator in the 160" mill, considered the crème de la crème of the U.S. Steel rolling mills; i.e., the general belief was that it would be around forever. The very same week, the elected Slab and Plate grievance representative Nat King suddenly and unexpectedly grew ill and shortly thereafter died of cancer. A mini-battle ensued over who would take his place. Dozens were vying for this coveted "super-seniority" position,[1] all with a lot more time and seniority in the mill than I had. Some of the right-wingers in the union, not to mention the Slab and Plate management, were not too happy that I was back to work. In the end Ronnie, on John O'Toole's advice, prevailed and put me on. When asked why I was chosen over the other dozen or so battling for the job, John said, "It was a no-brainer. You were organized, a hard worker, and a fighter."[2] By mid-1981, both Weisen and O'Toole knew there was a major battle brewing.

As the newly appointed Slab and Plate griever representing two thousand workers, I was determined to use the "system" and grievance procedure to serve and protect the members, as well as getting them involved with the union and their own fight. Between my grievance job and new utility crane operator job in the premier rolling mill, I started to get to know people from all departments. I appointed some new assistants, guys like Billy Barron in the 160" Shipping Department, Rick Koza in the 160" Maintenance Department, Gary Kasper in the 45" Slab Mill, and Warren Rudolph in the 100" Shipping Department. To make sure the displaced 48" mill employees were represented, I added George Hunter in the 160" mill Flame Cutting Department. George, like other 48" mill workers, such as Joe Derry, didn't get bullied or pushed around. My criteria for someone to be a griever were: know how to think, know the contract, and don't take shit from or get bullied by the bosses. I kept several of the former African American assistants on, including Ron Lee and O.B. Horn, who not only fit the criteria but demonstrated I was determined to make sure African Americans were represented on my watch.

With only four years in the mill, I had the most powerful position among the zone grievers and super-seniority. Knowing I had something to prove, I dug into my job like a maniac. I put a flyer out in the mill and an article in the July and September 1981 issues of the local union newspaper:

Slab and Plate Members—A Message from Your New Zone Grievanceman

My name is Mike "Kentucky" Stout and I have been temporarily appointed as Head Grievanceman of the Slab and Plate Division (100", 160", 45" Mills and Slab Yard.)

I am here to support and represent *all* Slab and Plate members and to fight your grievances and for your rights as best as humanly possible. *I don't make deals* behind the backs of rank-and-file union members. *You*, the membership, are the backbone of this local union. You don't need a grievanceman that parrots the bosses and sounds more like management than management. You don't need a grievanceman that sides with the company against you in grievance meetings. You don't need a grievanceman who says "There's nothing I can do for you" or "Well, did you do it?" You don't need a union official who gives you a harder time than the company does. I'll fight every instance of Company harassment, every contract violation, and I'll fight every attempt by the company to eliminate your jobs.

Brothers and sisters: You are now paying $25–30 a month in union dues. 60 percent of this goes to the International and you

Slab and Plate office building behind the 160" Plate Mill, where the bulk of my grievances were fought.

get next to nothing for it. As for the 40 percent that goes to your local union, I'll work my hardest to give you the best union representation possible. I'll keep you informed of all union activities, layoffs and major grievances, as well as defending you against specific instances of harassment and exposing them through the pages of this paper.

Please join with me to fight the Company's job eliminations. Don't work overtime while people in your department are laid off. Report every contract violation and join your local union in the fight against plant shutdowns and the battle to bring democracy back to our union. If you need to get a hold of me, you can leave a message 24 hours a day at: 462-2522 (union hall), or call me at work: 412-464-2126.

Thank you,

Mike "Kentucky" Stout

I began to put articles in the newspaper informing workers of their contractual rights, how to file grievances, and how to "cover their asses." Under our contract, we had no paid "sick" or "personal days." I instructed workers how to take off work when necessary, without getting disciplined or getting docked any pay. Absenteeism was one of management's favorite ways to get rid of workers they didn't like.

As noted earlier, John O'Toole had been handling Homestead cases at fourth step and arbitration since 1980. Most of the cases he handled involved going to "mini-board arbitration," which heard disciplinary cases. These cases were usually expedited within a few weeks or months, and decisions were immediate; whereas "big board" arbitration handled discharges, job eliminations, crew cuts, seniority violations, contracting out, etc. It took months, sometimes years, to get through the procedure, get an answer, and get it implemented if we won. From mid-1981 on-job eliminations in one form or another dominated the grievance procedure.

As soon as I became griever, O'Toole started letting me handle mini-board cases for Slab and Plate. In fact, he encouraged all grievance representatives to handle their cases, but I was the only taker. Going up against my own bosses and winning at mini-board was energizing and empowering; I immediately got their attention and respect. Also, these quick wins encouraged the members to file grievances and stand up for their rights; it started to change the entire relationship between workers and management. The bosses feared a real union that fought for its members and, quite frankly, weren't used to it. Management tried both to intimidate me and to kiss my ass at the same time. They actually assigned a foreman named Allen Keyes (we called him "Carrot Head") to follow me around. I wasn't intimidated and let them know it; in fact, I started following him around.

The first discharge case I encountered immediately after I took office was a black worker from the 45" Slab Mill named Kenny Williams. Prior to the 8-B Hearing,[3] I was called behind closed doors by the Slab and Plate labor contract administrator (LCA) "Country Bumpkin" Jim Brown and then superintendent "Whiskey" Bob Frazier (it was rumored he always kept a half pint in his right-hand desk drawer; I can personally attest that the rumor was true, as I took a sneak peek).

They proceeded to tell me they were going to put the grievant back to work after three days without pay, but they wanted to "scare him— shake him up a little and put the fear of the Lord into him." When I told them I wouldn't agree to this, and that their days "game-playing" with the union were over, they both got red in the face, and Kenny was fired on the spot. The Company's case was weak, as Kenny (per my prior advice about "covering your ass") provided ample written

Jim Brown, Labor Contract Administrator of Slab & Plate, has been nominated ▪▪▪▪ of the Month. If either one of his two heads will step forward we'll give him the Award.

1397 *Rank and File* newspaper, September 1981.

documentation justifying his absence. He was back to work by the third step hearing and didn't miss a day's pay.

When I was an assistant griever and would go into second step meetings with Nat King and Jim Brown, they were always buddy-buddy, talking about their wives and home life, shooting the bull, and slapping each other on the back. Brown would play the down-home country bumpkin character, one of the good ol' boys. When the meeting started, he would turn into a shrewd and cunning corporate lawyer. They would then proceed to decide the fate of the grievant without his or her presence. Nat usually bowed to Brown's authoritative and intimidating presence. When I came in, all that stopped. They were scratching their heads, trying to figure out where the hell I came from and what "my

Jim Brown's Going-Away Party . . . GOOD RIDDANCE!

1397 Rank and File newspaper, January 1980.

angle" was. They even spread rumors I would be offered a white hat (foreman's job) before too long.

Within a few weeks of my taking office, Slab and Plate contract administrator and hatchet man Jim Brown saw the writing on the wall and decided to retire. I gave him a nice sending off in the newspaper.

Grievance Wars Escalate

In the 160" Maintenance Department where I worked, my main mill boss and archnemesis was general foreman Bill Fecko. He was smug, cocky, and smoked his cigarettes like Milton Berle, puffing his lips out with every exhale of smoke he blew in your face. When I introduced myself to Fecko for the first time, in May 1981, at his office, he said snidely, "Oh, this is going to be interesting, having a *real* in-house grievanceman." His attitude toward the workers was we were all in some class way beneath him.

My first big case, other than discipline, came in the fall of 1981. A huge layoff hit less than six months after I came back to work. The date was September 25, 1981. At Homestead, 1,800 workers were laid off, most never returning. Every department was devastated. Many people with more seniority than I had were laid off. Only my "super-seniority" grievance position kept me working. At the same time, older employees with more seniority transferred from other closed U.S. Steel facilities to Homestead, which created friction among the workers. In early October, a white millwright who had transferred from the U.S. Steel wheel and axle facility in McKees Rocks to the 160" mill, had an epileptic seizure at work. As the Company was in their "get rid of jobs" mode, the general foreman Bill Fecko told this millwright he was either bumped back from his craft position to a storeroom clerk (from a job class 16 to job class 4, with a huge pay cut) or "you're out the door." In a grievance meeting with Fecko, the wheel and axle transfer threatened, "Oh, yeah, well I got this black guy I work with named Courtney Senior, and he's been working for five years after numerous epileptic seizures. You didn't fire him. I'm filing discrimination charges against you." So how does the Company respond? They throw black millwright Courtney Senior out on the street.

Filed on October 16, 1981, it took close to a full year to get this grievance through the procedure. While, ostensibly, the board of arbitration was supposed to be neutral and impartial, it always appeared to give the benefit of the doubt to the Company. In my experience, when it was an employee's verbal testimony against someone in management, arbitrators usually believed management—kind of like when you're dealing with a cop in traffic court. Also, just like in real court, the arbitrator, Company lawyers, and union staff representatives would often meet behind closed doors and set parameters of cases out of earshot of the grieving employee and witnesses. Paperwork and documentation, much of which only the Company had access to, often decided the case.

Entering uncharted waters with my first big board arbitration case, I wasn't deterred one bit; I asked O'Toole if I could present the Courtney Senior discharge case in arbitration. He said, "Sure, why not?"

The word around the union hall was that no one had ever beaten U.S. Steel's medical department. I poured through the Company medical records on Courtney. I took him to the state and federal buildings, researching the laws and regulations on the legal rights and case histories of epileptics. Generally, the rule was after an initial period of a seizure, the epileptic was allowed to perform normal work functions as long as he was taking medicine and his epilepsy was under control. Courtney Senior had been put back to work for five years on his millwright job, because his epilepsy was under control. The Company had established a "past practice" for dealing with employees with epilepsy, covered under the 2-B Local Working Conditions section of the contract. This grievance appeared to be that old clichéd "slam dunk" to me.

On June 29, 1982, the case was heard by a black arbitrator whose name was Keith Neyland, a very attentive and fair-minded judge. When District Union staff representative George Myers announced I was presenting the case, the Company protested, claiming I had no right or jurisdiction. After conferring with the chair of the arbitration board Al Dybeck, Arbitrator Neyland told the Company representatives, "Only the union will decide who handles their case. The union makes that decision, not you."

With a gallery of six or seven craftsmen from the 160" Maintenance Department, including several witnesses ready to attest how well Courtney performed his job with no physical problems, I presented the mountains of documentation I had amassed. Fellow millwright Bob Collins, a Vietnam veteran, attested to Courtney's ability to perform his job after his seizures, with the proper medication. Several Company doctors, Assistant General Foreman John Halko, and Slab and Plate Maintenance Superintendent Dick Natili testified for the Company; none of them attempted to refute my "past practice" claim that they had allowed Courtney to work with his condition for five years. In fact, they just ignored my argument, as though I didn't know what I was talking about.

On September 29, 1982, the arbitrator ruled in the union's favor. We kicked their ass. Courtney was put back to work at his millwright job, with full back pay.[4] It was as though the Company gave him a yearlong all-expense paid vacation. Their shock at losing to an uneducated nobody worker with no formal legal training was written all over their faces. It would have been even bloodier had they known I was stoned on marijuana when I beat them. With Courtney back to work, word spread around the mill. Grievances came pouring in.

From this point on, I started handling all the Slab and Plate cases from the second step through arbitration, winning my first four cases.

To ensure continuity and transparency, I would make sure the grieving employee was present at every step of the procedure. Most of these grievances were individual job elimination cases, as the Company's cost-cutting measures intensified. After I won my first four cases, the Company started to counterattack, beating me the next three cases, relying on documents to which only they had access. After a hearing for one of these cases, I discovered that the Company (Fecko again) had altered a work schedule in his possession that was used as evidence to beat us. After the case was heard but before the decision was issued, I asked Al Dybeck, the board of arbitration chairperson, to reopen the hearing. In the privacy of his office he responded almost in a whisper: "There is nothing I can do about this. Once a case has been heard, it's been heard. Just like court. If I allow you to reopen a case that's been closed, it will open up a Pandora's box." After this episode, it became clear what I needed to do to beat the Company in arbitration: get access to their written documentation, as well as developing my own paper trail.

Throughout 1982 and 1983, the severity of the layoffs, crew cuts, job combinations, and contract violations intensified. Every department in Homestead was devastated. All through the Mon Valley the Company was shutting down entire departments and even entire mills, including the Edgar Thomson Works in Braddock. The devastation was shattering lives and families. The mill was on its last legs. The corporate bosses downtown put the word out to all the foremen and superintendents: "Get your production down to four man-hours per ton of steel produced, or you're finished." (At that point, they were at around ten man-hours per ton.) Management at every level started eliminating jobs. It was a massacre. Crews were cut down from twelve to two or three people. They knocked off second and third shifts, forcing those still employed to work overtime and ten-hour days. The contract was being torn to shreds. The Company violated it at will, in complete disregard for the people they were hurting. This situation was particularly heart-wrenching for me, as all the young workers I hung out and partied with were now in the streets. While for many Americans these were just statistics or blips on the evening news, for me they were friends—my mill family. Their pain was my pain. It just made me want to fight this lawless corporation even harder.

CHAPTER 17

THE BEGINNING OF THE END FOR STEELMAKING AT HOMESTEAD

I n July 1979, the local had 6,822 dues-paying members. By August 1981, only 5,824 remained, a loss of 998 members. With the layoff of 1,800 workers on September 25, 1981, the workforce at Homestead had lost over 2,700 jobs in just two years. By this stage, it was clear U.S. Steel had no intention of modernizing its antiquated steelmaking facilities or upgrading any equipment at Homestead. In November 1981, U.S. Steel announced the purchase of Marathon Oil at a price tag of over $6 billion, a move that shocked the people in the Monongahela Valley, as well as U.S. Steel employees around the country. Why, with its steel plants deteriorating, would U.S. Steel spend that kind of money to "branch off" into other industries? It seemed clear that it viewed the oil industry as more profitable than upgrading steel facilities and didn't really give a shit about its employees; it was that simple. Chairman David Roderick once told Congressman Peter Kostmayer from Eastern Pennsylvania, who had asked him to be part of a committee to explore ways of making the Fairless Works more cost competitive: "Look, I don't want one of those goddamned committees coming in here—a priest, a Boy Scout, and a housewife—telling us what to do. We're here to make money. You guys can't get that through your heads."[1]

For years, Roderick had lied about the corporation's plans to invest in the steel mills of the Monongahela Valley. In May 1979, after reaching a pollution reduction agreement with the EPA and the Carter administration, Roderick publicly stated, "Although this is a demanding package, it clearly demonstrates that U.S. Steel is committed to remaining in the steel business in the Monongahela Valley. . . . It can

1397 Rank and File newspaper, December 1981.

now act aggressively to revitalize our Pittsburgh-area operations."[2] In March 1980, in testimony before the Allegheny County commissioners, he claimed, "Right now we are reviewing plans to install a modern basic oxygen shop or other new steelmaking technology here in the Mon Valley to replace the present open-hearth steelmaking facilities at the Homestead Works." Nothing more was ever said or done about this "proposed" modernization plan. In December 1980, U.S. Steel sold coal reserves to Standard Oil for seven hundred million dollars, and Roderick publicly claimed that at least half this money was going to be used for modernization of steel mills. A few days later, he said the money from the coal sale would be used to purchase a new continuous caster for the Edgar Thomson Works in Braddock. Then at the annual shareholders' meeting on May 4, 1981, the plan was scrapped.

Roderick and U.S. Steel claimed that the purchase of Marathon Oil would not affect their plans for modernization of their steel mills. Even legislators did not understand this logic. Senator John Heinz, chair of the Senate steel caucus, was quoted as saying, "I don't know why U.S. Steel would want to spend six billion dollars on an oil company. My

May 5, 1981 Tri-State Conference on Steel Demonstration at U.S. Steel Stockholder's Meeting. Lynn Morton and Molly Rush (on left).

Moureen Trout, B.J. Buchannon, and Mari and Candice Wargo.

Barney Oursler keeping the pickets moving.

biggest concern is what this means for the company's modernization and expansion plans and, most important, area jobs." Senator Howard Metzenbaum, an Ohio Democrat, and another member of the Senate steel caucus, suggested that U.S. Steel was subverting the intent of Congress: "The purpose of relaxing taxes and environmental regulations for the steelmakers," Metzenbaum said, was to "give them money so that they could start producing more and start modernizing their facilities."[3]

On May 5, 1981, more than 150 members of Local 1397 and the Tri-State Conference on Steel (TSCS) (which at the time included those steelworker activists from other Mon Valley mills who would later form the Mon Valley Unemployed Committee) demonstrated against these disinvestment decisions outside the U.S. Steel stockholders meeting in downtown Pittsburgh. Meanwhile, inside the meeting, Ron Weisen and TSCS activist Father Rich Zelik, who both had proxy votes, confronted Roderick directly. In front of the hushed stockholder gathering, Roderick remained defiant and callous.

Unfortunately for the steelworkers in the Mon Valley, no "modernization" would come until late 1987, after a lockout in 1986 and long after 90 percent of the Valley had been shut down. Seven years after it was first promised and following a six-month lockout, the continuous caster meant for the Homestead Works was eventually installed at the Edgar Thomson Works, far too late to help prevent the demise of large-scale steel production in the Mon Valley.

By the end of 1981, the layoffs and shutdowns in the Pittsburgh region and around the nation had reached crisis levels. More than ten thousand basic steelworkers from U.S. Steel mills in the Mon Valley were on indefinite layoff. Nationally, one in four steelworkers was out of work, with steel plants operating at 50 percent of capacity. Employment in the domestic steel industry had plummeted to its lowest level in forty-eight years. On December 3, 1981, U.S. Steel announced it was closing the last two furnaces, nos. 3 and 4, at Carrie Furnace, located across the river from the Homestead Works, in Rankin. The furnaces had been operating since 1884; as recently as 1970, four huge furnaces, each over one hundred feet tall, had been producing pig iron for Homestead's Open Hearths. Homestead's "iron arteries" had now been completely severed.

While this tsunami was hitting industrial communities like Mon Valley and Turtle Creek Valley, looking like the depression that ravaged the U.S. in the 1930s, most of the country and many of my friends and relatives in other states, including New York, Kentucky, California, and Florida, seemed oblivious to what we were experiencing.

When the Rust Belt collapsed, most of the country was not immediately affected. The coasts with their imperial and global concerns remained largely indifferent, as did most of the political class. Technological development, the computer revolution, and the creation of the Silicon Valley and other high-tech centers were all in full swing. Coupled with the deregulation of interstate banking restrictions after the elimination of the Glass-Steagall Act by President Clinton, dollars from every state and mom and pop local bank were now flowing into derivatives and the global market. Debt became the standard, as credit cards became as accessible as televisions.

While a number of area politicians from the Mon Valley and Turtle Creek Valley worked conscientiously to mitigate the consequences of mass unemployment, they were far outnumbered by the ones basking

Gantry crane and water treatment facility, the last major upgrade by U.S. Steel at the Homestead Works. Installed in 1979 and brought into operation in 1982. Today, only the gantry crane remains, sitting between two hotels at the Homestead Waterfront Mall.

at the lobby feast of the New World Order. Only a handful understood that the demise of the basic production of goods people need to live, distinct from weaponry and fossil fuel–related manufacturing, linked us inexorably to an imperial global economic order. The untenable nature of this economic system, because of its environmental, military, or political consequences, is the problem facing us today.

Homestead management seemed completely clueless about downtown's real plans. At a January 1982 review meeting with Slab and Plate superintendent "Whiskey" Bob Frazier, he said, "I know it was a rough year, but things are looking up," pointing out the window to a new water treatment unit and giant gantry crane that had recently been installed along the river behind the 100" mill. The water treatment unit was never put into operation, and, to this day, the gantry crane sits idle, rusting behind the Waterfront strip mall, a relic of a forgotten past. The suspicion started gnawing at the back of my brain that this could be the beginning of the end for the entire Homestead Works.

CHAPTER 18

UNEMPLOYED ORGANIZING, FOOD BANKS, AND ROCK CONCERTS

A s the job loss ratcheted up, so did the unemployed organizing and activities of the more militant and outspoken steelworkers at every local. After six months at the griever job and over a year with the unemployed committee, a small group of younger workers banded together, becoming good friends in the process. This group had the support of Ron Weisen and the resources of the local union. Mike and Mari Wargo were two of these friends. We had been hanging out and partying together for several years. When Mike Wargo lost his job in the slab yard in December 1981, their doubts about the mill closing, which I had been preaching, turned to apprehension and anger; they were ready to rev up the fight.

We were at a Christmas party at the Wargos' house on December 26, 1981, when the food bank idea was born. With my knowledge of the "fight, don't starve" unemployed campaigns of the 1930s, I threw out the "worker's food pantry" idea to the hard-core partiers still there after midnight, including Jay Weinberg and Artie Leibowitz. Instead of the usual rolling of heads and changing the subject, everyone was at full attention. When the discussion turned as to where the financing was going to come from, Artie blurted out, "Hey, let's have a rock concert to raise the money." Having witnessed the connection of music to the movements back in the 1960s, I thought Artie was dead on target. Music was the fixer and elixir we needed.

We started listing local bands we knew. Mike Wargo's friend John "Ziggy" Seiger said he knew the Granati Brothers, four Italian blood brothers from Beaver County just north of Pittsburgh whose band had made it to the semi–big time, opening for Van Halen on a national tour. The ball was rolling.

Within several weeks, Mike called me and said the Granatis were on board; apparently, they had family and friends in steel who were losing their jobs and were more than sympathetic. They also agreed to contact other bands for us. Within a month, Joe Grushecky and the Iron City House Rockers and rhythm and blues singer extraordinaire Billy Price had jumped on board to volunteer their services. An African American quartet with killer harmonies and on fire percussion section, Rare Experience, was added to the lineup. Of all these fine musicians, Grushecky and the Granati Brothers were my cup of tea, especially the Granatis with their upbeat tempos, hard-driving rhythms, exquisite harmonies, and jumps in the air. Along with the House Rockers, these bands rocked. To say the least, I was geeked. The combination of rock and roll with labor organizing and grievance fighting was the ultimate elixir to carry me through some troubled times.

We immediately sprang into action. Jerry Laychak, along with longtime friend and Granati Brothers' cousin Paul Carosi, took responsibility for PR. (Paul and his wife Mary Anne later became two of my closest friends and biggest music supporters.) We contacted Pittsburgh radio stations for sponsorship, and rock station WDVE immediately jumped on board. Their popular morning show duo Steve Hansen and Jimmy Roach volunteered to MC the show. But to secure the Stanley Theater venue in downtown Pittsburgh, as well as do the initial advertising and outreach, we needed five thousand dollars. At the March 1982 local union meeting, under the auspices of the unemployed committee, I introduced a resolution requesting the money. The resolution stated the money would be paid back after the benefit. When three or four of the conservative wing of the local spoke out against the resolution, they were completely outgunned, as sixty workers who supported it had shown up. I'll never forget how elated I was to see Mike Wargo and his whole shift from the slab yard (many who were on layoff) ready to tango. Most importantly, Ronnie had earlier told the executive board that he was backing the idea, and they voted unanimously to support it, sealing the deal. When the vote came in the local union meeting, the "ayes" had it overwhelmingly.

For the next several months, we concentrated on outreach and ticket sales. At first, it appeared like we weren't getting much interest;

Author Mike Stout jumping two feet in the air, at the Local 1397 food bank benefit rock concert, April 14, 1982.

that attendance might end up less than five hundred. Then the two weeks before the show, WDVE pumped the shit out of it and ticket sales snowballed. On April 14, 1982, close to three thousand fans showed up; every band tore down the house. More than ten thousand dollars was raised, on top of the five thousand we paid back to the local. Every major network and news outlet covered the event. A few days later, I got a call from my dad in Kentucky saying he had just seen me on the *Today Show*, musing, "I'm not sure what you're doing, but it sounds like a good thing."

In between the Granatis and Joe Grushecky, I got to give my stump speech on the dire economic and political situation and why we needed a food bank. As the Steelers mascot, along with Steve and Jimmy (both over six feet tall—the top of my head barely reaching their chins)— looked upward in disbelief, I gave one of my best flying rock and roll leaps and yelled, "Are you ready to rock?"

The Food Bank Starts
Flush with success and start-up funds, several dozen of us met and set up our organization to get the food bank off the ground.

With Jay, Artie, and Jerry doing the networking, lobbying, and PR, the bulk of the preparation and distribution work was done by women

Our Organization

In order to maintain and expand the Food Bank effort, we have set up the following structure:

FUNDRAISING	FOOD-RAISING	ORDERING & DISTRIBUTION	ALL FOOD PICKUPS
Jerry Laychak	*Steve Minnaji*	*Barb Weibelt*	*Mike Wargo*
Jay Weinberg	*Art Leibowitz*	*Moureen Trout*	*Rich Mizak*
Jim Thorhauer			

	OVERALL COORDINATOR	
TREASURER	*Mike Stout*	SECRETARY/STAFF
MUSA	462-2522	*Sheila Stall*

Original food bank organizational chart.

mill workers, led by Moureen Trout, Barb Weibelt, and Sue Harakal from Slab and Plate. The women volunteers numbered over fifty and included the wives of steelworkers like Mari Wargo and my first wife Kena. Mike Wargo, Rich Mizak, and O.J. Simpson (yes, we had a white steelworker by that name) headed up a transportation crew that picked up the food from the Pittsburgh Strip District and got it to the distribution point in a timely fashion.

Like a well-oiled machine, within a month, on May 12, 1982, we had our first distribution at the Steel Valley Council of Governments (SVCOG) building on 17th and Maple Streets, ten blocks up the hill

The Slab and Plate food bank women, including Local 1397 Secretaries Darlene and Cheryl (top row).

Coordinating the October 1982 food bank distribution in the basement of the SV COG Building.

from the mill. By midsummer, we were handing out two full bags of groceries to 1,200 laid-off workers twice a month. Each distribution included milk, meat, cheese, cereals, and other nutritious food. We took pride in the type of food we were giving people, avoiding junk food whenever possible. In a short period of time, five other locals joined our food bank. I'll never forget the solidarity, comradery, and love I felt with this group. The decision-making process was familial, informal, and democratic.

A few months before our Local 1397 food bank started, activists at Clairton, Edgar Thomson, Irvin, and Duquesne Works started another food bank just as big as ours. But unlike at Homestead, which had the support of the local union administration, these activists had to pool their own resources and do independent fundraising, as their local unions did not officially or financially support the effort.

Initially part of the Tri-State Conference on Steel (TSCS), in 1982, this group would evolve into the Mon Valley Unemployed Committee (MVUC). They would wage an uphill but ultimately successful battle to

MVUC activists joined the TSCS and Local 1397 march through downtown Homestead, Labor Day, 1982.

slow down and curb mortgage foreclosures, passing and funding the Pennsylvania Homeowners Emergency Mortgage Assistance Program.

Working with other unemployed groups around the country, the MVUC was instrumental in extending unemployment and Trade Readjustment Allowance (TRA) benefits for the long-term unemployed. The Local 1397 Unemployed Committee joined in lobbying and pressuring Congress to reform and extend the TRA program that Reagan tried to destroy. The May 12, 1982, MVUC demonstration attended by thousands in downtown Pittsburgh was, in my opinion, the high point of their efforts, as the buzz of activity and protests up and down the Valley got more pervasive and louder.

In the summer of 1984, another important group that included laid-off Edgar Thomson worker Bob Anderson, his then

MVUC demonstration, downtown Pittsburgh, May 12, 1982.

UE steward Joe Jurich revs up demonstrators at the anti-Reagan demonstration outside the Hilton Hotel, April 6, 1983.

wife Theresa Chalich, a nurse, and community activists, including Delores Patrick, branched off the MVUC to form the Rainbow Kitchen on 8th Avenue and Amity Street in Homestead. Not only did the kitchen provide food and a breakfast program to laid-off steelworkers and feed the hungry, it was a hub of political activity in the area, with a free health clinic run by Chalich.

Nearly a year later, on April 6, 1983, a cold, rainy day, President Reagan came to town to tout his new retraining program. The MVUC joined with Local 1397, the United Electrical, Radio and Machine Workers (UE), and TSCS to organize more than four thousand angry workers—many on permanent layoff—to greet him at the downtown Hilton Hotel in a pouring down rain. When it appeared Reagan was exiting the Hotel, thousands rushed the front doors, giving the finger en masse, chanting: "Screw Nancy not the workers." Needless to say, the president had to sneak out the back door to avoid what was the most hostile workers' demonstration I had ever attended in Pittsburgh, rivaled only by the Pittsburgh Press lockout ten years later.

Unfortunately, as people's unemployment compensation (UC) benefits ran out, the number of volunteers and demonstrators dwindled, with workers having to find new jobs, many leaving the area. Building a sustained organization in steel communities experiencing

Joe Grushecky, Jay Weinberg, Artie Leibowitz, and Mike Stout, April 1982.

Mike Stout and Artie Leibowitz with members of the Granati Brothers and Rare Experience.

rapid job loss was like no other movement. As Staughton Lynd noted during the Youngstown shutdown fights:

> A plant closing struggle is totally unlike, say the struggle for the right to vote in the south, or resistance to the Vietnam War. There, no matter how small a movement's beginnings (one person in one town refusing to go to the back of the bus, four young men sitting in at a lunch counter), one could proceed with some confidence that the same causes which led the first person to resist would also prompt more and more resistance with the passage of time.
>
> In a plant closing struggle the movement may grow weaker rather than stronger as time goes on. When the closings in Youngstown were first announced there were, in each instance, angry mass meetings at which young workers especially talked about chaining themselves to machines, or blowing things up. With each shutdown, there were fairly militant actions in the first days or weeks after the announcement. . . . But as time goes on, collective outrage dims and personal survival takes over. The failure to produce a quick change leads to a mood of resignation and a focus on looking after oneself. The rhetoric of struggle is replaced by a rhetoric of benefits. Since each union member is slightly differently situated with respect to the benefits available, the pain of the plant closing becomes privatized and personal.[1]

During the initial year of the layoffs, the food bank distributions hummed along, with continuous concerts and fundraising activities.

We had every type of benefit concert from hard rock to blues to country. Not only did dozens of local groups, including the April 14 lineup and stars like the late great B.E. Taylor step forward, but national acts were tapped, including Corbin and Hanner. A former steelworker friend and supporter from Republic Steel, Lee Ballinger, knew Springsteen biographer and *Born to Run* author Dave Marsh,[2] who called in a favor and brought in rockers Molly Hatchet for a benefit at the Stanley Theater on June 2, 1983. In addition to the concert fund-raising, in an effort to create a steady stream of incoming funds,

Slab yard employee Rich Mizak helping at the first food bank distribution, May 12, 1982.

we initiated a "payroll deduction" program with the Company, so that those still working could donate directly to the food bank out of their paychecks. This idea actually originated from a group of older workers still on the job. After a phone call from Ronnie to plant superintendent Harry Dolan, hundreds of those still working were supporting their brothers and sisters on the street.

CHAPTER 19

UNION ELECTIONS—THE INTRAUNION BATTLES INTENSIFY

B y the next local union election in May 1982, Ron Weisen and our Rank and File Caucus local were at their strongest. Committees were at peak activity, the food bank was getting off the ground and, with two of us handling cases in arbitration, the grievance committee was fighting to slow down the job eliminations. By the time of the election, my grievance efforts were so strong and successful, no one dared run against me for the zone grievance position, which had super-seniority status. Hundreds of workers with more time than me were on layoff. With not even five years in the mill, I ran unopposed.

With Ronnie's continuing vitriol against the union bureaucracy's lack of response to the shutdowns, the International made a concerted effort to defeat us at the polls. Just prior to the election, the International audited the local and found that some of the officers had received improper expense payments. Ronnie was charged with a "fictitious" claim of $1,372 for airline flights. Apparently, he and four other officers had submitted reimbursement claims to the local for flying business class to the 1980 convention in LA, and then flew at a cheaper coach rate or drove out and back by car. When the audit was released on March 26, the red-faced officers immediately paid back the difference. It was wrong but chicken shit compared to the waste going on elsewhere at the upper echelons of the union.

Meanwhile, the International lined up those they thought were the Rank and File Caucus's strongest nemeses in the local; John Balint would run as vice president and former local president Mike Bekich would again run for president against Ronnie. At the local union

WEISEN'S A LOSER!!!

Vote Like Your Job Depended On It

THE RANK AND FILE WRECKING CREW

With the *1397 Rank and File* newspaper cartoons so wildly popular, the Job Protection Team opposition attempted to use cartoons of their own. Their "cartoonists" were given an "F" rating by the membership.

meeting a week before the election, they passed out a four-page report on the audit trashing the Rank and File Caucus officers, calling us thieves and telling the membership to throw us out of office.[1] With the local elections less than a week away, the purpose and timing of the audit were all too obvious.

In typical fashion, Ronnie's defense was to counterpunch with a strong offense. Our local sued the International for compensatory and punitive damages, accusing them of illegally interfering and attempting to influence the election process. To top it off, after we won reelection, we held an informational picket line downtown in front of the International Union's fortress at Five Gateway Center. This was always guaranteed to garner maximum publicity from the local press—and it did.

The International's ploy completely backfired: Weisen would be the first two-term president at Local 1397 in at least fifteen years. In a four-man race, he received 1,682 votes to only 836 for Mike Bekich, whom he had defeated three years earlier. Independent candidate Ray Anderson received 337 votes, while Billy Joe McCallister received 154. Balint got creamed by Ingersoll, 1301 to 809. The only reason he didn't lose by a larger margin was because Ron Mamula, another Rank and File Caucus member who didn't like Ingersoll, ran and received 715 votes. The election was a clean sweep, in spite of the constant barrage by both the Company and the International. Their attacks only tightened Ronnie and his Rank and File Caucus team's control of the local. Not only did we still hold all the top union posts, but we took control of the entire grievance committee. The Rank and File Caucus candidates who won included Frankie Boyle, who defeated John Balint in Open Hearth no. 5 (OH5), John Deffenbaugh in the Forge Division, Terry Bernh in the Structural Division, and Gregg Mowry in the zone 1 Inspectors Division. In zone 3, former Rank and File Caucus supporter Bob Stevenson, who lost the grievance chair job to O'Toole in the rerun back in 1979, didn't even run. Weisen ally Sam Spence demolished three other candidates. I'll never forget seeing Sam campaigning outside the mill and union hall in freezing temperatures. While snow was coming down, he was wearing a short-sleeve shirt and not even shivering—another steelworker with iron in his veins.

In spite of the convincing victory and sweep, the barrage of smut pieces that came out on the Rank and File Caucus deeply tarnished its image and dampened member participation in the union. As Brett Reigh told it:

> Even though their victory was an easy one, there were many "scandal sheets" printed up by the opposition. These flyers portrayed the leaders of the Rank and File as militants who wanted to, as one sheet said, "Make a Revolution, Kill the Union, Kill the Company." They showed Weisen as a boxer, punching out at everything, destroying the Homestead Works, and taking money from the union treasury. The sheets also mentioned the audit done by the International numerous times. So even though they had easily won the elections, there was still opposition to 1397 Rank and File present at the Homestead mill.[2]

On top of the propaganda barrage, the International also continued their tactic of forcing election reruns to bleed the local financially, make it look inept, and shut Weisen up. Longtime friend and future printshop co-owner, newly elected zone 1 griever Gregg Mowry, was a prime example, having to rerun on two different occasions. As Gregg told it: "They wanted us to spend our money. I mean, they wanted to bankrupt us, basically was their object, keep on running these elections and consuming our funds, if there were less than fifty vote margins."[3]

As in earlier elections, reruns always produced the same result as the previous election, with the Rank and File Caucus candidates easily

1397 Rank and File newspaper, front page, March 1982.

reelected. The majority of members saw the International wasting our money, not the other way around.

With the layoffs mounting and union dues dwindling, only two issues of the *1397 Rank and File* newspaper came out in 1982. They were full of news reports about the layoffs and dire warnings about the direction the Company was going in. That year, the Homestead mill was integrated into the Mon Valley Works, along with Edgar Thomson, in Braddock, and the Irvin Works, in West Mifflin. As promised before we were elected to office, the yearly salaries and lost time of all union officers were once again reported in the newspaper, and committees gave detailed reports about their activities.

The front page of the March 1982 issue was a major article on the local's intervention in an EPA Clean Air Act lawsuit against U.S. Steel, in an attempt to ensure that the Company complied with the ruling obliging it to clean up the river and its facilities, comply with its promise to modernize, and not use the court ruling as an excuse to shut down its operations.

The "Plant Plague" section was hard-hitting and truthful but also sarcastic and hilarious, especially when reporting management's

1397 Rank and File newspaper, March 1982.

stupidity. My favorite in the March 1982 issue was about a 45″ mill foreman who brought in a fancy expensive six-by-eight-foot white shag rug from home, put it in a mill washing machine, turned the water on extra hot, and completely destroyed it in the process. Other cartoons were just as hilarious but truthful; the "phantom shitter" struck again. The list of worker submissions for the "Dumbest Foreman in the Mill" continued to grow.

The September 1982 "Convention Edition" newspaper was extremely critical of the upcoming United Steelworkers of America (USWA) convention in Atlantic City, which I attended as an elected delegate. Its front-page article decried the lack of democracy, predicting Local 1397 delegates would be "ruled out of order." In fact, for several days of the convention, the Local 1397 delegates table was surrounded by gun-toting International staff, whose job was to stop other delegates from talking to us or getting copies of our newspaper.

Other articles decried the International's lack of response to the mounting layoffs and steel crisis, as well as their talk of granting wage

Local 1397 rank-and-file delegates elected to attend the 1982 USWA Convention in Atlantic City, New Jersey. (From bottom left) Tom Jugan, Jack Bair, Ron Weisen, Mike Stout, Dave Horgan, Jim Kooser, Ron Funk, Sam Spence, Joe Ruscitti, Terry Bernh, John Ingersoll (Missing from table) Barb Weibelt.

and benefit concessions, which we argued would in no way stem the tide of shutdowns. My grievance report once again lambasted the outmoded grievance procedure, announcing changes we would be proposing at the convention. We reprinted a letter from R.L. Schneider, vice president of U.S. Steel's eastern operations, ordering all management personnel to "avoid, wherever possible recalling laid-off employees, since by doing so will re-entitle them to benefits that might otherwise have run out."[4] Our newspaper launched a major petition drive and campaign against working overtime while thousands were laid off. Both Ronnie and I got disciplinary slips and warnings of further punishment if we didn't "cease and desist" from our campaign. We didn't. I started filing overtime grievances for every department.

THE FOLLOWING IS A PARTIAL LIST OF FUNDS AND FOOD RAISED OR DONATED TO THE MUSA/1397 FOOD BANK SINCE APRIL OF THIS YEAR:

$10,500 - Stanley Theater Benefit, 4/15	$900.00- Union Railroad Credit Union	$ 2,000 - I.E.W. International
1,300 - Foggy Bottom C & W Benefit, 7/30	$1,037 - Homestead Gate Collection,4/25	$495.00 - (+ 5 Truckloads of
5,000 - Homestead Credit Union	(+ 40 boxes of canned goods)	canned goods: Pgh.
1,500 - 1397 Pensioneer's Assoc.	1,900 - Homestead Gate Collection,6/17	Pirate fans, 9/6)
175.00 - St. John Mark Lutheran Church	(+ 60 boxes of canned goods)	100.00 - Homestead Park
875.00 - St. Mary Magdaline	350.00 - Stagehands Union, Local #3	Methodist Church
265.00 - Carrie Furnace Collection	2,200 - AAP Promotions	2,700 - Personal donations

LOCAL 1397 WOULD LIKE TO EXTEND OUR DEEPEST THANKS AND WARMEST APPRECIATION TO THE COUNTLESS INDIVIDUALS, CHURCHES, UNIONS AND ORGANIZATIONS WHO HAVE DONATED FOOD, MONEY OR TIME TO OUR FOOD BANK, ESPECIALLY THE EMPLOYED MEMBERS OF LOCAL 1397.

List of earliest food bank donors, summer of 1982, 1397 Rank and File newspaper, September 1982.

- NOTICE -

The following results are from the General Election
Of Local 1397 held on Tuesday, April 13, 1982:

President: Bill Joe McCallister, 154; Ray Anderson,
337; Ron Weisen 1682, Mike Bekich, 836.

Vice-President: John Balint, 809, Ron Mamula, 715,
John Ingersoll, 1301.

Recording Secretary: Tom Jugan, 1440,
Vicky Talton, 950.

Financial Secretary: Joe Stanton, 1530,
Andy Masco, 928.

Treasurer: O.B. Horn, 327; Ed Wargo, 895;
Ron Funk, 1478.

Guide: Bill Rager, 565; Frank Domagala, 1120;
Gene Garbowsky, 816.

Inside Guard: Dave Horgan, 1368;
Bill Burkes Jr., 913.

Outside Guard: Bob Chasko, 965; Jim Kooser, 1345.

Trustees: Brian "Red" Durkin, 624; Gary Kasper, 1068;
Marty Hanchak, 166; Ed "King" Hamlin, 1122;
Joe Ruscitti, 564; Jim "Cuts" Cannon, 1120;
"Big" John Richards, 767; Andy Zavinsky, 784.

Journal Agent: Ollie Madison, 839; Don McKinney, 1399.

Zone 1: Gregg Mowry, 116; Wendell Brucker, 91.

Zone 2: John Rossi, 188; John O'Toole, 208.

Zone 3: Don Kline, 25; Sam Spence, 339; Ron Pryle, 34;
Larry McGuigan, 113.

Zone 5: Dan Barbarino, 260; Terry Bernd, 286.

Zone 6: John Balint, 74; Frank Boyle, 122.

Zone 7: John Deffenbaugh, 207; Joe Nestico, 101.

- NOTICE -

The following is the results of the election for
Delegates to the USWA 21st Constitutional Convention,
Held Thursday, August, 26, 1982, at the 139 Union Hall.
(The winners are underlined)

1A	Bill Moutz	27	1B	Jack Bair	270
2A	Gregg Mowry	37	2B	Mike Stout	304
3A			3B	Henry Hester	17
4A	Bill Kersell	13	4B	Warren Rudolph	18
5A	Sam Palotti	114	5B	Don McKinney	53
6A	Joe Ruscitti	241	6B		
7A	Terry Bernd	243	7B		
8A	Jerry Laychak	28	8B	Ron Funk	279
9A	Tom Jugan	289	9B	Barb Weibelt	211
10A	Bill Burkes	67	10B	Bob Chasko	74
11A	M. Gassettee	14	11B	Mike Bekich	53
12A	John Rossi	47	12B	Ron Lee	18
13A	Dave Horgan	46	13B	Larry McGuigan	63
14A	Frank Foster		14B	Sam Spence	249
15A	Art Leibowitz	21	15B		
16A	Andy Zivinsky	16	16B		
17A	Andy Macso	18	17B	BJ McCallister	28
18A	Ron Mamula	121	18B	John Ingersoll	281
19A	Jim Kooser	241	19B	Vicky Talton	92
20A			20B	Ollie Madison	109
21A			21B	Bob Hamlet	7
22A			22B	Ray Anderson	150
23A	Don Jackson	19	23B	Ed Hamlin	31
24A			24B	Paul Lampone	23
25A			25B	OB Horn	69
26A			26B	John Balint	105

Local union and convention election results. (Note: There were no election results for Slab and Plate zone 4, as I ran uncontested). *1397 Rank and File newspaper, September 1982.*

The September 1982 issue also contained a major report on the food bank benefit concert, as well as the first distributions. To eliminate any possibility of financial wrongdoing and make sure all funds contributed and raised were used for food, the bookkeeping was handed over to the Methodist Union of Social Services, a local United Way community organization.

The September 1982 issue also contained the results of the local union election, as well as the results of the election for delegates to the upcoming USWA convention. And most importantly, Ronnie and I wrote another diatribe against granting concessions, which we were convinced were no answer to the steel industry's woes.

Not only was the Rank and File Caucus still popular in the mill, its strength and resistance at Homestead increasingly attracted outside

Molly Rush, c. 1985.   **Charles McCollester, c. 1980.**

interest and support, as the union hall further opened its doors to groups like the Tri-State Conference on Steel (TSCS). On February 25, 1982, the Thomas Merton Center held its annual New People's Award dinner at our local union hall, honoring Poland's Lech Walesa and his Solidarność (Solidarity) movement. Organized mainly by Charlie McCollester and anti-war mother and activist Molly Rush, the dinner was attended by more than three hundred people. We were fed a smorgasbord of Polish food. Charlie gave the keynote speech, drawing the parallels between the goals of Poland's Solidarity movement and ours: democracy and a voice in the investment decisions. There was dancing by the local Duquesne Tamburitzans, and I performed two of my new songs, including "Flowers of the Working Class" about Youngstown heroes Ed Mann and John Barbero and one in honor of the Polish Solidarity movement titled "I Think You Need Some Solidarity:"

> When you're bogged in the dog-eat-dog,
> When looking out for number one won't do;
> When you're broke, at the end of your rope,
> The whole world is caving in on you.
> I think you need—some solidarity.
>
> When you're trapped, under attack,
> When the vultures are circling over you;

When you're in hock, hit bottom rock,
All the vultures are circling over you.
I think you need—some solidarity.

They rule the seas, they're the powers that be,
You'll never beat them alone, you see—
The only damn thing that's gonna break these chains,
Is when we stand up together again—in solidarity.

When you're on strike, in the middle of a fight,
About to crack, your back's against the wall;
When you've been burned, got nowhere to turn,
Teetering unsteady, getting ready to fall,
I think you need—some solidarity.

Mike Stout singing "I Think You Need Some Solidarity" at Merton Center dinner, February 25, 1982.

That same year California Newsreel, an independent film outfit, came to town and produced their classic documentary *The Business of America*, about the decline of the steel industry, focusing on Homestead and its workers.[5] While a number of us usual suspects appeared in the film, it also featured two good friends—Moureen and Paul Trout. Both former Reagan Republicans, they were going through economic shock and awe, radicalized by Moureen losing her Homestead 160" mill job and Paul losing his job at Mesta Machine. When it was initially released, the documentary aired nationwide on PBS stations—everywhere except here in Pittsburgh. With the release of this film, reporters poured into Homestead.

The coalescing and joint activity with the Thomas Merton Center continued for the next several years. In the summer of 1983, a major forum was held at the Local 1397 union hall, sponsored by the Center and our local union on U.S. intervention in El Salvador and Nicaragua. It was attended by more than a hundred people, including many Homestead steelworkers. To

Moureen and Paul Trout, c. 1998.

understand how radical this move was, you have to know just how "prowar" Homestead steelworkers had traditionally been through every war, including Vietnam. A large portion of the work done at our mill came from military contracts. For example, we made armor plate for tanks, ships, and other military hardware.

In the summer of 1984, I posted an 11" × 17" poster on the 160" mill bulletin boards with a map of Central America, detailing how much of our tax-funded dollars were going to support dictatorships in these countries, including El Salvador, Nicaragua, Guatemala, and Honduras. At the bottom of the poster, in big bold letters it stated: **"$175 million for Central America, $0 for Homestead!"** Not only did the posters not get torn down but a handful of workers met to try and figure out how we could make a twenty-foot long banner of it to hang from the Homestead high-level bridge! Many workers were beginning to see who the real enemy was.

CHAPTER 20

ENVY AND JEALOUSY–WRECKERS AND SPLITTERS

By late summer in 1983, another unnecessary fissure developed in the ranks of Local 1397. By this time, I was fighting hundreds of grievances at every step, coordinating the Tri-State Conference on Steel (TSCS) effort with the local union, singlehandedly doing the grunt work of typing, formatting, and laying out the newspaper, and coordinating the biggest local union food bank. Displaced steelworkers were being scrutinized like a "soon to be extinct" species on the Audubon Society list. After being interviewed for a leading front-page article in the *Post-Gazette* on November 27, 1979, about the upcoming 1980 presidential election, cameras and news reporters were constantly in my face, hounding me for stories. Out-of-town newspapers and publications, including the *Los Angeles Times*, the *New York Times*, the *Washington Post*, the *Nation*, and the *Village Voice*, were regularly showing up at the union hall. Shining the national spotlight on what was going on in the steel industry was critical to our strategy for educating the general public, as well as for establishing ties with others around the country facing the same prospects. While Ronnie was doing his share of interviews and stories, many of these publications were approaching me directly as a result of recent appearances on the *Today Show* and elsewhere, as well as for my coordinator role at the food bank. Ronnie didn't like anybody grabbing more headlines than him.

Several friends in the local told me that people were "pissing in Ronnie's ears" that I was getting too much power and too much coverage. Some were spreading rumors that I planned to run against him for president, which was patently untrue and absurd. The local union president presided over monthly meetings, chaired committees, met with the Company every three years on local issues and contract negotiations, and voted on the national contract. This kind of stuff was right up Ronnie's alley. As a zone griever who fought my own arbitration cases, I was winning day-to-day tangible victories for workers—putting money in their pockets, saving their jobs (at least temporarily), winning benefits they were owed, and helping their families. Why would I want to trade that job for the president position, especially when it was being held by someone as strong and popular as Ronnie? I didn't give a damn about or want to be president—ever!

By mid-1983, as the red-baiting subsided and grew increasingly ineffective, right-wing forces switched gears and started spreading new rumors: now I was a "cocaine addict" and was "stealing from the food bank" to support my habit. Anybody remotely close to me or who hung out with me knew these rumors were total slanderous bullshit. Not only was marijuana my only drug of choice, but the few bouts I did subsequently have with cocaine were a nasal disaster. Having had sinus troubles my whole life, cocaine merely exasperated my breathing problems, making it impossible to sleep. Several episodes of this bullshit were enough for me. I never paid a penny for cocaine in my life or ever did it again.

For me, the last straw on the psychological warfare front came in March 1985, when I got a phone call from an old radical friend of mine, Lenny Shindel, who was chairperson of the grievance committee at Bethlehem's Sparrows Point mill in Baltimore. Lenny was attending a Labor Notes conference of some five hundred radical and reform-minded labor activists in Detroit, Michigan.[1] After hellos and catch-ups, Lenny said, "You aren't gonna believe this—when I asked your local president [Ronnie Weisen] how you were doing, he said, 'Mike's got a bad coke habit.'" I couldn't believe Ronnie was running this slander at a national labor conference!

With a full grievance plate and TSCS activity intensifying, this kind of nonsense was the last thing I needed. I met face-to-face with Ronnie in his office and asked him to stop spreading the slander, emphasizing that there was not a shred of proof it was true. He refused to tell me who he heard the rumors from, so I could confront them. This whole episode was a real slap in the face. I was putting in hundreds of volunteer hours coordinating the food bank, never asking for a penny

United Steelworkers of America

Local Union 1397

RON WEISEN
PRESIDENT

JOHN INGERSOLL
VICE PRESIDENT

TOM JUGAN
RECORDING SECRETARY

————AFL-CIO————

615 McClure Street
Homestead, Pennsylvania 15120

JOE STANTON
FINANCIAL SECRETARY

RON FUNK
TREASURER

TELEPHONES
462-2522   462-2523

October 6, 1983

Dear Food Bank Members,

On Monday, October 17, 1983, there will be a meeting of Food Bank Recipients at 8:00 pm at the Union
Hall. Attendence is mandatory because we will be updating our register. Those who do not attend will be
placed in our in-active files and will not be eligible
for future distributions.

Thank-You

Ron Weisen

Ron Weisen
President
USWA Local 1397

On the instructions of Chuck Honeywell, this letter was sent to Local 1397 food bank recipients, most of whose UC had expired.

of compensation, and then getting accused of bullshit like this. When the slander persisted, I resigned as coordinator of the food bank. I had more than enough to do without putting up with this nonsense. I put the word out that if I caught someone spreading these rumors any further, I would file charges and sue them for defamation of character. No one ever said a word to my face, and the character assassination retreated to a whisper behind closed doors.

The lesson of this whole episode was the destructiveness of the envy/jealousy factor—a horrible disease that can turn friendships sour, sow divisions, crumble movements, and destroy causes. Ronnie was persuaded that I wanted to take his job, fake news and views he was getting from a few other jealous union members. He let the cat out of the bag one Wednesday night while drinking at the Coral Lounge Bar after bowling (we were on the same last-place team with the highest handicap in Local 1397 history). After a few beers, I guess he forgot that I was one of his targets when he blurted out: "I can't hit people with my fists anymore; I get sued. So now I just wage psychological warfare on them."

This unnecessary split really hurt our efforts and struggle. By the time I quit the food bank, dozens of others, including most of the women, had already started fading away, food rations had dwindled, and the fundraising had dried up. Outside of two checks from Bruce Springsteen in 1984 and 1985, all the grassroots fundraising and concerts ceased. With the workforce in the mill dwindling nonstop, payroll deductions ceased. In addition, unemployment compensation (UC) had expired for most of the food bank volunteers, forcing them to look for work elsewhere. Another nail in the food bank coffin came in late 1983, when Denominational Mission Strategy (DMS) leader Chuck Honeywell came to a food bank gathering and threatened to cut off food rations unless recipients joined his organization's protest actions. With this threat, over half of the recipients stopped coming for food. So who was this DMS guy Chuck Honeywell?

CHAPTER 21

COALITION WITH THE DENOMINATIONAL MISSION STRATEGY

At the end of December 1982, a piece appeared in the *Pittsburgh Post-Gazette* about a press conference held by a group of Protestant ministers, calling on the governor and state to come to the aid of laid-off steelworkers.[1] Calling themselves the Denominational Mission Strategy (DMS), they requested to meet with Senator Arlen Specter, Governor Thornburg's office, and other high-level public officials, demanding that they proclaim the Valley a disaster area and grant laid-off and dislocated steelworkers federal emergency aid. Of course, as usual, the calls fell on deaf ears. After returning from a Christmas holiday trip to Kentucky and seeing this article, I noticed one of the ministers was Jim Von Dreele from the St. Matthews Episcopal Church on 10th and McClure Streets, two blocks from the union hall. Knowing him previously through Tri-State Conference on Steel (TSCS) activity, I went to meet with him, proposing a coalition between the ministers, our local, and other organizations in the Valley fighting the shutdowns.

The paid staff organizer for the DMS was Chuck Honeywell. He had migrated to Pittsburgh from Buffalo, New York, in 1975, to work for a community organizing project affiliated with the late Chicago activist Saul Alinsky's Industrial Areas Foundation. It had been founded in 1939 to empower the unemployed through confrontation and direct actions. Within five months of getting the job, he was fired. Ed Chambers, the foundation's executive director described Honeywell as "incompetent and unaccountable" and said, "If Alinsky was alive, he wouldn't approve of Honeywell's kamikaze tactics."[2] With local church memberships drying up with the avalanche of job losses, a group of protestant ministers, including the Lutheran and Presbyterian bishops, hired Honeywell to help them address the massive unemployment problem. At the time, I was dealing with Von Dreele, and Honeywell's background was unknown to those of us at Local 1397.

I arranged a meeting with Ron Weisen at Local 1397. A week later, I brought together a number of groups for a giant powwow, including the DMS, the TSCS, Mike Bond from Local 2227, the Mon Valley Unemployment Committee (MVUC), activists who later made up the Rainbow Kitchen, concerned local businesspeople, and some local borough officials and community activists. We called ourselves the Network to Save the Mon Valley. (I'll refer to this organization as the "Network" for short.)

The initial focus of this coalition effort was demanding government aid for displaced workers. At the same time, we advocated for more militant tactics in an attempt to stop the bloodletting. If the government wasn't going to respond as the corporations continued the shutdowns and banks continued redlining local industry, while investing in steel facilities overseas, then we had to intervene and stop the damage with direct action.

The first tactic we came up with, a takeoff from a campaign to save a Nabisco plant a few months earlier, was for people to threaten to withdraw their money from banks abetting the shutdowns by signing pledge cards to stop doing business with them. It was the TSCS activists who proposed a strategy of focusing on the disinvestment policies of the corporations. The TSCS and Local 1397 had been hammering U.S. Steel and other companies about importing foreign steel for well over a year in our newspaper and the press, as had Bob Anderson, who was laid off from U.S. Steel's Edgar Thomson mill. It was Honeywell who suggested aiming our campaign at Mellon Bank. On top of seeming to have some kind of personal dislike for Mellon, Honeywell had organized an incredible cache of information on Mellon and its overseas ventures, including their investments in Japan's Sumitomo Industries. He had also detailed personnel links between Mellon, LTV Corporation, U.S. Steel, and their foreign partners, cataloging their interlocking corporate directorships—all on 3" × 5" index cards. For instance, Tom Graham, a former LTV chair and then U.S. Steel vice president and the main hatchet man directing the plant shutdowns was also president of Mellon Bank. Having observed "corporate campaigns" conducted earlier by a hired gun named Ray Rogers,[3] I was all on board with this plan of action.

The Bankruptcy of Mesta Machine Company

Mellon Bank, with an array of junior partners, bought Mesta Machine Company in 1978 with a twenty-million-dollar loan, then systematically disinvested and drove Mesta into bankruptcy. At the same time, in a consortium with eight other banks, Mellon invested some twenty to thirty million dollars in Sumitomo Industries in Japan, which, coincidentally, by 1983, replaced Mesta as the number one producer of steel mill machinery in the world. For more than fifty years, Mesta Machine Company, right up the road from the Homestead mill in neighboring West Homestead, was top dog. It was so well-known that when Soviet Union leader Nikita Khrushchev came to speak before the United Nations in 1959, there were only three places he wanted to visit: Disneyland, a mechanized farm in Iowa, and Mesta Machine Company.

After declaring bankruptcy, Mesta withheld over five hundred thousand dollars in workers' back pay and severance pay, as well as pensions in escrow, and refused to release it. Twelve hundred workers with an average seniority of twenty-five years were thrown out into the street. Independent of the DMS/Network, the TSCS had pulled together another group and formed the Save Mesta Machine Coalition in West Homestead.

When the TSCS initiated the Mesta campaign and coalition in early 1983, for the first time, there was a positive response from some borough officials, local union officials, and citizens to the idea of forming a Steel Valley Authority (SVA) with the power of eminent domain. One of Local 1397's strongest points in this period was that we always had an "inside-outside" strategy. From 1980 through 1984, our local union hall was the de facto home for the TSCS, with Ronnie's full support and involvement.

As the volunteer TSCS and Local 1397 liaison meeting with the ministers, I approached Honeywell and proposed that our coalition combine the disinvestment issue with the shutdown and bankruptcy of the Mesta Plant.

Eminent Domain and the Steel Valley Authority

The TSCS had made a number of attempts in 1982 to convince public officials to establish a Steel Valley Authority (SVA) and exercise the

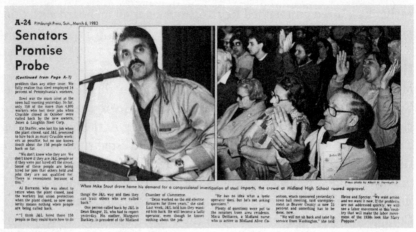

When Mike Stout drove home his demand for a congressional investigation of steel imports, the crowd at Midland High School roared approval.

Pittsburgh Press.

right of eminent domain to stop plants from closing and being dismantled. The idea for an SVA was first proposed by Staughton Lynd in 1980, based on the same principle as the Tennessee Valley Authority (TVA), established in the 1930s, when thirty-two private utility companies failed to provide electricity for that impoverished Appalachian region. (The TVA is a perfect example of the "socialism" I described in the introduction.)

The first meeting of the Pittsburgh-based TSCS was held in December 1980, at St. Stephen's Church in Hazelwood, where Father Gary Dorsey was pastor. The meeting was held in response to the shutdown of LTV's Hazelwood strip mill and the loss of over a thousand jobs. At this gathering, former J&L local union president and former state legislator Frank O'Brien gave meat to the SVA proposal with the example of J&L using eminent domain under the recently enacted Municipal Authorities Act of 1956 that cleared the neighborhood of Scotch Bottom to expand the mill (which never happened). Both Staughton and Frank opined that we could use this law to turn the guns around, using eminent domain to *save* mills and jobs, instead of destroying communities. The idea started to gain momentum.

In the summer of 1982, we were invited by the Midland mayor and borough council, the local union at Crucible Steel, and church officials in the town of Midland, north of Pittsburgh, to do a presentation on reversing the shutdown of Crucible Steel, which was throwing five thousand people out of work. I had introduced the town and local to the TSCS when I went to a town hall gathering on March 5, 1981, and shared the stage with Pennsylvania Senators John Heinz and Arlen Specter. When both senators decried unfair foreign imports, blaming them for our layoff and shutdown problems, I embarrassed them with a barrage of facts on the import of foreign steel by U.S. Steel and other domestic steel companies, demanding a full-scale investigation in front of five hundred cheering, angry workers and citizens. At the invitation of local officials in Midland, in June 1982, TSCS activists, including young attorney Jay Hornack, made a presentation proposing the use of eminent domain by local officials to rescue the Crucible facility. Unfortunately, the idea was much too big and scary for them. Longtime labor priest and Local 1397 friend Monsignor Charles Owen Rice, who headed up our TSCS delegation, noted afterwards, "This is no time for small minds."

The Save Nabisco Campaign

The next time TSCS had a chance to talk about or introduce the idea and tactic of using eminent domain was in December 1982. A group of women who worked at the local Nabisco Plant had won a major discrimination lawsuit and forced Nabisco to give them 385 thousand dollars in back pay. Nabisco's response was to announce they were going to shut down their Pittsburgh plant, even though it was making a profit. At that point, a group called the Save Nabisco Coalition was initiated by future state senator and community activist Jim Ferlo, community organizer Rick Flannigan, Pittsburgh city councilman Tom Flaherty, and Sam Papa, president of the Bakery and Confectionary Workers Local 12. A mass meeting was pulled together in East Liberty on December, 21, 1982. The meeting was attended by some 1,500 people, including Local 1397, the TSCS, a dozen other unions, a number of church and civic organizations, Pittsburgh city council members and Pittsburgh mayor Richard Caliguiri. The TSCS attorney, Jay Hornack played a pivotal role behind the scenes advising the Save Nabisco Coalition on the use of eminent domain. At that meeting, the coalition came out with a three-point strategy:

- they would immediately institute a boycott of Nabisco products, including the crackers and cookies that were produced at the plant;

- they (with city council and the mayor of Pittsburgh joining in) would look seriously into using eminent domain to take the plant from Nabisco and run it under new ownership;
- they passed out forty-five thousand pledge cards to the people in the audience and told them all to go get a friend, neighbor, coworker, or whomever to sign a pledge card to take their money out of Equibank, which had someone on the board of directors of Nabisco and was Nabisco's biggest banking partner.

Nabisco was so shaken by the action—which included the mayor of Pittsburgh threatening a boycott of all Nabisco products, the involvement of the city officials, and a sizable coalition—barely two weeks later they came out and publicly announced they had cancelled all further plans to shut the Nabisco plant down. The threat to use eminent domain combined with a boycott appeared to be a major factor causing them to reverse their decision. It was a great victory for the people of the Pittsburgh area—650 jobs were saved, at least temporarily.

In 1998, the Nabisco Corporation returned to the question of leaving Pittsburgh. The factory was leased to the Bake-Line Group of Oak Brook, Illinois, which declared bankruptcy in 2004 and phased out the plant. According to company officials, the building, constructed in 1919, was too old and too far from highways and railroads. Pittsburghers around the city boycotted Nabisco products, but it was not enough. With tens of thousands of steelworkers and their families having left the area with the wave of steel shutdowns, any effective boycott had been severely blunted. The old Nabisco building remained vacant for a few years and was declared "blighted" by the city of Pittsburgh in 2006. As with so many other former manufacturing and mill sites, it's now home to a shopping mall.

Nevertheless, the December 1982 Nabisco town hall meeting sowed the seeds for the pledge card and bank boycott ideas soon to be adopted in our steel shutdown battles. But unlike a cookie and cracker plant like Nabisco, the Mesta Machine and steel mill shutdowns presented a much bigger problem: the amount of capital required to save and modernize the mill was substantially larger. The struggle to save facilities like Mesta or the Homestead mill would have to be much more concerted and broader. With the examples of the previous Youngstown effort, we were well aware that an investment campaign of that magnitude could only be spearheaded by the federal government, and getting the federal government involved would require a massive and radical push.

Taking on Mellon Bank

When Mellon drove Mesta into bankruptcy in February 1983, it was very clear to the steelworkers angered about losing their jobs and ready to fight who the main enemy was. Public meetings were called in early 1983 at various churches in McKeesport, Homestead, and Duquesne. The meeting on January 12 in McKeesport was attended by close to five hundred people, representing dozens of unions and churches, and including borough council officials from up and down the Valley. Over ten thousand pledge cards were distributed, with signers threatening to withdraw their money from Mellon.

With Honeywell and the Network's research, Mellon's economic and political influence in the region became crystal clear:

> Mellon Bank . . . was at the heart of nearly all [economic] decisions in the region. Its directors sat on the boards of most Pittsburgh-based corporations, including hospitals and universities. . . . Mellon owned outright or controlled as one of the top shareholders of Alcoa, Gulf Oil, Koppers, U.S. Steel, Westinghouse, Pittsburgh Plate & Glass (PPG), LTV Corporation, Armco, Allegheny Ludlum Steel and others. . . . They were the major influence in such policy groups as the Allegheny Conference on Community Development and the Regional Industrial Development Corporation.[4]

We kicked off the campaign with a media blitz against Mellon. In early March, Von Dreele and I were flown to New York City to appear on the *Today Show* to explain the campaign to a nationwide audience. Whether it was monikers like "Smellin' Mellon" or slogans like "A neighbor you *can't* count on," Mellon deserved every invective and diatribe we threw at them.

In reaction to our campaign, Mellon didn't mince words, publicly declaring they could care less about steelworkers losing their jobs. Mellon CEO David Barnes, declared he "saw nothing wrong with an investment policy that sacrificed local jobs for foreign jobs as long as it yielded a higher rate of return."[5] Mellon officials made bombastic

TSCS activists and staff, including Bob Anderson (second from left), Father Gary Dorsey, Mari Wargo, Bob Warfield (far right), and Artie Leibowitz (center kneeling).

public statements like: "People need to give up and either move out or accept lower paying jobs."[6] Heading into the spring of 1983, the campaign continued to grow. More and more people were pledging to take their money out of Mellon Bank if they didn't meet our two demands: give the Mesta workers what they were owed, and invest our monies back into basic industries in this area. Meanwhile Honeywell—through a series of back and forth letters with United Steelworkers of America (USWA) International president Lloyd McBride—somehow convinced the USWA International to become part of the boycott campaign. While McBride kept himself at arms distance from Honeywell and the coalition, he put out a call—a mailing—to 120 thousand area steelworkers and retirees, urging them to withdraw their money from Mellon Bank if the Mesta workers did not receive the monies owed. The letter was signed by McBride and all three area District directors.[7]

When there was no response from Mellon by early May 1983, I pushed the coalition to up the ante, arguing, "A 'pledge' is not enough, it's time to actually go and withdraw money from Mellon Bank and show them we are serious." Weisen, always up for a fight, didn't hesitate to give his approval and make sure it happened. A motion was passed at the local union executive board meeting in May to move our money out of Mellon to PNC Bank. A press conference and demonstration were planned for June 6, 1983, the anniversary of the 1944 D-Day invasion of Western Europe at Normandy; except our D-Day was called "Disinvestment Day."

Pittsburgh Post-Gazett

TUES AY, JUNE 7, 1983

Mike Stout, left, of United Steelworkers Local 1397, speaks in rally outside Mellon Bank's Homestead office. With him are the Rev. John Gropp, center, of Denominational Mission Strategy, a union-clergy group, and the Rev. Paul Himmelman of the Lutheran Synod of Pittsburgh.

No deposit

Mesta asks court to free back wages in Mellon boycott

We put out a small press release, hoping maybe 50 people would show up, but, much to our surprise, over 250 people showed up, including representatives from three other local unions, ministers from a dozen churches, borough officials, and steelworkers from the Homestead and Irvin Works. Local 1397 and other individuals withdrew approximately 250 thousand dollars from the local branch, including the certificates of deposit we had there.

Untold others were also going into various Mellon Bank branches and taking out their money. There was no way to get an exact count on the funds removed, but it gave Mellon quite the scare. Our withdrawal/ bank boycott campaign received such favorable publicity that several days later the Pittsburgh city council voted unanimously to sever their dealings with Mellon Bank if the Mesta workers didn't receive what they were owed. Then County Commissioner Cyril Wecht announced he was introducing a resolution to have the county boycott Mellon Bank. Various state representatives were also pledging to do the same. The movement took off like wildfire; within three days on June 9, 1983, Mellon Bank agreed to release every penny of the monies owed to the Mesta Machine workers.

The bank boycott and withdrawal showed the potential power of our movement, as well as the effectiveness of the tactic. It was so powerful because it directed fire at the system and the very institution that was orchestrating the disinvestment of the Valley. It was an action that the average citizen, the unemployed, retirees, union members, townspeople, or local institutions and churches could take part in. Anybody could walk into Mellon Bank, shut down their checking and

Local 1397 officers, financial secretary Joe Stanton, president Ron Weisen, and treasurer Ron Funk (left to right), withdrawing our money from Mellon Bank.

savings accounts, and inform the bank they're going to another financial institution that was more responsive to the community. And it was nonviolent!

Meanwhile, the coalition to save Mesta picked up steam. The West Homestead borough council actually began the process of forming the SVA. At TSCS urging, Local 1397 president Ron Weisen, who was a life-long resident of West Homestead, ran for and was elected to West Homestead borough council. With TSCS's legal assistance, he convinced four out of seven West Homestead borough council officials to establish the SVA. But once the Authority was voted on and established in August 1983, it was vetoed by the mayor, John Dindak, who at the time was in management at U.S. Steel and had strong ties to the business community, including Mellon Bank.[8] At the same time, unbeknownst to us, Mellon had promised several union officials at Mesta a sweetheart deal, saying they would assist them in setting up an employee-owned operation at Mesta. It was more bullshit and diversion.

Within a short period of time, this phony employee stock ownership plan (ESOP) venture fell apart, and the three union officials

TSCS attorney Jay Hornack (far left), Monsignor Rice (center, seated), and council member, Ron Weisen (second from right) at West Homestead Council Meeting, August 1983.

involved were forced to pay back a large portion of the money they were fronted—seven hundred thousand dollars. Mellon had promised a seven-million-dollar loan to get the project off the ground. Not only did it renege on this promise, it reneged on a promise to repave Route 837 (the previously mentioned pothole-riddled main road in front of Mesta that kept me up all night for four months).

Instead of an ESOP with former employees or dealing with the TSCS, they opted to go with the Park Corporation, an outfit run by a scrapper and funded by Mellon. Within a year, Park moved in and set up a nonunion operation, WHEMCO (West Homestead Machine Company), which at the time employed approximately fifty people, taking work away from the roll processing and machine shops at the Homestead mill. These departments were phased out in 1983, throwing over five hundred people out of work. At nonunion WHEMCO, the hourly wage was half of what steelworkers were making. Mellon's seven-million-dollar bait was actually just that: bait to suck the local union in and squash the efforts of the TSCS. And it worked.

After the Mesta workers received their monies owed, Mellon officials and their minions in the government and the press moved to separate the back pay and disinvestment issues. Right in sync, Lloyd McBride and the International reasserted their "you can't tell the

Company what to do" posture, bowing out of the campaign once the Mesta workers got their benefits. Mellon counterattacked in numerous ways: a media barrage of full-page newspaper ads to polish their image that cost tens of thousands of dollars; a weekly op-ed forum in the *Pittsburgh Post-Gazette*, where supporters touted the economic advantages of Mellon's overseas investments; conservative local chambers of commerce deluging newspapers with letters to the editor not only supporting Mellon's disinvestment but blasting our efforts as harmful, claiming we were discouraging other investors. At the same time, in three weeks in July 1983, Mellon donated some 750 thousand dollars to approximately nine different charities, to buy them off and further polish its image. It was a nice crash course in going up against big money.

The Coalition Crumbles

It was at this juncture that the TSCS and other community forces and activists had a major falling out with DMS and withdrew from the Network coalition. After Mellon counterattacked, Charlie and I, as well as others in the coalition, argued that we should counterattack Mellon by taking them on in the public and political arena, that we should hold forums and town meetings and educate the public by debating the disinvestment issue. I vehemently argued that we should continue the withdrawal movement to get more individuals and institutions to shut down their accounts at Mellon bank, that we should stay focused on the bank boycott, barely a month old. DMS paid organizer Chuck Honeywell disagreed. He asserted we should expand our campaign to attack churches, businesses, and unions that didn't join our effort. Outgunned by Honeywell's mini-army of ministers and a handful of union officials, we lost the argument at the next Network meeting. A little over a month after our successful bank withdrawal, a number of us left the coalition, warning that Honeywell's approach would not only isolate the Network but would end up attacking many people and institutions that were potential allies.

My personal split with the DMS occurred at the second to last Network meeting I attended on July 6, 1983 (the ninety-first anniversary of the 1892 Homestead Strike), at Von Dreele's St. Matthews Episcopal Church. Honeywell began the meeting by announcing he had set up a "new hierarchy" (that's exactly what he called it), telling the

Chuck Honeywell (left), with his three "generals" Darrell Becker, Ron Weisen, and Mike Bond (left to right).

rest of us in the audience that anyone who wanted to address him, had to go through his "chosen generals": Ron Weisen, Mike Bond, president at Irvin Works Local 2227, and Darrell Becker, president of the militant Dravo Local 61 on Neville Island. He then proposed that along with attacking the banks and corporations, the Network should also attack union leaders, church officials, and local businesses that did not side with us. He and some of the ministers put a leaflet out on 8th Avenue in Homestead, telling small businesses that if they weren't publicly *with* the Network, then they were *against* it, stating:

> What we are doing now is putting together a public list of those businesses that are clearly supporting Mellon's policies. If you are only listening to Mellon's side and not requesting DMS research, then you are in fact on Mellon's side and we will let the public know that you're an ally of Mellon. . . . It is simple enough, whether you are for or against us. No response or a neutral response is support for Mellon.[9]

In addition, Honeywell instructed his "generals" to inform laid-off workers that if they didn't attend Network activities their food

Network Mellon Bank demonstration, October 3, 1983.

bank rations would be cut off. I walked out of the meeting in disgust. At the last meeting of the Network I attended, in August 1983, at the Irvin Works Local 2227 union hall, activist leaders, including Barney Oursler, Bob Anderson, and me, were red-baited from the podium by Honeywell. We were labeled "enemy stooges" and sellouts for not acquiescing to his new strategy. As he ran his divisive crap to a silent but attentive crowd, I calmly uttered loud enough for people around me to hear: "Bullshit"—just as Ed Mann had done five years earlier. I was surrounded by three hulking DMS ministers, including John Gropp and Douglas Roth, who kept telling me to shut up. But I wasn't intimidated and kept it up through his entire speech. After the meeting, I confronted Honeywell face-to-face about his new strategy, explaining why I thought it was doomed to failure. He told me point blank that "the way you get people and institutions to side with you is by attacking and coercing them, embarrassing them." In all my years of organizing, I had never heard such crazy bullshit!

On October 3, the Network called a demonstration at the Homestead branch of Mellon Bank, in which I refused to participate. Unlike the June 6 money withdrawal event attended by two-hundred-plus

Network Monessen Demonstration, October 19, 1983.

people, only around fifty people participated. After picketing outside, most went inside the bank with bags of pennies to deposit. Two of the workers, United Electrical Workers Local 610 officer Robert "Joe" Jurich and Homestead's Artie Leibowitz had their heads busted by the cops and were arrested. At a separate demonstration at the Mellon Bank branch in Monessen later that month, with about the same number of people, Ron Weisen was pummeled with a nightstick. During the entire October 3 Homestead action, Honeywell hid at the Local 1397 union hall across the street while all the ruckus was going on inside and in front of the bank. From that point on, the ranks of the Network and the DMS began to rapidly shrink; they became more isolated, their actions more destructive and pointless in the eyes of workers and citizens, and public opinion turned against them.

In publications, articles, and news stories following the rise and fall of the DMS and the Network, writers and reporters focused on DMS tactics as proof they were the most militant and confrontational group in the Valley. From a tactical point of view, this was certainly true. Speaking for others and for myself, as someone active in the plant shutdown struggle, we liked and participated in many of their tactics: putting dead fish in safety deposit boxes; using pennies to disrupt business as usual; spreading diluted honey and bags of popcorn all

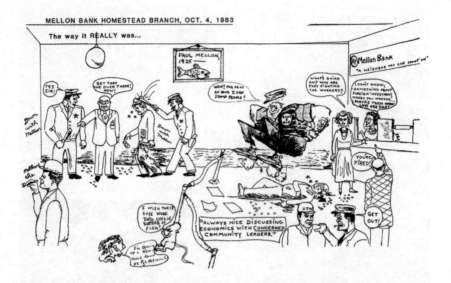

over the sidewalks in front of bank entrances. It was not their tactics we deplored, it was where and at whom they were aimed. Instead of attacking anyone in the community who did not agree with them, these tactics should have been directed squarely at the corporate and financial bosses downtown. Continuing the bank boycott should have been our main focus; it was popular, nonviolent, and very effective.

On Easter Sunday, April 22, 1984, DMS members, including the three "generals," invaded and disrupted a Shadyside Presbyterian Church service. The DMS claimed this was the church attended by Thomas Graham, U.S. Steel and Mellon Bank's chief hatchet man. However, church members hadn't seen him there in years. On Good Friday, before this Easter Sunday debacle, Jay Weinberg and I met with Ronnie in his office, begging him not to take part in any disruption of church services, warning him both that attacking a church would be perceived as attacking people's religion and that focusing on the church would take the public eye off the cue ball, which was Mellon Bank and its disinvestment policies. Ronnie agreed not to join the action. By Easter Sunday, however, Honeywell had talked him back into joining them. Subsequently, both Jay and I were placed at the top of the DMS enemy list.

In spite of Ronnie's hostility after this split, I tried to keep the focus on U.S. Steel and Mellon and their disinvestment policies, as well as promoting the practical solutions being proposed by the TSCS.

Along with a number of articles denouncing the concessions contract signed in 1983 by U.S. Steel and the USWA, in the March 1984 issue of the *1397 Rank and File* newspaper, I wrote major articles that detailed Mellon's overseas investment policies and the real reasons we were fighting against them, with a cartoon satirizing the senseless beating of the two demonstrators. Another major article in this issue explained the TSCS plan and the reasons for forming an SVA.[10]

In addition, knowing the banks and corporations would take full advantage of any split in our ranks, activists both within our local union, as well as within the TSCS and the MVUC, went out of our way to not criticize the DMS publicly. Unfortunately, ignoring their antics and "attack everyone who doesn't agree with us" strategy was becoming next to impossible.

Being the initiator of the coalition, I felt obligated to attempt to salvage it. Knowing that the effects of Honeywell's wrecking and splitting tactics would prove disastrous, in the summer of 1984, I convinced TSCS leaders Charlie McCollester, Father Rich Zelik, and Father Gary Dorsey to sit down with DMS leaders for a powwow, to see if we could reason with them and come to some kind of working agreement.

We met in the basement at the Saint Stephens Church rectory in Hazelwood. Honeywell came to the meeting with two DMS ministers, wearing his standard white raincoat—his cloak and dagger apparel. As he strolled into the room, he was beating a rolled-up newspaper in his hand. He sat down, looked around the table, and said, "First, let's get something straight: at the top of every army, there's only one general, and I'm that general." We were dumbfounded. While I'm sure some of us were itching to have a knockdown argument with him, convincing Honeywell he wasn't a king or a five-star general was not worth wasting our time and energy.

In hindsight, Honeywell's authoritarian, hierarchical style was not that much different from President Donald Trump's, with his "I know best" blusters. Also, like Trump, within a short period of time, Honeywell had nicknames for all of us who opposed him. For instance, Father Dorsey was labeled "Gary Do-little Dorsey." Father Rich was called "Father Zelig." Jay was called "Whineburger." I was called "Roderick's whore" and a "communist." I didn't know what political schooling Honeywell had, but I could certainly attest that browbeating and attacking people and treating allies like the enemy was *not* going to win them over to your side. The political infighting and name-calling must have had the powers that be sitting back and laughing with delight.

On December 16, 1984, Network goons in gasmasks invaded a church Christmas party, hurling skunk oil–filled balloons at children. One of these masked marauders was laid-off Homestead worker Dale Wharton, who was now head of the Local 1397 food bank. With this action, the Network lost what little public sympathy it had left. The YMCA, which had been brought on a year earlier to administrate and handle the booking and finances to keep the food bank legitimate, dropped their sponsorship and administration of the Local 1397 food bank like a hot potato.

With the DMS strategy of focusing on the churches, Ronnie's popularity and support in the mill plummeted. The local union elections were fast approaching. A mere handful of workers now supported Ronnie's activity with the DMS. But even they made it clear their allegiance was to Ronnie and not the Network and their focus on attacking local churches or tactics like throwing skunk oil balloons at little kids.

Within a short period of time, the DMS and the Network were banned from most union halls up and down the Valley. The only union meeting I missed in six years, while preparing for an important arbitration case in August 1985, was invaded by Network ministers (with Ronnie's blessing). Darrell Becker carried a guitar, deriding and mimicking me singing, while others passed out a flyer labeling me "Roderick's whore."[11] According to the flyer, my major crime was fighting workers' grievances, which the DMS and Honeywell considered a "distraction." I felt like I was in a B movie.

The members at the meeting were sickened by this backhanded bullshit. Several days later, at the insistence of other union officers, I called a special meeting at the union hall, where it was voted ninety to zero to ban the Network from the Homestead union hall. Even Ronnie Weisen couldn't vote against the motion in the face of such overwhelming opposition, so he abstained. The *Pittsburgh Press* followed up shortly thereafter with an editorial telling Honeywell and the Network it was time to pack it up. Honeywell's hierarchical style wasn't much different from the very people he was fighting: top-down, dictatorial, and undemocratic. He just didn't have their money and power. At first, his approach to people he thought were potential leaders was flattery, such as calling you a "general" or someone he would help to "go down in history." Then, if you didn't go along with his program, it was character assassination and slander. He ruined people's lives, using them up and spitting them out.

In February 1983, Honeywell invited me to one of his "Team 60" meetings. There were approximately twenty-five or thirty Protestant ministers in attendance. With his opening remarks and scripture reading, I got the feeling I was at some kind of a cult gathering. A few minutes later, he suddenly zeroes in on one of the ministers, browbeating and berating him, exclaiming, "Somewhere down the road, they will come for me. Are you going to be there for me, brother, because I don't see it in your eyes, and I want to know why?" Honeywell harangued the poor minister for a good ten minutes. At first, I couldn't tell if it was real or role-playing. It was real. I should have heeded my own instincts—I was dealing with a cult.

Further proof came in April 1983, after we had organized the successful town hall meetings in McKeesport, Duquesne, and Homestead. Honeywell invited me to dinner at his house. I was leery from the start; the way he spoke to his wife and ordered her around—I thought I was watching a cross between *Father Knows Best* and *All in the Family*, TV shows from back in the 1960s where the father of the family ruled, whether soft-spoken or loud and crass. After dinner, Honeywell took me up to his attic to show me his research, including his meticulously organized and well preserved 3" × 5" index card filing system. I was impressed. All of a sudden, he calmly asked, "Do you want to be the leader?" I gave him my best "what the fuck" stare, without answering. He followed, "No, I don't mean *a* leader, I mean *the* leader; the one who will go down in history as saving this Valley." I shook my head, shrugged, and wryly said, "Not really." I got the hell out of there. I know some readers out there are asking, "After these two experiences, why did you work with him?" While I highly suspected by this time he was a looney tune, I guess I thought he was just another quirky, behind-the-scenes egghead who had done a lot of good research, and someone we could handle. Wrong! I had no idea at this time that he was a self-declared five-star general and supreme leader! The announcement of his new hierarchy at the July 6, 1983, meeting at St. Matthews confirmed my worst fears.

The reputations of his three union "generals"—all decent union men who wanted to fight the banks and corporations—were severely tarnished, and they lost elections or were cut off from their base at their local unions. All of them explained in oral history interviews that they eventually left the Network because of Honeywell's obsession with focusing on the churches. As Ronnie summed it up a few years later to a *New York Times* reporter, "It became a church battle, that's what happened."[12]

While doing anti-war, community, and labor organizing over a thirty-year period, I always adhered to a fundamental principle and strategy: unite all who can be united against the common enemy. We called it the "united front" approach. Honeywell's approach was exactly the opposite: attack everyone who doesn't agree with you, and they will then somehow see you are morally right and join you.

During the 1980s, as plant shutdowns and deindustrialization wreaked havoc on the Mon Valley, entire communities around these mills and plants were devastated. Boroughs and towns lost their tax base. Dozens of churches lost congregations and closed. Small businesses went bankrupt in droves. And, of course, local unions were dissolved as millions of dues-paying members were lost. These institutions and people should have been our allies not targeted as enemies. The enemy was Mellon, LTV, U.S. Steel, and their inhumane system that put profits before and at the expense of people. Of course, there were those in businesses, churches, and the union who sided with the banks and corporations, and when they did so, we should have taken them on. But to blanket all of these constituencies and their people from the very beginning of the struggle with a "you're either with us or against us" mantra, especially without any real effort at education, was beyond ludicrous and self-defeating; it was political suicide.

Words can't express the frustration and disappointment I felt at the breakup of our coalition as a result of Honeywell's divisive, movement-wrecking strategy. If we were to have a prayer at salvaging any jobs, changing the investment policies of the banks, or building an ongoing people's movement in this area, we needed *everyone* working together and coordinating our activities. This included the DMS, the TSCS, the MVUC, local unions, concerned community support groups, local governments, and local churches. Had we maintained the bank withdrawal and boycott, as well as intensifying our education and organizing around their anti-worker/anti-community disinvestment policies, at the very least, some real concessions could have been wrung out of them and an ongoing organization built. Then the more radical tactics of the DMS would have made more sense. I'm not going to sit here and Monday morning quarterback, claiming we would have won the battle and the war, but we certainly would have gotten a lot more accomplished!

CHAPTER 22

JOB ELIMINATIONS AND GRIEVANCE BATTLES ESCALATE

Meanwhile, for the grievance representatives, the battles inside the mill intensified. Ninety percent of my grievances were filed from late 1981 through 1984. Prior to this time, most grievances had taken five to six months to get to the board of arbitration and

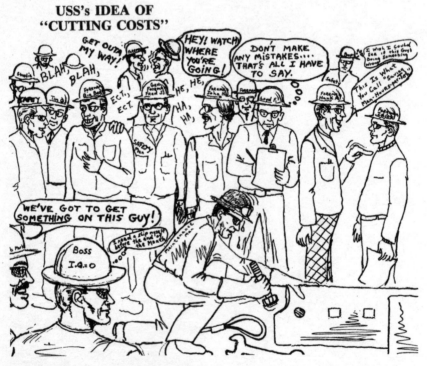

1397 *Rank and File* newspaper, March 1983.

usually another five to six months to get an answer from the board and resolve matters. Now the system started really getting bogged down. Management openly sought to clog it and back it up with hundreds of cases. By late 1983, it was taking most grievances two years or longer to get to arbitration, receive a decision, and be resolved. Local management was continually under the gun to cut their man-hours per ton. They clearly began to violate the contract at will, deciding to take their chances later in court.

The vast majority of grievances I filed were job eliminations of some sort: job combinations, crew cuts, and using overtime instead of recalling laid-off employees. Every time they had to recall someone from layoff, it gave that employee a new seniority date and renewed health care and other benefits. In the 160" Maintenance Department where I worked, I had a good assistant griever named Rick Koza, a rocker who lived up on "Hunky Hill," which was the ninth ward of Munhall at the top of Whitaker Avenue. Rick was a real "do your homework" investigative type who kept meticulous records. When he filed a crew size reduction grievance for the millwrights and motor inspectors in early 1982, he was immediately laid off by the Company. Management's thinking likely was his layoff would be deterrence to any other workers joining his grievance or fighting back. Unfamiliar with our fighting spirit, stubbornness, and persistence, they were sadly mistaken.

Expedited to the second step, I filed what is known in contract and grievance jargon as a minimum assigned maintenance crew size grievance.[1] It took three full years to win the case and get the final back pay award implemented on November 30, 1985—eight days after the 160" mill was permanently closed. Rick and most of the younger workers were now on the street. Winning the case was going to be a real challenge.

The concept "minimum assigned maintenance crew size" meant there had to be adequate maintenance personnel to safely cover the different departments during operating shifts when the mill was rolling, and that these crew sizes were a protected local working condition under Section 2-B of the contract. At the end of December 1981, the 160" maintenance crew was cut in half, with no reduction in production for the two shifts still operating. To even have a chance at winning, I had to find workers on layoff who not only had the guts to take on the Company, but had the connections with coworkers still on the job that would let us know what jobs were being combined, what overtime was being scheduled to do the work of those laid-off employees, etc. Along with Rick, two other maintenance workers, Ralph Budd (who for a while was considered so diligent by management he was made a vicing foreman, i.e., temporary but still in the union and paying union dues) and Bob Collins, a Vietnam vet, stepped up to help in their own case. All three of these maintenance men knew their involvement with the grievance would be a strong incentive for the Company to never bring them back to work. They weren't intimidated; they did what was right.

Very early on I found that the key to winning cases was the employees, the members themselves. The grievance procedure was merely their instrument. Koza, Budd, and Collins were around my age but had at least ten years or more seniority in the mill. They were diligent, persistent, and would give Perry Mason detective Paul Drake a run for his money. Most importantly, management didn't intimidate them. They started keeping records, calling those still working daily, and getting information to support the grievance.

Meanwhile, I started digging, researching, and reading through hundreds of old arbitration cases (remember, this was pre-computer days with everything on paper), I found only one of more than a dozen cases that ruled in the union's favor on this issue.[2] I scoured it closely, looking for the similarities with our case. Accompanying the three workers who really carried this case, we amassed a heap of written documentation and evidence to prove our allegation.

My approach to and appearance at arbitration was, to say the least, pretty uncanny. Prior to the hearing, I stayed up studying three nights in a row, organizing files and evidence, and memorizing our defense and summation. In defiance of their suit and tie dress code, I came into the arbitration hearing blurry-eyed, with a sleeveless black-collared shirt, white tie, blue jeans, and rock and roll boots. Since they thought I was uncouth and uneducated, I dressed the part. I invited the entire maintenance department to watch. A half dozen of them showed up, with several testifying on our behalf. For them, watching me take down the bosses who had treated them like shit since anyone could remember was a joy. In the role of union lawyer, my years reading about Clarence Darrow were instructive and inspirational.[3]

On December 28, 1983, a decision was issued, and we won the case. The arbitrator ruled there was a past practice of having so many maintenance people at each level of operation, and management couldn't just unilaterally reduce it.[4] Never before in the history of Homestead had a case like this been won. Fecko and Natili were so shocked we won the case, that when I met with them to talk about implementing the award (which would bring ten or fifteen maintenance employees back to work with back pay), they refused to talk to me.[5] I said, "We won the case." They said, "Mr. Stout, we have nothing to say; get out."

I immediately filed unfair labor practice charges at the National Labor Relations Board (NLRB), which then called up the Company and ordered them to meet with me. When the Company representatives did finally meet with the four of us, General Foreman Fecko smugly said, "We are not going to implement it." We then had to go back to arbitration to force them to comply with the decision. This is where my three assistants were most instrumental. They had been in the 160" Maintenance Department since the day they were hired. They knew every coworker. They were able to document every single hour that someone laid off should have been working and who was doing their job while they were on the street. At a follow-up second arbitration hearing on January 22, 1985, we kicked their ass again. The Company had to pay 330 thousand dollars to nineteen maintenance guys, as well as vacation pay and sub-pay, and give them back the seniority time they had lost.[6] During scattered weeks until the 160" Plate Mill was shut down on November 22, 1985, at least a few of these millwrights and motor inspectors were temporarily called back to work, renewing their seniority time and benefits.

This case clearly demonstrated the importance of keeping written records and the involvement of the workers themselves. We had to convince those still on the job to see their involvement and help as an expression of support for their brothers and sisters on the street. It's called "solidarity."

In this grievance, as with so many others, the Section 2-B: Local Working Conditions clause in the contract was my major weapon for protecting jobs and crew sizes. In fact, it protected just about everything to do with life in the mill, down to the type of speech used. My all-time favorite disciplinary grievance case involved another 160" millwright, "Captain" Ray Kondas. Ray was what we called a "curmudgeon." His vocabulary around other workers in the mill was extremely limited.

When he came to the safety meeting first thing in the morning and fellow workers said hello to him, his response was universal: "Go fuck yourself." In fact, it didn't matter what you said to him: "I love you, Ray" or "How was your weekend, Ray?" The response was always the same: "Go fuck yourself."

In the summer of 1984, a new foreman was hired straight out of college. He had snowy blond hair, and his name was Larson, probably only around twenty-two or twenty-three years old. One hot, sticky day he went down to the 160" Mill Plate Treating Line maintenance shanty at 3:15 p.m., when the maintenance men traditionally knocked off and headed for the showers. This young foreman, still green around the ears and almost as young as Ray's three daughters, told Kondas that he had to go repair a roll that had broken on the plate treating line. As always, Ray responded, "Go fuck yourself."

While I was in a grievance meeting with General Foreman Fecko a half-mile away in the 160" maintenance office, Larson came running in all out of breath and said to Fecko, "A millwright, Ray Kondas, just told me to 'go fuck myself.'" Fecko responded in between two long drawn out cigarette puffs, "So what else is new; you think you're something special?" Larson said, "I don't have to put up with this treatment." Fecko said, "Do what you gotta do." So Larson gave Kondas a disciplinary slip and three days off for insubordination and cursing at him. Meanwhile, Kondas had already gone with another millwright and fixed the roll while Larson was complaining to Fecko.

When we got to mini-board arbitration, I claimed a "2-B past practice" justifying the captain's language. There was no "insubordination," as the repair job had gotten done. I only had to put one witness on the stand, fellow millwright Courtney Senior, whose case I had recently won. I asked Courtney how Ray greeted him every morning. He answered, "He says, 'Go fuck yourself.'" I asked Courtney, "No matter what anyone says to Ray, is that his standard reply?" Courtney replied, "Yep." I asked Courtney how long this had been going on. He replied, "Since I've been working with him; oh, I guess around twenty-five years." I then challenged the Company lawyer to produce any previous discipline examples for Kondas's foul language. Nada. Zip. While the decision wasn't officially issued until several weeks later, the arbitrator indicated right on the spot that he was going to rule in our favor, telling the Company labor contract

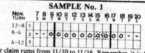

On Filing For 6th & 7th Day Overtime Claims; IT'S YOUR MONEY!

Over the past year our union employees are losing *thousands* of dollars from their pay checks because they either don't know HOW to file 6th and 7th day overtime claims, or are simply AFRAID to file them.

Under Section 11-C-1-d (page 78) of our contract, it states that you have to file a written claim for a 6th and 7th day where they cross a payroll week, in which the first 5 days were worked. This means ANY 7 consecutive 24 hour periods or 168 Hours, but if their is a shift change, it shortens to 152 hours.

Below are samples on how to file a claim, and examples of when you are eligible. Many people are under the mistaken impression that you have to actually work all 6 or 7 days straight. This is not true.

Even if there's a 24-hour break AND a shift change, as long as "the first five days were worked" in the 7 consecutive day period, and the 7th day falls within 152 hours, you are still eligible for a 7th day overtime claim.

Many employees have stated that they are "afraid" to file, explaining that the bosses will 'come down on them', or they won't be able to get any 'favors', schedule changes, etc. off of management if they do.

Filing a 6th or 7th day overtime claim is not like filing a grievance protesting this or that. IT IS A RIGHT *guaranteed* under the contract. It is a guard against the Company putting up all sorts of abnormal, weirded out schedules, not working you 5 (on) and 2 (off) like they are obligated to. In many cases, if the Company can work you 9, 10 or 11 days in a row, it keeps them from having to call back employees from layoff. Not filing simply encourages management to put up any type of illegal schedule and do whatever they like.

With times so bad and the money situation so tight, it is inconceivable how employees could be throwing so much of THEIR money away. In the 160" Maintenance Department alone, Millwrights, Motor Inspectors and Rollhands lost more than $4,000.00 DOLLARS in pay during the Month of November alone because they didn't file 6th and 7th day claims.

SAMPLE No. 1

Your claim runs from 11/10 to 11/16. Remember, it is ANY 7 consecutive day period. It does not have to begin on the first day you worked in a payroll week. Often, the 6th or 7th day falls on a Sunday, which the company does intentionally, because Sunday is already time and a half. Just move your claim back one more day.

168 Hours = 21 Squares
152 Hours = 19 Squares

You Must File Separate Claims For The 6th and 7th Day.

SAMPLE No. 2

Your claim runs from 11/10 to 11/16. Here there is a shift change, lowering the 7 consecutive day period to 152 hours (19 squares). A careful count shows that both the 6th and 7th day fall within "7 consecutive 24 periods", beginning at 8:00 a.m. on Wednesday, November the 10th (8:00 a.m., Wednesday - 8:00 a.m. Thursday = 24 hour period, 8:00 a.m. Thursday - 8:00 a.m. Friday, another 24 hour period, etc.)

SAMPLES No. 3 and No. 4

From 1978 to 1984, the *1397 Rank and File* newspaper was a valuable tool for educating members about their rights under the Basic Labor Agreement.

administrator (LCA) that he was ordering the slip pulled and Kondas paid for the time off.

The hearing had been held at 9:00 a.m. It was over by 10:30 a.m. As we left the hotel to get a bite to eat, Courtney turned to Kondas and said, "I guess you're gonna have to buy me lunch, Ray, since I won your case for ya." To which Kondas responded, "Go fuck yourself."

While the battles raged against the job eliminations, with the Basic Steel Contract toothless to stop the onslaught, demonstrations in the streets and the grievance system were all we had. For several of the more militant workers, such as friend Paul Mervis, arbitration saved their jobs more than once. And while I won a majority of the cases filed, things didn't always go as planned. When the Company eliminated all but one janitor for the entire mill, and locker room conditions went all to hell, a grievance was filed by janitor Kenny Bergert, again under Section 2-B. Kenny, who was handicapped, was one of hundreds laid off illegally just short of his twenty years and early retirement pension eligibility. At the dry run through before the hearing, the lone janitor left working, John Venable, who was also a reverend and had more than forty years in the mill, agreed to testify that it was impossible for one janitor to cover ten departments across several miles. We must have gone through his testimony five or six times. So when we get to the hearing, what does the good reverend do: he proudly boasts his workmanship in covering every department. We lost the case, but luckily I had Kenny covered with two other grievances and got him his back pay and early retirement pension.

Though I stayed involved in umpteen activities outside the mill, I came to the conclusion that the majority of my energy would be best spent using the grievance system to defend and organize the workers in their own fightback. I realized I was in a unique position to win some real justice and help the workers get through the worst effects of the shutdowns and devastation that was wrecking their lives.

CHAPTER 23

UNION-COMPANY RELATIONS TAKE A TURN FOR THE WORSE

W hile the union gave some monetary concessions to the Company in the 1980 national contract, for the most part nothing really changed on the shop floor. On the main concessions the Company wanted— to eliminate Section 2-B, the right to legally contract work out to nonunion shops, and the right to combine jobs and seniority units—there was no agreement. They also wanted the leeway to schedule ten- and twelve-hour shifts, without paying overtime. It started to sound like 1892 all over again. With demonstrations and industry-wide rank-and-file resistance, the International could not just roll over and play dead. The natives were getting angry and restless.

Business Week magazine, July 12, 1982.

On June 24, 1982, the great open hearth furnace, OH5, built during World War II at taxpayers' expense was shut down, with 250 employees put out of work. While the bosses called it "temporary and indefinite,"

Homestead OH5, closed June 24, 1982.

a handful of us knew it was permanent. On that day, our attorney Staughton Lynd traveled in from Youngstown to meet officers and OH5 workers at the union hall to file an injunction against the closing and any removal of equipment. Only four members showed up for the meeting: President Ron Weisen, the newly elected OH5 griever Frankie Boyle, his assistant and longtime rank-and-file activist Red Durkin, and me. Looking around the empty union hall, Staughton sighed, set his oversized briefcase down, and began the meeting. The disappointment washed over his face. The shocked majority of OH5 workers did not want to believe the shutdown was permanent. It was. The writing on the wall was as plain as could be.

When signing the contract on March 1, 1983, the International Union gave the Company more than four billion dollars in wage and benefit concessions, in an attempt to stop the bloodletting of the endless job losses. For U.S. Steel, this was not enough. When the union again refused to budge on the major issues of contracting out, job combinations, forced overtime, and elimination of Section 2-B, the Company's legal and financial bosses downtown made a strategic decision to sign the contract, then systematically ignore and violate it. The ink had barely dried when they began doing whatever they wanted, regardless of any legalities or contractual obligations. The way they figured it, if the union filed grievances, management would just tie them up in court for months or even years. In a lawsuit we filed several years later, I saw the script of a power point presentation the corporate overlords downtown had sent out with a SWAT team of Company lawyers. It instructed management personnel on how to circumvent and violate the contract: how to cut crews, combine jobs, schedule illegal overtime shifts, and contract work out, and how to best attempt to legally cover their asses while doing so. Their duplicity was sickening; the damage it caused to workers and their families was devastating.

With the grievance procedure our last and only real line of defense, I put a guerrilla network of those still working into action. Janitors were going through trashcans to retrieve documents. Office clerks took information for me out of the bosses' offices. Workers who delivered internal documents to the bosses gave me copies before the bosses saw their mail. I would make copies of the documents on *their* copy machines at work (while I was on the Company clock) before they arrived at the office. The clerks would then put the documents back in their envelopes for delivery to management with their morning coffee. I had their instructions and intercompany memos before they did. I knew every move they were making every day. It was a war of written information.

In late 1983, I really hit the "information jackpot" while arguing with then Slab and Plate labor contract administrator (LCA) Maureen Clark about a job pay issue. Maureen was the first Company LCA I dealt with that didn't treat me like dirt. To bolster her argument, she brought out computer generated statistics sheets. They were the spreadsheets sent to the pay center at Muriel Street on the south side of Pittsburgh to generate paychecks for all U.S. Steel employees. All these forms contained were numbers designating the cost center (i.e., department), job center (i.e., job and pay scale), and check number (i.e., employee). Across the top of these computer sheets was typed Sunday through Saturday. For each day it had the number of hours worked by each employee and a letter code designating how they were paid: regular, holiday, overtime rate, or Sunday premium.[1] I asked her if I could have access to copies, and she said yes, establishing yet another favorable local working condition under Section 2-B of the contract.

As an information source to track grievances, these pay sheets were a gold mine. Every time management used somebody on an overtime basis to keep workers on layoff, it showed up on the pay sheets.

Company weekly statistics pay sheet, 100" Plate Mill.

If younger employees were brought across seniority lines to work the jobs of more senior employees out on the street, their check number showed up on these forms. I could tell everything that was going on in the mill from those sheets; it was like having a minute by minute view of every foot of the mill.

At an early 1984 job eliminations arbitration proceeding, I presented the pay sheets as evidence to back up my assertions in the case. The Company objected. The arbitrator ruled that I could use them. After I used them in the case, the plant-wide Company LCA said I could no longer have access to them. I filed National Labor Relations Board (NLRB) charges and regained access to them. It was tit for tat with this outlaw company just about every day of the week.

Even with all this written documentation, there were still several other obstacles I had to overcome to win grievance cases. For one, the guys still working were generally in their late forties to early sixties, most with enough time in the mill to retire with a full pension. The last thing they wanted to do was rock the boat and jeopardize what little time they had left by helping me with grievances. The only way to get their help was to file grievances that also won money for them. This gave them a stake in helping those on the street. Second, I had to keep up the spirits of the people laid off. When their unemployment checks dried up, they wanted to quit, give up on their grievances, move on, and look for work elsewhere. My personal sermons and pep talks encouraging them to stay the course were never-ending. The other major problem I had to deal with was the way the seniority system pitted worker against worker; whenever there were seniority disputes, someone would always lose and get shoved out in the street. Very often I would have to play both sides against the middle; keeping the younger workers on as long as possible, while filing and winning back pay awards for the older workers. It was a risky approach; either way it would always seem someone was getting hurt.

From 1981 until 1984, my biggest case ever in Slab and Plate involved the Company's refusal to implement the area labor pool. As noted earlier, with the shutdown of the 48" mill on November 27, 1979, the area labor pool, a local seniority agreement for the Slab and Plate Division, allowing laid-off senior employees from one Slab and Plate department to bump junior job class 3 or 4 employees in other departments. Seeing this agreement as a disruption to their long-established work crews, management in every department simply refused to implement it. This problem became even more pressing after the 1983 Labor Contract was signed, and the Slab and Plate area labor pool was expanded to encompass the entire mill and include job class 5 positions. Anyone laid off throughout the mill could now bump a junior person in a job class 3, 4, or 5 anywhere in the mill, as long as they had "the relative ability" to do the job.

From 1982 up until the 100" mill closed on June 30, 1984, the Company retained a scrap-cutting crew (job classes 3 and 4), whose workers had six to nine years of seniority. Right next door in the 100" Shipping Department, there were employees with seventeen or eighteen years in the mill being laid off, including hookers, car blockers, and expediters (job classes 6–10). Under the Basic Steel Contracts at the time, if you had a least eighteen years of service and were past your forty-third birthday, you had two years on layoff to accrue seniority time and roll into your Rule of 65 early retirement pension. You would have a pension check roughly the size of an unemployment check and medical insurance until you became eligible for social security. And back in those days, there were no copays and deductibles. Everything was covered, 100 percent. It was the difference between keeping your head above water and drowning.

My assistant griever for the 100" Shipping Department was Warren Rudolph. He filed a number of grievances when the job eliminations started and was immediately tossed out into the street. He enlisted nine of his coworkers to sign the grievance. Warren was a smooth operator. He knew how to do the proper research, keep accurate records, and pull the Company's chain at the same time. Warren chewed on cigars when he wasn't smoking Lucky Strikes and had no fear of management. Another big helper on these cases was his friend and fellow expediter John Burkhardt, who became a good friend of mine through this fight. Both were excellent witnesses at arbitration proceedings. In addition to the area labor pool violations, Warren and John also filed grievances around overtime and the elimination of expediter, car blocker, and hooker jobs they should have been working. In addition to Warren's organizing and meticulous record-keeping abilities, I had those infamous pay sheets. Scrutinizing them regularly, I discovered that every single week they were scheduling the junior scrap crew employees from the sheer bay on overtime to cover the work of the laid-off senior shipping employees. It was right there in black and white.

It took two years to get the area labor pool case to arbitration, as the Company employed the big stall. Every time this grievance would get to the fourth step, on the eve of arbitration, the Company lawyer from downtown, Walter Payne, would order the local Homestead Company LCA to, "Get back and settle this," because it was such an obvious violation. Back at the mill, the Company LCA would refuse to settle, claiming he lacked the authority to settle something that costly. Finally, we got the case to arbitration.[2] It was another slam dunk that ended up costing the Company some three million dollars in back pay, vacation pay, sub-pay, medical benefits, and early retirement pensions for eighteen employees. With the pay sheets as backup, it was like playing poker with a marked deck, and I was the dealer. The pay sheets clearly showed management's blatant violations over a two-year period. Some weeks, management was using 200 to 250 illegal work hours. Winning justice for so many workers and saving their pensions was another shot of adrenaline that kept me going.

The Job Slaughter Continues

By this time, it had become apparent U.S. Steel was permanently shutting the mill down department by department. Like clockwork, at the end of each quarter the announcement would come: the Forge Division on December 27, 1983; No. 1 Structural in April 1984; the 100" Plate Mill on June 30, 1984; the 45" Slab Mill in September 1984, etc. With the massive and militant resistance experienced during the Youngstown shutdowns, the Company had learned a valuable lesson and attempted to kill three birds with one stone: cut costs, give workers false hope their departments would reopen, and turn them against each other, fighting over the scraps and few remaining jobs. For a worker to receive severance pay (usually the equivalent of seven to eight weeks of pay), their department had to be declared permanently shut down. To avoid making this payment, management labeled these incremental department shutdowns as "temporary and indefinite." It also delayed for at least two years those eligible for an early retirement pension. Once workers were laid off for two years, their seniority time stopped accumulating; out in the street after five years, they no longer had recall rights and were not owed severance pay. Calling the shutdowns "temporary and indefinite" also served to keep workers divided and gave them false hope that their department might reopen. Morale was slowly being suffocated. The betrayal workers felt was written on their faces. It didn't matter whether an employee was a good "company man" and the hardest worker on the job or a union radical—everybody got their throat cut! The "they'll never close Homestead" bombast rang hollow inside the union hall, replaced by the new reality painted on an outside Structural Mill wall: "the party is over."

In my home department at the 160", from 1983 through its closing November 22, 1985, only one or two shifts were working, with the third shift on indefinite layoff. At a meeting with Slab and Plate superintendent Gene Nethamer in the fall of 1984, I was told the third shift would never come back. He asked me to agree to schedule the remaining two crews on twelve-hour turns, three days a week (without paying them overtime). When I gave him a resounding no, the general foreman called a meeting at 3:45 p.m. right in the middle of the rolling mill, when the 8:00 a.m. to 4:00 p.m. shift was going home, and the 4:00 p.m. to midnight shift was coming in. Management called me at the union hall around 3:00 p.m. about the meeting, with no advance warning. Facing the entire 160" production workforce, the Company told the crews that if they didn't convince me to "let management do what it had to do," they were all goners. I refused to do it. There was a huge heated argument between some of the older employees and me. These guys argued it was "feast or famine," so why not let them earn the extra money while the getting was good. I said, "No, because these are your fellow workers who are laid off and I represent them too." It got really ugly, as I stormed away in anger, refusing to cave in to this cutthroat, divide and conquer crap.

1397 Rank and File newspaper, December 1981.

This was neither the first nor the only time the Company tried to turn worker against worker, rank and file against the union. That little song and dance was constant. After I had been elected grievance chair in May 1985, representing the entire mill, Fecko would schedule me on the 4:00 pm to midnight turn, knowing I was working at the union hall all day. This move would knock another friend of mine, crane operator Chuck McCann, off the schedule and out on layoff. When the schedule came out on Thursday, I went into Fecko's office, berated him, and said, "I'm wildcatting." Fecko responded in a threatening tone, "What did you say?" I said, "I'm calling off union business until further notice." By the following Monday, McCann was back on the schedule.

On another occasion, 160" shipping employees, all with an average seniority of twenty-five or thirty years, most of who were African American, were told I was bringing in workers from other parts of the mill on layoff to take their jobs. When I heard about the rumor and walked in to their lunchroom at noon, they were in a conversation about how they were going to kill me. I nipped the rumors in the bud. I learned early on that when someone was spreading rumors or slander about you, the best tactic was to confront it head-on, face-to-face. When I confronted these workers with the truth, I found out that the rumors originated at the union hall.

The main contract violation utilized by the Company was illegally contracting out work to nonunion shops (some of which had been set up by former foremen). The cost savings were huge, as they did not have to pay subcontractors medical benefits or pay into their pension funds, and subcontractors were compensated at a pay rate far below union employees.

In late 1984 and early 1985, I formed a strategic alliance with the Production Planning, and Accounting Departments, which were a separate salary union (Local 3063) at Homestead. Many of our Local 1397 union officers looked down on the salary union members, I guess because they were "white-collar" or whatever. But these workers were critical for tracking all the paperwork of every single job being contracted out. They became valuable allies in the struggle to compensate hundreds of workers who were displaced because of this illegal contracting out.

After the signing of the 1983 contract, it was like a full-scale war in the mill, and I was on the front lines daily. Also, my personal life was in shambles. When I got my crane job back and was appointed the zone griever job in April 1981, my family moved back to town, and I bought a nice house on Orchard Street, up by the Munhall Borough building.

As the economy continued to worsen and inflation soared to 16.5 percent, I was unable to make the mortgage payments. Though I had a good paying super-seniority grievance position, with the massive loss in dues monies, the local could only pay me one day a week. By early 1983, the bank (Mellon, of course) foreclosed on me, and I lost my second home. I was also separated for the second and last time; we filed for divorce, and the family again temporarily moved back to Kentucky.

Barney Oursler, c. 1982.

Shortly thereafter, I had to declare bankruptcy. I was averaging four hours of sleep a night. With the loss of their jobs, all my friends and coworkers were losing their families, homes, and dignity. Instead of calling in the state militia like they did 1892, the Company was clobbering us with computers and lawyers.

I often felt like I was on a battlefield with casualties all around me. Premature deaths and suicides became a common occurrence. In February 1985, as I headed to the locker room to change into my work clothes at 7:45 a.m., Fecko told me to head over to the abandoned Open Hearth and join the search party for a foreman who was missing. Dave Sapos, thirty-nine years old with nineteen and a half years in the mill, had not returned home that morning after working his 10:00 p.m. to 6:00 a.m. night shift. His wife had called the police, who called plant security. The night before, when he came to work, his supervisor told him to clean his locker out in the morning, that he was no longer needed. By the time I caught up to the search party, which included Homestead mayor and former machine shop superintendent Steve Simko, Homestead police chief Chris Kelly, and plant protection head Lt. Joe Morton, Sapos was lying on the ground dead. They had found him suspended from a high beam between two ladle buckets. He had hanged himself with a steel cable, after neatly placing his work gloves in his back jeans pocket and his goggles in his white safety helmet on the ground. You could see the cable marks around his neck when the cover over him slipped as the coroner loaded him into the morgue wagon. I was glad I only had coffee before coming to work, as I was retching all the way back to the 160" locker room.

Another legal obstacle we encountered with the grievance system was that every time we won in arbitration, the Company went out of its way to limit its liability and pay affected employees as little as possible. They found a buried 1965 agreement signed by I.W. Abel, the International president of the Steelworkers Union at the time, which provided that if the union won a back pay award, the Company could deduct any outside earnings during the covered period, including unemployment compensation, sub-pay, temporary jobs, etc. In addition, the Unemployment Compensation Act allowed the Company to reduce a back pay award by any UC received. UC was roughly half of what you made when you were working, and back then it wasn't taxed. Sub-pay took you up to two-thirds of what you made while working. From 1983 to 1986, when workers needed this sub-pay the most, the fund was completely dried up.

By the time I won the 100" shipping grievances, most of the eighteen grievants who were owed back pay and seniority had been laid off for more than two years. My assistant griever and the most senior grievant, Warren Rudolph, was awarded seventy thousand dollars gross in back pay. Seven more grievants got thirty thousand dollars or more, and another eleven received between two and twelve thousand dollars. With UC, sub-pay, and Trade Readjustment Allowance (TRA) deducted from their back pay awards, what they actually received was a fraction of what they lost. For example, Warren's seventy-thousand-dollar award shrunk to a net of seventeen thousand dollars after deductions. The massive reductions fueled their anger and demoralization. But right on time, a Pennsylvania Supreme Court case came along that would solve this problem.

Outside the mill I had developed a good working relationship with the Mon Valley Unemployment Committee (MVUC), especially with their help around UC and getting TRA benefits for many of our displaced members. Barney Oursler and Paul Lodico, the two main workhorses on the committee, both good friends, introduced me to the

MVUC lawyer and board chair John Stember. John and the MVUC had challenged a number of UC and TRA rulings in the state unemployment system, which administered UC and federal programs like the TRA. The Pennsylvania Supreme Court accepted one of their cases, *Cugini*, to decide what happens to a UC claimant when payment of money he or she is owed, such as severance pay, is delayed due to circumstances beyond his or her control, such as bankruptcy.

After Joseph Cugini lost his job at Mesta Machine, the Company filed for bankruptcy. Bankruptcy delayed receipt of severance pay that should have been received at layoff. The question was whether to count the severance as received when it should have been paid or when actually received. If counted from when it should have been paid, Cugini would be eligible for a second UC claim; if counted from when received, he would not. The Pennsylvania Supreme Court ruled that Cugini's severance should be counted from when it should have been paid and directed that he receive benefits.

Two years later, in the case of *USX Corp. v. UCBR*, the Pennsylvania Commonwealth Court extended the ruling in *Cugini* to the major grievance we had just won, involving union stalwarts Joe Nestico, Ron Lee, Warren Rudolph, John Burkhart, and the fourteen other grievants. When the union showed that the layoffs were improper, the arbitrator issued substantial back pay awards, which USX paid in lump sums. USX then claimed: (1) receipt of a lump sum made grievants ineligible for UC they were then collecting; (2) the lump sum had to be counted when it was paid, which made them ineligible for any further UC claim. The court was not persuaded. It ruled that the grievance award should be counted as received in the quarters U.S. Steel should have paid it—and not as a single lump sum—which meant that grievants were eligible for new UC claims.

The court ruling also meant that grievants' UC and TRA benefits would be calculated as if they had worked and were paid on time. For instance, even if UC offset a back pay award, grievants were eligible to open new UC and TRA claims based on when the back pay they were awarded should have been paid. In short, it gave me the legal means to recoup monies USX deducted from back pay awards, by making former employees eligible for new UC and TRA claims. This meant that grievants could receive up to another two years of UC and TRA and paid schooling.

On top of being a good union man, Warren was a good friend with good business sense. By the time we won this case in April 1986, I had been grievance chair for a year. The chairman's pay rate was equal to the highest in the mill—job class 27. But, as previously noted, because the local was being drained of dues money from layoffs, I was cut back to one paid union day a week. When the 160" mill closed on November 22, 1985, there was nowhere in the mill I could work. Realizing I was on UC and doing the work of a lawyer for next to nothing, Warren organized a dinner at Poli's Restaurant across the river in Squirrel Hill. Poli's was kind of a swanky place, and, back in the day, a lot of bosses ate there. When union folks did, it was a special occasion. Five grievants came. After dinner each handed me an envelope with five hundred dollars inside. I was humbled. While I know your average lawyer makes that much in a couple of hours, their solidarity and generosity left me speechless for one of the few times in my life. It made me want to fight for their UC and TRA even harder.

In a grievance with power and fuel employee Chuck Brantner, I won forty thousand dollars in back pay when his job was illegally contracted out.[3] He invited me to Lapko's Bar, where he handed me two thousand dollars cash for winning his case. On permanent layoff, with the local unable to pay me, I could not have stayed on as grievance chair without the kindness and generosity of these fellow workers.

Perhaps the most significant case Barney, Paul, John Stember, and I worked on is also among least known and appreciated. Once again, our lead claimant was a Local 1397 worker John Jakiela, who worked in the 160" Mill Shipping Department and was also a member of Braddock borough council. The problem we confronted was that while TRA provided up to two years of additional cash benefits, paid training, and job search and relocation allowances, the Reagan administration interpreted the eligibility periods in a way that meant no one—and I mean no one—in the entire country could receive the benefits. According to the Reagan administration, their eligibility periods expired before they were able to collect them.

Jakiela was our test case to challenge this ruling. It was a major campaign that John Stember later told me was among the most significant things he was ever involved in. To generate publicity and momentum, at the referee's hearing before Florence Godich, we had Senator John Heinz testify. He was then a member of the Senate finance committee, which had written the trade act that included the Trade Adjustment Assistance (TAA—the schooling part of the TRA) and the TRA. Senator Heinz was asked to explain what his committee meant by the statutory language. He explained it in a way that supported our position. When a Democrat, Robert Casey, was elected governor, he appointed Harris Wofford, later Senator Wofford, as head of Pennsylvania's Department of Labor and Industry, which had jurisdiction over UC, the TAA, and the TRA. When Wofford was greeted by 125 angry steelworkers who had had their TRA benefits stolen from them as he entered office on his first day, he got on board—though we felt our chances were pretty good when Referee Godich asked for a picture with Senator Heinz.

While we waited for rulings, thousands of individual appeals piled up. We worked out a procedure with the Casey administration so local unions, including Homestead's, could designate the Mon Valley Unemployment Committee and John Stember as their representatives, so no appeals would fall through the cracks. Huge boxes filled with appeals began arriving at the Mon Valley Unemployment Committee every day.

Both the referee and the Unemployment Compensation Board of Review ruled in our favor. Because Wofford supported it, Pennsylvania did not appeal. What followed, however, was a massive operation to implement the decision with the thousands of dislocated workers from the steel, electrical, railway and other import affected industrial facilities throughout Mon Valley and Pittsburgh region. There was also a strange incident where John Stember and I were summoned to the International and told we were wrong and threatened with removal from United Steelworker cases. The truth was that they were wrong. While we had some consults with the United Steelworkers of America's outside lawyer, they were not in familiar waters and politely backed off.

While the Casey administration did not appeal the Jakiela decision, the Reagan administration blew a gasket. All state UC systems, including Pennsylvania's, must be certified by the federal government as in compliance with federal law. Compliance means that a state will be reimbursed by the feds for *all* administrative costs of the UC system and receive a major tax credit for employers against their federal tax liability. No state had ever been decertified, but the Reagan administration threatened to decertify Pennsylvania. A later federal audit demanded reimbursement of all TAA and TRA benefits paid.

For the next several years, Stember and the MVUC went up and down the Three Rivers doing case after case to implement the Jakiela decision. Appeals that had piled up were processed and paid. They handled many individual claims for training, some of which were unusual—taxidermy, gunsmithing (particularly popular in Johnstown)—or far flung (helicopter repair training in Arizona). Thousands of dislocated workers received TRA cash and were retrained as nurses, teachers, etc.

We would end up taking more than three hundred UC and TRA cases for Homestead workers through referee hearings and before the Unemployment Compensation Review Board. I got so well-known at the unemployment office that the referee, Florence Godich, had coffee waiting for me when I showed up and told state workers to make any copies I needed. The MVUC won more than eight thousand TRA appeal hearings for workers in 1988 alone.

Up to the closing of the 100" Plate Mill, on June 30, 1984, there were numerous grievances, as the Company attempted to cut their losses. Warren alone filed five different grievances: one in response to the elimination of his expediter-loader position; two grievances for the elimination of the car blocker and hooker jobs he was entitled to work; one addressing less senior sheer bay workers who were crossing units to do his job on an overtime basis; one as part of the big area labor pool grievance. He couldn't get the back pay for everything he won in arbitration, as the weeks for each grievance he won overlapped. Throughout the rest of the Slab and Plate Division, almost every department had job class 3, 4, or 5 positions filled by younger people than those on the street. These jobs were the dirtiest and lowest paid—at the bottom of the ladder—but precious at this juncture. The Company ended up paying so much back pay that the U.S. Steel lawyer from downtown, Walter Payne, and a Homestead LCA were demoted. In addition, winning these grievances meant dozens of employees illegally laid off were now eligible for early retirement pensions, as their new seniority dates (last day worked) gave them twenty years of service. A Rule of 65 early retirement pension was guesstimated by the Company at 250 thousand dollars over its lifespan.[4] It was a sip of sweet justice in the middle of a slaughter.

One of the grievances most gratifying to me personally was won in December 1985. The Company had reopened the mold yard in OH5, but instead of bringing the employees who should have been working these jobs back from layoff, they brought over a crew from another department that was already working. As noted earlier, OH5 had been permanently closed on June 24, 1982, but dozens of its employees elected to remain on active status, in the hope of getting called back to work in another department. One of these employees was the former OH5 zone grievance representative John Balint, who for seven years had been calling me a communist and generally giving me a hard time. He used to hum the "National Anthem" and "Battle Hymn of the Republic" every time he came around me in the union hall.

John Balint was a good union man; a cursory reading of his articles in early issues of the rank-and-file newspaper proved that. His view just got poisoned and distorted by the whole red-baiting virus. I felt his hostility had no basis in the real world. I was determined not to respond to him with more hostility or indifference. I was determined to treat him like a union brother should be treated—with dignity, respect, and solidarity.

Shortly after I was elected to the grievance chair position in May 1985, Balint came marching into the grievance chair's office late one afternoon with five other guys and a menacing glare on his face. It was after 5:00 p.m., and the place had cleared out. He demanded I file another grievance. I said, "No problemo." Apparently, these former OH5 employees had filed a complaint with O'Toole a month earlier when John was still grievance chair. But with Balint red-baiting Ronnie regularly, Weisen made sure the grievance went straight to the trash can. I looked forward to fighting this one in court.

On December 9, 1985, the night before the case was to go to arbitration, the Company called me at home and settled; Balint received $10,000, and the other grievants each received $7,500. With new last-day worked seniority dates, they all had their medical insurance renewed and became eligible for unemployment claims and the TRA, which I won for them a few months later. With new seniority dates, Balint and a few others were now able to slide into a Rule of 65 early retirement pension or transfer to another mill. After the lockout ended in 1987, Balint ended up at Edgar Thomson, his seniority intact.

The same thing happened with these employees as happened with the 100" shipping guys and Chuck Brantner. Balint and five other grievants invited me to a bar on Route 51 south of Pittsburgh called Molnar's. I brought my 38 snub-nosed pistol, as Balint's past behavior toward me wasn't exactly sociable; I guess I was a little paranoid. When I entered the bar, all six of them handed me envelopes with $150 in them. It was another humbling experience. I walked out to my car, all choked up. Several weeks after the settlement, Balint's wife Marsha called me at the union hall with some insurance questions. In the course of the conversation, she said, "I guess my John's gonna have to take back all those bad things he said about you, huh?" I answered, "That would be nice." With this case especially, I was out to prove that as a union representative you fought just as hard for the people who didn't like you personally as the ones who did, that the union represented *all* workers not just the clique that was in power. Several times after the mill had closed, I ran into John at Steel Valley High School football games (my son played; his daughter was in the band). We shook hands and hugged like brothers—the way it should have been all along.

Arbitration preparation and hearings were a weekly occurrence. I was literally deluged with grievances of all kinds. With no department, worker, or foreman untouched by the layoffs, getting information and witnesses was no problem. Having mastered the system, I was winning the majority of cases. Unfortunately, this was a mere pittance relative to the number of jobs lost at Homestead and other steel mills. With such a massive shutdown, coupled with the uncertainty about whether or not their jobs would still be there, many workers grew extremely demoralized; just getting them to file grievances was a monumental task.

CHAPTER 24

WEISEN'S 1983 PRESIDENTIAL BID AND THE DECLINE OF THE RANK-AND-FILE MOVEMENT

Ron Weisen announces his candidacy for USWA International president.

In late 1983, at the pinnacle of his popularity and prior to his Denominational Mission Strategy (DMS) church invasions and antics, Ron Weisen announced his candidacy for president of the United Steelworkers of America (USWA) International. The election was to be held in March 1984, to finish the term of the deceased Lloyd McBride. Running as a "rank-and-file" candidate, Ronnie promised to shake up and change the direction of a union, which was, for the most part, standing idly by while plants were being closed and thousands of union members thrown into the ranks of the unemployed. He also spoke out strongly against any "concessions" to steel corporations, which were being accepted or condoned by other USWA officials. In the March 1983 Basic Steel Contract, the union had agreed to massive wage and benefit concessions. Weisen warned that the concessions were a "union-busting tactic," that the contract "was nothing more than a sellout to the greed of the big steel companies for higher profits." He went on to point out that "none of the billions of dollars in concessions given up by our members had been reinvested back into the mills and plants."[1] Weisen argued that both of his challengers, Frank McKee and Lynn Williams, would not be tough enough on the companies, which, in his opinion, were walking all over the union. In a flyer and press release announcing his candidacy, he stated:

> As President of the USWA International, I will mobilize the entire resources of our great union to protect the interests of our members, and defend them from the constant attacks on their standard of living. I have been called a militant by the International, and if fighting both the Companies and the International to protect our members is considered "militant," then I am proud of that title.[2]

Unfortunately, Ronnie never made it through the nomination process. He received only 75 of the required 111 nominations needed from USWA locals to be included on the ballot. In shades of the Sadlowski campaign, he won most of the big locals in basic steel but lost the small locals that were controlled by District staff representatives and beholden to the International for their financial solvency. Ronnie also failed to distance himself from Frank McKee's jingoistic "America First" campaign. As a result, Canadian locals joined the union staff and hierarchy across the border and voted overwhelmingly for native Lynn Williams. As had been the case in the Sadlowski election, we suspected some of the locals had possibly been stolen, if the experience we had in Aliquippa was any indication.

At Aliquippa's Local 1211, there was a nice size group of young rank-and-file activists, including Denny Trombulak, Bob "Boo" Bauder, and others, who were friends and Weisen supporters. When Jay Weinberg and I went up to work the polls at the union hall with

Ron Weisen, c. 1983.

Local 1211 rank-and-file activists Denny Trombulak (top) and Bob "Boo" Bauder (front).

them on the nomination election day, it looked to us like the vote was extremely close; if anything, we had the edge. When the votes were counted, Weisen lost 3–1. After smoking a joint and hitting a local watering hole to cry in our beer, we ran into then District 20 staff representative Billy George, a Lynn Williams supporter. He bought us all a drink. When we complained about the vote count, George bluntly blurted out, "Everyone that came to the polls for my candidate got three ballots; that's how you lost." Ronnie protested the nomination process but to no avail, as there was no paper trail or hard proof that the votes were stolen or ballot boxes stuffed.

Though our relationship was extremely tense with the "cocaine addict" slander going on behind my back, I worked hard on Ronnie's campaign. We visited numerous locals together, pursuing every contact we had in the union. With the massive job loss and shutdowns all around us, it felt like we were out on the high seas in the middle of a horrible storm. The boat was taking on heavy water, and Ronnie was the only captain that had the guts to try and sail through it.

In February 1984, Weisen joined other rank and filers from around the country, as well as a dozen of us from Local 1397, and formed a "nationwide rank and file caucus."[3] On July 14, at the Local 1397 union hall, the USWA Rank and File Caucus held its first meeting and stated its purpose:

> To unite the grassroots fighters in our union, as well as those who have been laid off and have lost their "good standing," to challenge the treachery at the top of our union and provide genuine leadership on the burning issues facing steelworkers.[4]

Membership was open to any member of the USWA. The Caucus created a union-wide newspaper called the *Unifier*. The Caucus called for an end to concessions, the right of the membership to ratify contracts, unity of big and small steel and non-steel shops, cutting the pay of International officers, strengthening civil rights, a national policy to rebuild plants, and a major dues reform.[5] The Caucus, like Weisen's presidential bid, was doomed to failure, because of the developing split in Local 1397 over his DMS activities. In addition, most Caucus members lost their steelworker jobs, and when their benefits expired, they had to seek employment elsewhere. Later that year, with the subsequent alliance of the Tri-State Conference on Steel (TSCS) and the International Union around the Dorothy Six battle, the Caucus all but fizzled out.

In August 1984, elections were held for delegates to the International convention in Cleveland, Ohio, the following month. This time Ronnie opted not to run, going by acclamation, which was his right as local union president. The top two vote-getters were Ray Gottschalk, vice president in the former Bekich administration, and me; others who were lining up to oppose Ronnie also got elected. For the first time in six years Ronnie looked beatable. An opposition slate formed against him included former staunch supporters John Ingersoll, Tom Jugan, and Jack Bair. Despite their entreaties for me to join them, I opted to stay neutral. Ingersoll accused me of "playing politics" for refusing to take sides. Ronnie got really pissed, because I refused to campaign for him or denounce his opposition. Immersed in the many grievance fights at the time, and once again running unopposed for both the zone grievance position and the grievance chair, I saw this internal political strife as a senseless, no-win distraction. Taking sides would have been totally counterproductive and pointless. In spite of the falling out with Ronnie over his involvement with the DMS, he was still the only sure bet to not cave in to any concessions, which I was convinced would never save our mill. I felt really bad about this destructive split; I liked all of these guys. At this stage, we should have all been working together.

CHAPTER 25

THE CHANNEL 13 PBS AFFAIR

nother event took place in June 1984 that would totally change my trajectory in the local and my relationship with Ronnie and the newly formed national Rank and File Caucus. As noted earlier, Pittsburgh's PBS station, Channel 13, did not air the documentary *The Business of America* when it came out a month earlier.[1] In response, a group of us from Local 1397, the Tri-State Conference on Steel (TSCS), and the Mon Valley Unemployment Committee (MVUC) organized a picket line in front of the station in the Oakland section of Pittsburgh. When the station manager saw that Monsignor Rice was with us, he invited the Monsignor and several others from our ranks to come in and talk. To persuade us to call off the picket line and probable bad publicity, executive producer Herb Stein not only offered to air the documentary but also to host an hour-long panel discussion afterwards.

The panel would consist of Roger Albrandt, a professor from the University of Pittsburgh, Leon Lynch, International vice president for human affairs of the United Steelworkers of America (USWA), J. Bruce Johnston, U.S. Steel vice president in charge of employee relations, and someone from our ranks. At the insistence of J. Bruce Johnston, they specified that I was not welcome on the panel. Of course, they weren't going to tell us what to do, so we told them our spokesperson would be Barney Oursler. Then I showed up at the last minute as the panel assembled. Johnston just about hit the roof, refusing to go on the air. After a few tense moments and negotiations with the station manager, he agreed to go on if he was first given fifteen minutes by himself.

Johnston kicked off the panel discussion with a diatribe against the usual bogeyman, "foreign imports." Leon Lynch followed him stating, "This is one time I have to agree with the Company." When it got around to my turn, with a smirk, I stated emphatically, "The only import problem we have is downtown at 600 Grant Street." I then gave detailed examples of U.S. Steel's importing of steel and Mellon's foreign investments in a Brazilian steel operation that was supplying massive amounts of semi-finished steel to the U.S. market, as well as their massive investments in Japan's Sumitomo Industries. I pointed out the interlocking corporate ties between U.S. Steel and Mellon Bank, with the example of job elimination hatchet man Thomas Graham sitting on both boards. To his credit, this information had come straight from Honeywell's research and 3" × 5" index cards.

The panel moderator came unglued, quickly changing the subject. My microphone was cut off. Highly embarrassed by the whole affair, Leon Lynch approached me afterwards and said that "maybe we need to sit down and talk," that it was time to find out if there were ways to start working together. Somewhat startled and mildly surprised, I agreed. Within a few weeks, a meeting was hastily organized at the International headquarters that included Lynch, International union general counsel Bernie Kleiman, and several assistants to the International president. Charlie McCollester, Staughton Lynd, Jay Hornack, and I represented the TSCS. We hammered home the realities we were facing at Homestead and in the Valley, stressing it was time for the International Union to change policies and direction and stand up and fight for their members. As stated previously, for several years, U.S. Steel had been blatantly violating the contract and walking all over the union. My basic thinking at the time was that if we didn't *all* join forces, we were *all* going under. The coalition with the District and the International to save the Dorothy Six blast furnace in Duquesne was born at this meeting.

The move to form an alliance with the International to fight plant shutdowns put a destructive wedge between those of us in the local who were part of the TSCS, including Jay Weinberg and me, and Ronnie and the national Rank and File Caucus. Just for proposing working with the International, we were labeled sellouts and castigated. Of course, at the time, I didn't see it that way at all. I saw it as the International finally coming around to our way of thinking—that it was time for them to join the resistance. Ronnie was furious. Lee Ballinger and Dave Marsh stopped talking to me and Jay. Staughton Lynd was openly leery and let Charlie and I know it. In reaction to the split, dozens of local activists faded away. In hindsight, their arguments were not without merit; thinking we could maintain an independent voice in an alliance with the USWA International hierarchy turned out to be a bit naive.

To add insult to injury, while returning from an arbitration hearing in January 1985, District staff representative George Myers asked me to run for president against Ronnie, saying, in reference to the International Union, "We'll give you whatever support you need; money's no problem." The offer sickened me. The whole Valley was going through an economic holocaust, and these guys at the District were worried about Ronnie! With a distraught look on my face, I responded angrily, "No thanks, I got more important things to do."

CHAPTER 26

ART MEETS LABOR–SPRINGSTEEN COMES TO TOWN

The friction with Ronnie cost me a chance to meet one of my very favorite singer/songwriters. On September 21–22, 1984, Bruce Springsteen came to Pittsburgh for his momentous *Born in the USA* shows at the Civic Arena, selling out both shows in hours. In what became an ongoing staple to his concerts for years to come in every city he played, Springsteen donated ten thousand dollars to the Rainbow Kitchen and ten thousand dollars to the Local 1397 food bank. During a press conference announcing the donations at the Rainbow Kitchen, located on the corner of 8th and Amity, two blocks from the mill gate, Bruce was asked by Rainbow Kitchen cofounder Bob Anderson if he had heard of the Tri-State Conference on Steel (TSCS) and its efforts to stop the plant shutdowns. Before the "Boss" could answer,[1] he was interrupted by tour manager Barbara Carr, wife of Dave Marsh, who asked, "Oh, you mean that group fronting for the banks and International [Union]?" We were stunned. From that point on, Ron Weisen was the only person from our local invited to meet and talk with Springsteen. That evening, Jay and I attended his show as guests of Steve and Jimmy from the WDVE morning show. We cheered like maniacs when the "Boss" declared from the stage, "This song [Trapped] is dedicated to the Local 1397 rank and file." Ronnie got to watch the show from backstage, as he did when Bruce returned and played Three Rivers Stadium the following summer on August 11, 1985, and donated another ten thousand dollars each to our local food bank and the Rainbow Kitchen.

This whole ordeal was especially stinging for me personally, being a songwriter and musician who had played in New York City at places like the Gaslight Café, where Bruce started out. Since seeing Springsteen at the Bottom Line in New York City on August 14, 1975, I had been a huge fan. Just before I left New York and moved back to Kentucky, he had introduced his newly released album *Born to Run* to America. Springsteen was wild, working-class, and an incredible songwriter. His E Street Band rocked! We were born the same year, both raised Catholics, and my energy level was on a par with his. In subsequent years, I saw him more than thirty times live, including a dozen times with my wife Stephanie on his 1999–2000 reunion tour. We've seen him in

Stephanie Stout (on right) with the "Boss" and high school friend Doris Brown (on left) after Berkeley, California, show, June 1978.

numerous big cities, from Fort Lauderdale to L.A. to Toronto and all points in between. Springsteen concerts, especially in later years, were like rock and roll revivals, marathon performances lasting up to four hours. They really revved you up. Denied an audience with him when he came to Homestead ("my hometown" at the time) was a bitter pill to swallow.

A month later, on October 29, Ballinger and Marsh organized a "Labor Meets Art" event in New York City, attended by a number of national musicians, including another musical hero of mine, John

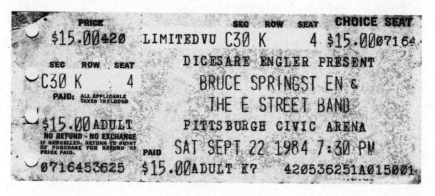

PRICE $15.00 420 LIMITED VU C30 K 4 $15.00 071 64
CHOICE SEAT SEC ROW SEAT
SEC ROW SEAT C30 K 4
PAID: ALL APPLICABLE TAXES INCLUDED
$15.00 ADULT
NO REFUND - NO EXCHANGE
IF CANCELLED, RETURN TO POINT OF PURCHASE FOR REFUND OF PRICE PAID.
0716453625 $15.00 ADULT K7
DICESARE ENGLER PRESENT
BRUCE SPRINGSTEEN & THE E STREET BAND
PITTSBURGH CIVIC ARENA
PAID SAT SEPT 22 1984 7:30 PM
420536251A015001

Cougar Mellencamp. Earlier in the summer I had been notified about the planning for this event and told to save the date; then I was dis- invited. The only steelworkers invited were Ronnie and Larry Ragan, president of U.S. Steel's giant Local 1014 in Gary, Indiana. I was getting red-baited from the right, slandered from the center, and blackballed from the left.

CHAPTER 27

THE DOROTHY SIX CAMPAIGN AND FORMATION OF THE STEEL VALLEY AUTHORITY

I n the latter part of 1983 through the summer of 1984, the Tri-State Conference on Steel (TSCS) devoted the majority of its attention and effort to developing and going public with its plan to establish a public industrial authority and exploring the takeover of abandoned plants. On October 29, 1983, the TSCS held a conference at the Local 1397 union hall. It was attended by approximately ninety people, including academics and steel experts from all over the country, along with local union officials and community and church activists. The nuts and bolts of our initial plan to form the Steel Valley Authority (SVA) through the local city and borough councils and to build a grassroots movement to accomplish this were explained in detail, and put in a booklet prepared by TSCS activist, Bob Erickson. The shutdowns and layoffs were accelerating at every plant in the area. This seemed like our last-ditch effort to stop the bloodletting.

Beginning in 1982, TSCS activists had begun lobbying borough officials in the area around the SVA idea. We attended borough council meetings, asking for feasibility studies and introducing the idea of eminent domain. These efforts mostly fell on deaf ears. Many officials took the position that what little salvation there was left lied with the corporations and somehow convincing them to remain open. At the same time, during this period, TSCS won some very progressive and important political supporters to our SVA idea, including Homestead steelworker, borough council member, and future mayor Betty Esper, 160" mill worker and Munhall council president Ronnie Watkins, Munhall mayor Ray Bodnar, Mon and Turtle Creek Valley state representatives Tom Michlovic, Dave Levdansky, and Mike Dawida, as well as Charles Martoni, the mayor of Swissvale. To our way of thinking, if we were ever to force the federal government's hand on reinvesting and saving some portion of these mills, we needed a giant community-based coalition that included both local and state elected officials.

On October 9, 1984, U.S. Steel officially announced they were demolishing the recently closed Dorothy Six blast furnace at the Duquesne mill. Seemingly all at once, union members, public officials, and an array of citizens realized the TSCS was the only game in town, and that it was time for action. On October 29, the TSCS called a meeting at the Swissvale Borough building. In attendance were eight state representatives and state senators, two county commissioners, and Pennsylvania senator Arlen Specter. In addition, representatives from the local union in Duquesne, the USWA District and International Unions, and Protestant and Catholic pastors were in attendance, as well as some sixty citizens and workers. The TSCS laid out its strategy for saving the Dorothy Six blast furnace, using a three-pronged approach:

> One: stop the demolition of the mill by legal or whatever means necessary;
> Two: involve the county, the city, and the International Union in funding a feasibility study to prove that Dorothy was economically viable, and that there was a market for its slabs;
> Three: use the announced demolition as the impetus to go into the borough councils and convince them to form the Steel Valley Authority, a legal entity which could take the mill from U.S. Steel and transfer the property to another entity.

Conditions were ripe for the struggle to catch fire. First, Duquesne Local 1256, led by the Mon Valley Unemployment Committee (MVUC), Local 1256 activist Jim Benn, local president Mike Bilsick, and the local's vice president Don Rudberg had a large core of activists and workers who were ready to fight for their jobs. Although their current president Mike Bilsick was no friend of Ronnie's, the local had twice supported Weisen for District director. These three Duquesne workers were at the forefront of this battle from beginning to end. Second, the Duquesne mill itself was a relatively new and modern facility, the basic oxygen furnace (BOF) shop and the blast furnace in particular. The BOF shop could produce four hundred different grades of steel

The idled "Dorothy Six" blast furnace just before it was demolished in January 1986.

and had a tremendous degree of flexibility. Dorothy Six had the greatest capacity of any blast furnace in the area. Also, the workforce was very knowledgeable and productive. In fact, in December 1983, a week before it ceased operations, the blast furnace workers were awarded the prestigious Iron Master Award. They were given jackets, a plaque, and had their pictures taken for the newspaper. Feelings of betrayal were rife in the workplace and the community.

The coalition immediately implemented the three-pronged strategy. A week later, in early November, a hastily organized bus tour included the three county commissioners, International and District Union officials, state representatives, TSCS activists, and local union people. At this stage, TSCS was in the driver's seat. After the tour of the blast furnace at Duquesne, county commissioners and the International Union were convinced the place was worth saving. Allegheny County, the City of Pittsburgh, and the United Steelworkers of America (USWA) International Union each put up fifty thousand dollars for the initial feasibility study. Duquesne Light Company, which had an obvious stake in seeing the mill saved, also put up fifty thousand dollars. Mike Locker and Locker-Albrecht, consultants out of New York City, were hired to do the initial study. In November, I went to New York City and obtained a $75,000 grant from the Stern Foundation,[1] which allowed the TSCS to hire three paid organizers, including Jim Benn, a MVUC rank-and-file activist from the Duquesne local, and Jay Weinberg from Homestead. With paid staff and an office, the TSCS now had the resources to go into a full-blown grassroots organizing drive. Together with the local union at Duquesne, we moved quickly to stop the demolition of Dorothy Six, save the plant, and organize for the formation of the SVA.

Jesse Jackson at rally to save Dorothy Six in Duquesne, January 30, 1985.

Jesse Jackson Comes to Town

On January 18, 1985, in snowy weather with a wind chill of -10°F (-23°C), approximately five hundred people appeared at a rally in front of the Duquesne mill. The main speakers were Jesse Jackson, who declared Dorothy Six the "Selma of the plant shutdown movement," and USWA International president Lynn Williams. Numerous public officials and congressmen attended the rally, all declaring they would do whatever it took to stop the permanent shutdown and demolition of the mill. In the 1984 Democratic Party primary, the Borough of Homestead and others up and down the Valley had endorsed Jesse Jackson for president. On more than one occasion, Jesse came to rallies in Homestead, staying at the Wargos' house on Custer Avenue in Baldwin.

Ron Weisen and Mike Wargo (far right) with Jesse Jackson at one of his many Homestead rallies.

Meanwhile, Duquesne's Local 1256 president Mike Bilsick provided a trailer for laid-off Duquesne workers, who held a twenty-four-hour-a-day vigil directly across the street from the main gate. Workers watched the mill to make sure equipment and machinery were not removed.

On January 28, 1985, the Locker-Albrecht feasibility study was released, stating the mill was not only viable but had potential customers and could be operated at a profit. On January 29, the TSCS organized a town meeting at the largest church in Duquesne (without the consent of Duquesne borough council officials) to present the results of the feasibility study. A meeting this size hadn't been seen in the borough since the Committee of International Organizations, later the Congress for Industrial Organization (CIO), drives of the 1930s. Nearly eight hundred people attended; hundreds of people were turned away from the meeting, because they couldn't get into the church or find any place to park.

A most dramatic event had taken place a month before, on December 8, 1984. Thirteen laid-off Duquesne maintenance workers, most of who knew they would never get their jobs back, entered the mill

Laid-off steel workers pumped 550 gallons of antifreeze into Dorothy Six in an attempt to save the condemned blast furnace.

on their own accord with their own tools and equipment. Providing free labor, they winterized the facility by pumping Freon into the pipes in the blast furnace, so the pipes wouldn't crack. U.S. Steel did everything they could to stop this from happening, declaring the coalition had to put up sixteen thousand dollars in insurance money in case somebody got hurt on their property. The money was fronted by the International Union and later repaid through an aggressive grassroots door-to-door collection campaign by the local union and the TSCS. At the same time, the TSCS and local union activists began going into the community to mobilize people to oppose the shutdown of the mill. We also began going into borough councils up and down the Valley advocating the formation of the SVA.

Formation of the Steel Valley Authority

Our first success came in January 1985, when a town meeting of approximately 250 people was held at Steel Valley High School, in Munhall. Munhall city council became the first to pass a resolution to form the SVA. This was the result of at least three or four meetings behind the scenes with borough president Ronnie Watkins (who worked in the 160" Plate Mill, where I was his coworker and grievance rep), U.S. Steel employee and borough mayor Ray Bodnar, and the borough solicitor.

Items sold by Dorothy Six coalition to raise funds for the Winterization Insurance.

TSCS board member and lawyer Jay Hornack played a pivotal role in convincing the borough officials our plan was legal, viable, and would not create any financial liability for the borough. Quickly, other boroughs followed suit, beginning with Homestead Borough passing a resolution to form the SVA the following month. This accomplishment was especially notable, as then council member and Homestead mill employee Betty Esper told me

Then council member and Homestead mill employee Betty Esper.

and other TSCS members before the meeting that she did not think she could swing one council member to vote to establish the Authority.[2] When I walked into the meeting with twenty-five steelworkers, including five from Betty's department at the 160" plate treating line who spoke out in favor of the TSCS proposal, the vote in favor of forming the Authority was unanimous.

Before the discussion ensued, to warm up the crowd, I pulled out my guitar and opened with my just finished anthem, "Valleys of Steel" (later renamed "Stand or Fade"):

Rusted hills, brown fields, broken wheels that used to roll out the best.
Boarded doors, closed stores, and ghost towns all across the U.S.
Broken dreams, abandoned terrain,
Silent machines of rusted remains,
Helplessness and hopelessness were drifting over the plains,
Masquerading as the agents of change.
Working mass where is your class, where is your will to survive?
Salt of the earth, where is the work of worth that kept you alive?
Your labor's lost, it's left in the cold.
The human cost is uprooted souls.
A slow-motion holocaust with invisible hands,
Spread like a cancer all over the land.

Stand, get up off your knees.
Stand, get back on your feet.
Let the struggle and resistance begin.
Let your love for life spread like the wind.
I said it before and I'll say it again—
(You better) *stand*, (you better) *stand*, (you better) *stand*,
Stand or crawl, stand or fall, before you fade and it's too late!
They disinvest, scrap the best, run off to some foreign land.
Mergerize, polarize all the wealth into just a few hands.
Corporate greed, capital flight,
Refugees of industrial blight,
Shattered, battered, tattered families and bankrupted lives,
For the victims of their free enterprise.

[*Chorus*] It's the only thing you'll both leave and take with you when
  you die.

In February 1985, as the vigil and campaign continued in the bitter cold, U.S. Steel sent a truck into the mill to remove a heavy piece of equipment. The vigil put phone calls out, and forty or fifty workers showed up at the mill entrance within an hour, ready to lay their bodies down if necessary. In fact, when the truck came out, local union officers forced the driver to allow an inspection to see what was on board. With the urging of then county commissioner Tom Forrester, U.S. Steel backed off and agreed not only to allow the union officials to inspect anything going out of the mill but to allow local union officials to walk into the mill on their own accord and do random inspections of the Dorothy Six blast furnace. Also, after the feasibility study was officially released on February 2, the second deadline U.S. Steel had announced for the demolition of the mill was delayed until June 2. This would allow the union and the TSCS the chance to do a marketing feasibility study. The Thomas Merton Center, through the efforts of Molly Rush,[3] began training workers and citizens in nonviolent sit-ins and resistance.

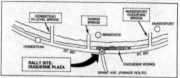

All through 1985, the TSCS continued its efforts to convince the boroughs to join together and form the SVA. For the next six months, I spent several nights a week with other TSCS activists, including Charlie McCollester and Jay Hornack, meeting behind the scenes with borough officials and solicitors and speaking at town hall meetings, in an effort to build public support. By June 1985, eight out of ten cities and boroughs we had targeted, including the City of Pittsburgh through the efforts of Charlie McCollester, had agreed to form the SVA and passed resolutions. Only the boroughs of Duquesne and Wilmerding, both with elected officials who were in management at U.S. Steel and American Standard's WABCO plant in Wilmerding, resisted.

In May 1985, the movement reached its peak, culminating in a rally in front of the Duquesne mill. More than a thousand people attended: there were fire engines, a high school marching band, congressmen, and many supporters from outside the area, including Staughton Lynd, Ed Mann, and a contingent of veterans from the Youngstown shutdown struggles. Even the Duquesne borough council reluctantly came out and joined the efforts to save the mill.

Rally and march to save Dorothy Six, May 1985.

The marketing feasibility study was conducted by Rosa Torres-Tumazos from Openheimer and Company, a prestigious Wall Street consulting firm. At the end of May, she released the second feasibility study, which confirmed there was a growing market in the United States for semi-finished slabs. It also identified and interviewed potential customers who would set up contracts with a slab producing mill at the Duquesne Works. Next, was a third feasibility study addressing financing, exactly what modernizations would have to take place, and what the costs would be to get the mill operating.

It was at this point, after May 1985, that serious mistakes were made. As a waiting game set in, mass activities waned. The project and third study were turned over by the USWA International Union to Lazard Frères, a major capital investment bank in New York City. Lazard Frères had orchestrated the New York City bankruptcy bailout in the 1970s. They also engineered the Weirton employee stock ownership buyout of

Weirton Steel from National Steel. The decision-making concerning the production process, marketing, and financing was completely taken out of the hands of the TSCS and the coalition and turned over to finance capital itself. The TSCS position up to this point had been that the Duquesne facility could only be saved in conjunction with saving some combination of other phased out finishing facilities in the Mon Valley and elsewhere. The list of possibilities included the 160" Plate Mill and Structural Mills at Homestead, the pipe finishing mills at National Works, and the finishing mills at Duquesne. Instead, Lazard Frères

Mike Stout, with guitar, sings his ode to U.S. Steel's Dorothy Six

***Pittsburgh Press*, May 4, 1985.**

confined their study to Duquesne as a purely slab-producing hot-end entity. This meant that at the very least a two-strand continuous caster would have to be installed to meet the diversity in the slab market. A continuous caster would add approximately 150 million dollars to the original cost. This approach pretty much sunk the deal.

Besides the formation and incorporation of the SVA, the only other TSCS bright spot that year was a benefit concert on November 22, 1985, at the beautiful (since torn down) Syria Mosque in the Oakland section of Pittsburgh. The performers included Joe Grushecky with his new Brick Alley Band, and John Cafferty and the Beaver Brown Band. Cafferty had done the music for the popular movie *Eddie and the Cruisers*.[4] Like the first food bank benefit concert held at the Stanley Theater in 1982, rock radio station WDVE's Steve Hansen and Jimmy Roach and I were the MCs. In between acts, I took the stage to say, "This is the first concert I know of in the United States for jobs instead of food,"[5] referring to our earlier food bank benefits, as well as national and international benefits such as Farm Aid. With 1,300 attending, Grushecky rocked the house, ending his set with "Stand Up in the Valley of Steel," co-written and a takeoff from my original "Valleys of

Steel" song. The concert, coupled with sales of the single, raised close to twenty thousand dollars. It once again showed the power of music in support of working people's struggles.

With all of TSCS's marbles thrown into waiting for the results of the third feasibility study, the grassroots movement dissipated. The vigil became harder and harder to man. Workers exhausted their unemployment compensation (UC) and had to seek other employment, many of them leaving the area. While U.S. Steel had backed down for the third time from demolishing the Duquesne mill and had extended the deadline indefinitely, during this period town meetings, rallies, and keeping the community informed and involved petered out, a major failure that really hurt our efforts. Between October and December of 1985, the TSCS got involved in a behind the scenes struggle to force Lazard Frères to come out with what we had heard through the union grapevine was going to be a negative study. At the same time, the permanent closing of American Standard's Switch and Signal plant in Swissvale (where Charlie McCollester was chief steward) in September seriously diverted TSCS staff and resources.

Over the summer, the TSCS convinced the City of Pittsburgh to provide an economic planner who actually began meeting with the TSCS and other project supporters. This city planner asserted that if the package was a under two hundred million dollars, she could put together a public-private buyout of the Duquesne Works. The buyout would include a consortium of approximately twelve banks putting up half the money, with the county, the City of Pittsburgh, and the state putting up the other half. Then all of a sudden, Lazard Frères upped the ante, claiming more than three hundred million dollars was needed for the startup. They told the International Union and public officials that the money could never be raised.

Another major disagreement we had with the Lazard Frères study was that it placed the burden for amassing the capital on the private sector. The TSCS's position was that only the public sector had the ability to step in and put together the package. This type of public-private partnership happened later when the City of Pittsburgh and Allegheny County officials stepped in to save Pittsburgh's sports teams and build new stadiums. Why not a steel mill? Lazard Frères recommended against putting any funds into trying to reopen the Duquesne facilities and said they would not assist in the effort. At this point the county commissioners, the City of Pittsburgh, and the USWA International all caved in and agreed to abandon the Duquesne project.

Over three decades later, it might easily be concluded that this campaign would never have been successful, in view of the odds we were up against. Nevertheless, TSCS organizers (including me) should never have accepted the capitalist logic of Lazard Frères that Dorothy Six could not be operated profitably. We should have voiced our opposition publicly. Both Charlie McCollester and I later admitted we were much too timid in challenging the status quo.[6] In terms of the numbers presented in the Lazard Frères report, they could have easily been reinterpreted to show the feasibility of a start-up operation trying to break even or making a modest profit. We should have struggled longer and harder for interest-free loans and grants from the government. Our campaign should have targeted the public and focused on a reorientation of government policy around rebuilding mass transit and our region's infrastructure. Too much of the Lazard Frères study was taken as fixed and accepted as unchangeable; the TSCS should have more vigorously challenged the Wall Street logic of the profit system. The funding and material support we were receiving from the International Union seriously compromised our voices.

When the USWA released their death warrant for Dorothy Six at a June 2, 1986, press conference, at the very least we in the TSCS should have publicly disagreed. The decision to rely on finance capital and their studies resulted not only in a negative conclusion about reopening the mill but served to demobilize workers and their community supporters. The form of losing made it more difficult for future struggles down the road, especially in the Mon and Turtle Creek Valleys.

A gargantuan effort followed the failed Dorothy Six campaign, when the TSCS mounted a major campaign to save LTV's two giant electric arc furnaces in South Side Pittsburgh. This effort went well beyond the Dorothy Six campaign. Our coalition was politically broader, the community and former workers even more supportive, and we were given a grant of 365 thousand dollars from Duquesne Light, which was used to establish a management team and prepare the appropriate feasibility studies. At least eight major customers who also agreed to help finance the plan were lined up. I chaired a "buyout committee" which coordinated the campaign for over two years. In the end, we were seriously sabotaged by LTV on the purchase of the equipment and property. Once again, Wall Street and the financial community redlined any possibilities for raising the start-up capital. The deindustrialization and globalization that was in full swing was an unstoppable stampede.

As I said at several TSCS and SVA meetings, "We should not have fought U.S. Steel and their multinational corporate priorities on their terrain of balance sheets and conservative economics. Rather, we should have challenged them with the strength of our organization, our mobilization of the workers and communities, and our vision that "people are more important than profit." It is we who should have redefined and made visible the criterion for investment and production—not them!"

CHAPTER 28

THE 1985 LOCAL UNION ELECTIONS: HOW DID WEISEN WIN AGAIN?

hrough 1984 and 1985, steel production in the Valley continued to plummet. By late 1985, the only departments working at Homestead were the 160" Plate Mill and No. 2 Structural Mill. With a skeleton Central Maintenance crew and only one janitor for the entire mill, the workforce had shrunk to 750, from a high of 7,000 when I started working. With no union dues coming in, all but one secretary was laid off. The one left, Cheryl Bacco, was put on part-time, paid only one day a week. Both Ronnie and I were cut back to one day, and the other officers stopped coming around, as their departments closed, their

Gregg Mowry, c. 1985.

John Deffenbaugh, c. 1985.

jobs were phased out, and their benefits expired. Most of the grievance committee was laid off, and some had to get on with their lives and find other jobs. Several, including Tom Farren, Gregg Mowry, and John Deffenbaugh, stuck around on their own dime to help me with the grievance backlog. These three grievers will always be my heroes.

With Ronnie's involvement with the Denominational Mission Strategy (DMS) and their skunk oil antics and battles with the churches, some on the local union executive board and his rank-and-file team turned against him, running an opposition slate for the upcoming local union election. Ray Gottschalk ran as their presidential candidate. Ray had formerly been vice president with the clique we threw out of office in 1979. Everywhere we went, working at Homestead was equated with skunk oil and disrupting church services. Our messages of bank disinvestment and corporate greed were smothered beneath the constant barrage from the media concerning the DMS and Network to Save the Mon Valley tactics. With the upcoming local union elections in April, it looked like Ronnie was going to lose for sure. However, something happened just before the election that would turn the tide in his favor.

One of the many grievances I was fighting at the time included one concerning the 160" Mill Plate Treating Line scheduling practices. A week or so before the local union election, I went into General Foreman O'Brien's office to get copies of schedules he owed to me. Busy in a meeting, he told his clerk Donny Radjenovich: "Get the schedules for him; they're on my desk." Donny and I were pretty tight, and he had been feeding me information for weeks. Donny went down to get the schedules for me. I followed him into O'Brien's office. I asked Donny to look in a stack on the right side of his desk, and I'd look in a stack on the left side. My eyes were like a computer, constantly scouring for documents to support my grievance cases. If I saw something I thought was pertinent, I'd try to take it in a heartbeat.

In the pile I was looking through, I saw a document sticking titled "Local Agreement." I pulled it out of the pile. It was a proposed "Fairfield-type agreement," similar to one that had been drawn up and signed at the U.S. Steel mill in Fairfield, Alabama. The International Union's District director for Alabama Thermon Phillips was notorious for granting concessions and giving the Company everything but the kitchen sink.[1] The "Local Agreement" had been retrofitted for

Homestead. It included provisions to eliminate Section 2-B, the section of the contract that protected crew sizes and other local working conditions. It gave management the right to combine twenty seniority units into two. Twelve-hour shifts, called "bookend" schedules, and forced overtime without overtime pay were also included.

When I saw this proposed "Local Agreement," I grabbed it and left. While Donny was still looking for the schedules, I made a hundred copies of the agreement on the Company's Xerox machine, stapled the original back together, and put it back in the pile without Donny seeing me do it (at least I don't think he did). I took the hundred copies and passed them out around the 160" Plate Mill. The workers hit the roof when they read it.

By the end of the shift at 4:00 p.m., management was aware we had access to their concessions proposal. The superintendent, Gene Nethamer, called a meeting at his office. He ordered the plant police superintendent, two departmental foremen, the Slab and Plate and plant-wide labor contract administrators (LCAs) to attend. Rank-and-file griever Tommy Farren was outside the door intently listening when the meeting took place. Nethamer demanded to know how the union got a hold of the secret contract agreement. It didn't take him two minutes to say, "It had to be Stout." It was now after 5:00 p.m. Nethamer phoned the 160" mill office clerk Donny Radjenovich at home and told him to come back to the office. The Company knew exactly who in management had been given a copy of the proposal. Nethamer ordered everyone to bring their copy with them to the meeting.

With all the copies now in the room, they looked them over and noticed that the one from O'Brien's desk had a staple that I had put back in it not quite in the same holes. Also, in the section of the proposal calling for "bookend 12-hour shift schedules," O'Brien had written a note on that page of his copy in pencil saying "This will never fly." The Xerox copies I made faintly picked up his written comments. They now knew it came from O'Brien's desk. Meanwhile, the clerk, Donny Radjenovich, had returned; they thought for sure they had me for stealing. Interrogating Donny, Nethamer asked, "When you came down here to get the schedules with Mike, did you see him take anything off this desk?" Donny vowed, with his right hand raised in courtroom fashion, "I swear on my mother's grave and God that Mike didn't touch anything on this desk." End of case.

By the following Monday, they had changed all the locks on the doors in the 160" office building. When I showed up at work, Superintendent Nethamer called me into his office. As he nervously chewed on his big stogie cigar, he spit out, "You cocksucker, you got me on this one didn't ya." I responded, "Why I don't know what you're talking about, Gene." He retorted, "If Weisen wins the election, we're finished." I knew this statement was total bullshit. According to the feasibility study I had lifted from his window sill earlier, we were already finished.

Several days before the May 13 local union election, my 160" Shipping Department assistant grievance representative Billy Barron called me over to a powwow with his work crew. Most of the people remaining in the mill had more than twenty years seniority, some more than thirty years; most preferred taking their pensions to working under a concessions contract, which would have them doing a number of different "combined" jobs, and working twelve-hour shifts. Knowing I had been taking a hands-off approach to the election, Barron spoke for the whole crew when he said, "Mike, do whatever you gotta do to make sure Weisen wins this election." I assured him with the concessions contract proposal circulating among the workers, Ronnie was a shoo-in.

At the local union executive board meeting just before the election, Weisen strode in like a boxer ready to rumble. He asserted in a loud, gruff voice, "I hear there's people here who don't support me?" He was looking straight at me, staring with an icy glare. It looked as though he was going to deck me at any moment. By this point, I didn't care; all the pressure was really starting to get to me. I responded defiantly, "And I think you better get an adoption lawyer, because you are going to be paying me for the rest of your life." As everyone else stared in disbelief, I continued: "You've been spreading rumors around that I have a cocaine habit, and I stole from the food bank to support it." As though I was defending myself in court, I then attested to the slander I was hearing, giving the names of several workers who told me Ronnie was spreading the rumors. I also related the phone call from my friend Lenny Shindel, to whom Ronnie had run this slander at the Labor Notes conference the previous month. I finished my defense with: "Well, let's see your proof; I'll resign [from my grievance job] right now if you can produce one witness or show me one iota or shred of proof."

To my utter astonishment, he backed off, looked around the room and said, "I have none." I said, "Thank you." There was a collective sigh of relief in the room. Local union inside guard and Weisen supporter Dave Horgan told Ronnie he should put a retraction in writing and give it to anyone who had been told these lies. Ronnie said he would. Nothing ever happened. In any case, it was a huge load off my shoulders. I hoped that maybe now we could get back to the business at hand: working together to fight the greedy banks and corporations and defend our members—as a team.

The proposed concessions agreement was the fuel that drove Ronnie's car to victory. Ronnie was reelected local union president for a third term by a comfortable three to two margin. While his DMS activities were a major pain in the ass and made no sense to most of us in the local, the workers knew he would *never* sign any concessions agreement that would adversely impact so many people. When I met with Superintendent Nethamer the day after the election, May 14, 1985, he said, as I walked in the door, "Go tell all your fuckin' asshole union buddies you just shut this mill down."

CHAPTER 29

FIGHTING TO THE END

There was another case I'll never forget that demonstrated the kind of extracurricular activity needed to win some grievances. The 160" Plate Mill was permanently closed November 22, 1985. By August of that year, everyone knew the shutdown was coming; I knew it would be permanent. In the 160" slab yard, an older worker named Baker passed away from a heart attack. The next guy in line to get called back to work was my friend Mike Wargo, who had been laid off since December 1981.

As explained earlier, under the Basic Steel Labor Contract, after you've been laid off for two years, you stop accumulating seniority time and all of your benefits have long since dried up. However, you still have recall rights for up to five years. When I walked into Superintendent Nethamer's office to confront him about bringing Wargo back to work, he gave me his standard, "What do you want, asshole?" I answered, "I want you to put Mike Wargo back to work." He looked at me and took his cigar out of his mouth saying, "Sometimes your fuckin' intelligence insults me. Knock, knock, Mr. big-shot union man, the mill's shutting down, and you know it, and I know it. I'm not bringing him back to work, and, quite frankly, I don't care if you file one of your fuckin' grievances and win it three years from now. I ain't gonna be here. Go ahead!"

That was on a Friday; I was fuming all weekend and really pissed off. The Wargos were friends of mine. In an angry trance while smoking a joint to calm down, the answer came to me. But to understand how I resolved the situation, I need to backtrack and tell you about another grievance that I fought at this time.

There was a 160" Shipping Department employee named Larry Coyne. Larry told the Company he lost his last paycheck and asked for a replacement. He didn't realize banks have cameras, and they had pictures of Larry cashing both of his paychecks. Shortly afterwards, I was called to the superintendent's office. Nethamer informed me that Larry was getting fired for stealing. At this point, my TV lawyer training from watching Perry Mason must have taken over. I started talking like we were in a movie; it was surreal. Plant Police Chief Lt. Joe Morton was present. I asked them, "Do you know who Larry's brother is?" Nethamer answered, "What do you mean." I said, "His brother is Jimmy Coyne." The new plant-wide labor contract administrator (LCA) John McCluskey said, "Yeah, so what." I answered, "His brother is the police chief of Munhall. You have trucks coming out of the plant loaded with slag, which I think we all know exceed the legal weight limit. Wouldn't you hate to see those trucks get pulled over, cited, and not have any access in and out of the plant?"

In reality, I hadn't talked to the police chief and doubt that he would have gone along with my plan to cite the trucks. It was a total bluff. Piercing me with one of his "I don't need this shit right now" looks, Nethamer dropped the discharge. Larry was back to work the following week.

While at this meeting, I cased the place for documents. I got up and walked around, strolling over to the window to stare out at the dirty, muddy Mon River. While there, I noticed sitting on the window sill a thick document labeled, "Mon Valley Feasibility Study." I walked back to my seat, pick up my yellow tablet, and headed back to the window sill. Thinking I was just pacing, as I frequently did during meetings, no one was paying attention to me. The third time I walked over to the window I put my yellow tablet on the report, picked it up, and took it home with me.

When I arrived home that evening, I pored through the feasibility study. In a nutshell, the study concluded that the Company would remain profitable only by permanently closing the Homestead Works and reopening the 44" Slab Mill at Edgar Thomson in Braddock. I had proof in hand that the shutdown at Homestead was permanent. To skirt their pension and severance liability, management was claiming the shutdown of the various departments was "temporary and indefinite." I hadn't quite decided what to do with the study—that is, until the Wargo case. The light bulbs started flashing.

Monday morning, I went in to Nethamer's office and said, "Hey, Gene, I wanna know if you'll join me in a press conference?" Gene crunched on his cigar saying, "What do you mean?" I explained, "Well, I'm going to have a press conference this Thursday, and I'm gonna announce that you've permanently shut down the plant." He impatiently retorted, "Stout you know something, you're a fucking looney tune. I don't want to hear your crap this early in the morning." I said, "Well, you don't understand." He said, "I don't care what you say in your fucking press conference; go ahead." I said, "No, you don't understand, Gene. I'm gonna show them this feasibility study." He went bonzo: "I knew you were the one that stole that, you thievin' motherfucker." I looked at him and winked, "No, Gene, it was delivered in a plain brown envelope to the union hall." I rattled on, "Nah, Gene, you don't get it. I'm going public with it." He said, "I don't care, go ahead, dipshit; see if I care." I said, "You don't understand, Gene. I'm gonna go public, and I'm gonna have four network TV channels there, and I'm gonna tell them that *you* gave the study to me and thank you for helping us get out the truth. How do you like that?"

Mike Wargo was back to work three days later; he worked off and on until the mill closed on November 22, 1985. All his benefits were reinstated. He received health insurance for another year. He was now eligible for a severance pay, a small pension payment, and unemployment compensation (UC) and Trade Readjustment Allowance (TRA) claims when the mill finally closed. His wife Mari sent me a nice thank you card for getting him back to work. In such a dog-eat-dog setting during a plant closing, simple acts of gratitude such as this were greatly appreciated and helped me carry on.

CHAPTER 30

RON WEISEN–HEART OF THE RANK AND FILE

Ron Weisen, c. 1982.

In the middle of all the grievance battles, turmoil, job loss, and personal tragedies happening, working with Ronnie was always an extra layer, a particular challenge. To say he was complex would be putting it mildly. He would love you and hate you all at the same time. In one breath he'd say I was the best grievance man in the union and in another that I was a cocaine addict. One day, you might be his closest ally, only to be his enemy the next day. As a fighter and rebel icon, I think he was simply trying to figure out how to be a militant union leader and, in that capacity, help his members. The power and notoriety that fell into his lap—well, he didn't always know how to handle it. All of us knew he was prone to doing whatever the last person told him to do. It didn't matter to him what the group, caucus, or local decided. John Ingersoll, who knew him the longest, put it best:

> You could sit down and have a meeting, with everybody in our rank and file and decide, well this is the way we're gonna do it. Ronnie would go into the bar next door, the Irish bar next door, and the last guy he talked to, it was like we didn't decide anything at all. Ronnie did it the way he wanted.[1]

He made up for his lack of polish, ego problems, and insecurity with his drive, sincerity, and courage. Whether his brain was right or wrong, he had a heart of gold, and it was usually in the right place and on the right side. He wasn't afraid of anyone or anything. His prowess as a boxer and fighter was no mere Homestead myth. After a late-night party at the union hall in 1983, witnesses watched him put 45" mill crane operator "Butchie" Kansas—who was a head taller and bigger than Ronnie—through a three-quarter-inch plate glass window with a single blow. All I could think about after this episode was the Bob Dylan line in his Rubin "Hurricane" Carter song, "He could take a man out with just one punch."[2]

For the most part, Ronnie knew who the enemy was, and he went after them like a pit bull. Sometimes he just got pointed in the wrong direction by people like Honeywell. He would get sidetracked by jealous workers like the ones who pissed in his ear about me "wanting to take his job." When I was with him on a picket line, at a convention, at a demonstration or some other action, I felt like I was with an army. When I was with him at the 1982 Atlantic City convention, we passed seven or eight Edgar Thomson delegates and International supporters in a hallway. As they glared at Ronnie walking past, he turned and faced them with clenched fists saying, "So what are you looking at?" They all walked away.

In a weird sort of way, I think Ronnie liked me because I wasn't afraid to disagree with him, even though it pissed him off when I did. In the mid-1981 to early 1983 period, he strongly relied on me to delineate the political landscape for him. When I couldn't get through to him, Jay Weinberg could, becoming one of Ronnie's closest advisors during this period. Dozens of leftists were hovering and descending on the union hall during his reign. If I told him Lee Ballinger was a good guy to work with, then Ronnie trusted him. When I was around Ronnie and working with him, which was constantly after I got the grievance position, I felt his power; his courage was infectious. His persona was like a magnet for anyone fighting the corporation or corruption in the union. Shutting down the mill and local union was the only way they would ever shut Ronnie up.

When he went off with the Denominational Mission Strategy (DMS) and Honeywell's "attack the churches" nonsense, it was very hard for me, because I didn't believe that what he was doing was right. I had to speak out, as did other of his former allies, including Tom Jugan, John Ingersoll, and Jack Bair. Our split was going to kill not only our local union's effectiveness but the struggle against the shutdown of our mill in general. While many of us felt his DMS-related actions were detrimental to the struggle of workers in the mill, Ronnie thought that what he was doing was *for* the people in the mill. His intentions and fight were always righteous; unfortunately, when he started swinging, sometimes he would hit the wrong people on the wrong battlefield.

Years after we were both out of union politics, Ronnie would visit and bullshit with me at the printshop I ran at the corner of the Homestead Grays Bridge and 8th Avenue. There was no tension or competition. We only reminisced about our past glory days of solidarity. Shortly before he died, his wife Jeanie stopped by the print shop. She asked me to watch Ronnie in their minivan while she dealt with a problem at PNC Bank. I always thought the world of Jeanie; the love and loyalty she showed toward her family was more than admirable. When their son Bobby had a swimming accident that paralyzed him from the neck down, he became number one on Ronnie and Jean's priority list, no matter what else was happening. As Jeanie returned and started up the car, Ronnie said to me, "Well Mike, at least we gave 'em a good fight, didn't we!" I told him I loved him; he nodded back in the affirmative. That was the last time I saw him; he died on January 12, 1998.

The funeral home was jammed with hundreds of activists, neighbors, and former coworkers. A group of us turned and noticed that J. Bruce Johnston, Ronnie's U.S. Steel archnemesis, was standing there all alone. Labor lawyer and friend, Mike Healey, said loud enough for him to hear, "Shouldn't we be throwing this bastard out of here?" It sounded like something Ronnie would say. His spirit was everywhere in the room. When the funeral service took place the next day, only two of us showed up from the union: his ever loyal secretary and good friend Cheryl Bacco and me. It definitely felt like the end of an era. When I returned to the printshop after the funeral, working there alone after hours, I quietly cried—not just for Ronnie but for the whole union democracy movement. Its most outspoken voice had just been silenced.

CHAPTER 31

THE LAST ATTEMPTED BRIBE

On January 2, 1986, the Mon Valley labor contract administrator (LCA) "Big" John McCluskey called me into a meeting during the holiday shutdown. In 1984, they started shutting down the mill for two weeks during the Christmas and New Year holidays. It was really cold and snowy that year. I was the only union representative at the meeting. It was in a dark, dank office somewhere up in the Structural part of the mill; an area I had never been to before. Present at the meeting were the Mon Valley Works superintendent John Goodwin, the downtown lawyer who was in charge of all labor contract matters, Butch Hansen, and of course McCluskey. Hansen spoke first; I can remember his little speech almost verbatim:

> All right, Mike, we are going to tell it to you like it is. This place is done unless we make some drastic changes around here. We don't need to involve Weisen. As chair of the grievance committee, under section 13-B-2 of the contract, you have the right to alter and merge seniority units; you have the right to sign internal local agreements. *You* have the right; Weisen doesn't. We don't need him. We have approximately 750 people working between the 160" Plate Mill and no. 2 Structural. There's a handful of Central Maintenance people that float in between the two operations. If you wanna see the 160" Plate Mill and the no. 2 Structural Mill keep operating, we need you to sign an agreement with us. The agreement would allow us to combine their seniority units. What we would like to do is run the same operations that we are

doing with 750 people, with only 375 people. What we will do for you, Mike, is give you 375 early retirement pensions and you can hand them out to whomever you want. We don't really care to whom you give them. They are yours to hand out. You can be king. Not only can you be king with the 375 still working but with the 375 people to whom you give the pensions. You have a win-win situation here. What's your answer?

I couldn't believe they were talking to me like this. I felt nauseated. The way they appealed to my ego wasn't much different than the experience I had with Honeywell at his house. They were asking me to sell out thousands, to keep several hundred working.

I told them I had a couple questions of my own: "What about the three thousand people out on the streets that still have severance and pension cases pending? What about all the grievances that are still pending? They are worth millions of dollars." McCluskey said, "Mike, why don't you start looking at the half loaf of bread in front of you and stop worrying about the half that's in the garbage. There is nothing you can do about them; they are gone." I then asked a second question: "If I sign this agreement, will you guarantee *in writing* that this place is still going to be working in five or ten years?" They began to fidget. Butch Hansen advised, "Why don't you stop this nonsense, Mike, and come to your senses." I glibly responded, "I have nothing else to say to you." On my way out the door, the Company LCA John McCluskey muttered almost under his breath, "Fuck you." I replied, "Fuck you," and walked out. They worked the No. 2 Structural with one shift up until May 25, 1986; then shut it down. It was the last gasp of one of the greatest steel mills in U.S. history. Meanwhile, I still had hundreds of grievances in the hopper; the war continued.

CHAPTER 32

THE 1986 LOCKOUT

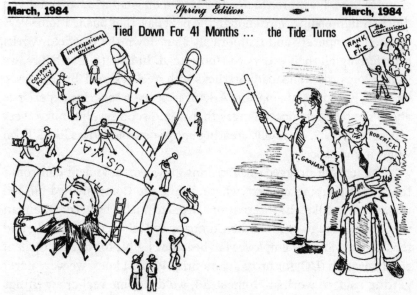

With their blatant, nonstop contract violations between 1983 and 1986, U.S. Steel made it clear they were out for war. After giving major wage and benefit concessions in the 1983 contract, rank-and-file steelworkers made it clear they were in no mood for further concessions, especially around the issues of contracting out and elimination of Section 2-B of the contract. On August 1, 1986, the six-month lockout began. It was very bitter. Unions were in a very weak position at that time in history. The Company held most of the cards. Importing semifinished steel from places like Brazil and South Korea was far cheaper than modernizing mills at home. The globalization stampede had only just begun. It would dramatically kick into hyper-speed when Clinton signed NAFTA on December 8, 1993.[1]

In addition, the computer revolution was unfolding. Technology was making it extremely easy for companies to move production around to different parts of the country and different parts of the world. As early as 1980, I learned about the technological revolution that was beginning to unfold. We were having absentee issues in the 100" crane department. At a meeting with 100" mill general foreman Lloyd Fenstermaker, he warned: "We have a serious absentee problem in Alabama. These southerners don't want to work. You guys have a problem here too. I'm not saying you're as bad as Fairfield, but you are getting there. I want to teach you a lesson on what will happen if you don't straighten up." Sure enough the next day, they pushed some keys on their computers and temporarily shut down the Fairfield Works, transferring all their orders to Homestead. In twenty-four hours, we were filling orders and loading trucks with steel destined for Tennessee, Georgia, Florida, Alabama, and Arkansas. It was a sobering experience about the technological changes that would soon revolutionize every aspect of the U.S. economy, creating entire new industries like Silicon Valley in the process.

The lockout dragged on. Tensions grew worse. Violent confronta-tions were popping up everywhere. While the Company had pushed the union to strike, the International legal team, led by Bernie Kleiman, was smart enough to force the Company to lock us out. This allowed tens of thousands of employees to become eligible for unemployment compensation (UC) for up to six months. While I knew we were never getting back to work at Homestead, we did some real crazy things anyway. On one occasion, Ronnie and I went with several Irvin Works local union officers to a giant warehouse in Leetsdale, Pennsylvania. Leetsdale is just up the Ohio River from Pittsburgh. In preparation for the lockout, U.S. Steel was using a giant warehouse there to store, stockpile, and ship rolled sheet steel produced at the Irvin Works. Going aisle by aisle, we ripped all the tags off the steel coil rolls. Now they would have no idea what was going where. We were chased off the premises by armed guards, guns drawn. During the lockout, no one accused us of "selling out" by working with the International. We were all in the same foxhole. In my opinion, this was no different than working with them around the Dorothy Six campaign. While I clearly opposed their antiquated policies, wasteful bureaucracy, and lack of democracy, the union was not the enemy.

From the beginning of the lockout, the International provided "strike benefits" to our local in the form of weekly food vouchers. The food vouchers were worth sixty dollars each. Anyone who had worked in the last three years was entitled to a voucher. In December 1986, while Ronnie was in Russia trying to get medical help for his son Bobby, several zone grievers and I were left alone to manage the food voucher distribution. Another task that fell in my lap was coordinating the manning of picket lines at the gates around the clock. It was an extremely busy time, with no pay.

In October 1986, in the middle of the lockout, Local 1397 officially went broke and was placed under trusteeship by the International (meaning they now controlled our finances). At a tense meeting with International president Lynn Williams and District director Andrew "Lefty" Palm, Ronnie and I were promised that none of the local union officers would be removed.

Late on Thursday afternoon, December 18, when only Cheryl Bacco and I were in the union hall, District 15 staff representative George Myers came busting into the building and announced that they were cutting off food vouchers for most of our members. He said that only a handful of employees from no. 2 Structural who had worked after January 1, 1986, would continue to receive vouchers. He demanded we give him our keys and vacate the hall. As I stared without budging, he pulled back his winter coat to show me his gun strapped to his waist. Mine was at home. When we handed him our keys, he yelled, "You're fired." I felt like I was in an old western oater (cowboy TV show). In hindsight, I'm glad Ronnie wasn't there; someone would have been killed. Of all the despicable things the International did to our members, this was the worst—it was Christmastime!

The next day, I called both the District and the International, ranting and raving. I threatened the legal department with the National Labor Relations Board (NLRB) charges. We demanded they give us a union hall. If not, we would take our "LOCKED OUT BY USX" signs, and change the USX to USW. We would call the media and picket in front of the International headquarters. The District office claimed they had the right to shut down the hall, as Local 1397 had been placed in bankruptcy. By late Monday, December 22, Director Palm ordered Myers to return my keys to the union hall. When I met him there, Myers told me: "Bacco and the other grievancemen aren't coming back; you're on your own." Our mail was redirected to a subdistrict office in Donora. There was no heat in the union hall. The office supplies had all been removed. It was virtually impossible to be in there, much less do my unpaid job.

Several grievers and I continued to barrage the District with phone calls about the deplorable conditions at the union hall. Director Palm finally backed off several weeks later. We were given a storefront ten blocks up the hill on 17th and McClure Streets. It was an empty, ramshackle building that once housed a greasy spoon, and it smelled like stale grease. There was a desk, two chairs, a file cabinet, and one phone line to service the entire workforce in the midst of a plant shutdown. Director Palm told us the union hall building at 615 McClure Street would never reopen.

All grievances were, of course, put on hold during the lockout. At that time, there were over two hundred grievances at some stage of the procedure. By the end of January 1987, the bitter cold having set in and the workers' UC expiring, both sides did the usual give and take. On February 1, a new contract was signed between U.S. Steel and the International Union. Four U.S. Steel facilities in the Valley— Homestead, Duquesne, National, and Christy Park in McKeesport— were permanently shut down. The only bone thrown the union's way was a continuous caster at Edgar Thomson. While this did mean Edgar Thomson would reopen with close to a thousand workers (including numerous transfers from Homestead), the floodgates were opened to outside nonunion contractors. They numbered in the hundreds. U.S. Steel employed some thirty thousand workers at their seven mills in the Mon Valley when I arrived in 1977. It now employed a little less than three thousand. The remaining workforce was spread among Edgar Thomson, Irvin, and the Clairton Coke Works. For anybody out there who flunked basic math, that's a 90 percent reduction—a slaughter, pure and simple.

CHAPTER 33

THE MILL IS GONE, BUT THE GRIEVANCE FIGHTS CONTINUE

After the contract was signed, the District Union directed me to settle the local grievances and issues still pending at the plant level. I entered into negotiations with Company labor contract administrator (LCA) John McCluskey. We met two to three times a week at several hours a clip. Through most of this ordeal, friends and fellow grievers Gregg Mowry, John Deffenbaugh, and Tommy Farren were right by my side. Luckily, with the help of Barney Oursler, I learned how to "work the system" and was able to open up a new unemployment compensation (UC) claim, as I was receiving no pay from the union up through and after the lockout.

A lot of the grievance cases involved one person. Some involved two or three people. Others involved dozens, even hundreds. Several of the cases involving five hundred people or more were about the denial of severance pay by the Company. McCluskey tried to wear me down on every case, with the settlement attempts dragging on for weeks.

February 1, 1987, was now the official shutdown date for the Homestead mill. The five-year recall period had ended for anyone laid off prior to February 1, 1982. Most of the 1,800 people who were laid off in September 1981 and through the rest of the year would not be eligible for severance pay.[1] It was a rip. For many of the Slab and Plate employees who fell into this category, I had filed other grievances that they eventually won. Since I didn't become grievance chair for the entire plant until May 1985, for the most part I knew very little about what was happening in other sections of the mill up to that time and had no jurisdiction to do anything if I did. Had I been grievance chair earlier, there would have been "backup" grievances filed for many more workers.

A perfect example was a case that was out of the Forge Division. Management axed a whole group of machinists with at least nineteen years and eleven months of service. These employees were callously put in the street a few weeks shy of their early retirement pension eligibility. Their home department, the Forge Division, was closed on December 27, 1983. It was criminal. These guys filed a lawsuit that I became involved in after becoming grievance chair. A federal judge dismissed their case, asserting they had not exhausted the grievance procedure. The only thing I could do for these workers was add them on to another grievance I had filed out of Slab and Plate, where the Company had refused to honor transfers to the Pittsburg Works in Antioch, California (named for nearby Pittsburg, California, not a misspelling of the Pennsylvania city's name). Seeing the betrayal these dedicated, hardworking employees felt was heart-wrenching.

Negotiations with McCluskey dragged on for about six weeks. One of my main goals was to get as many workers as possible an early retirement pension. Hundreds of workers had been working at Homestead for eighteen or nineteen years when they lost their job. Instead of back pay, I settled some grievances by getting the workers' "last day worked" date changed, making them eligible for an early retirement pension, as well as transfer rights to other mills. This also made them eligible for more UC and for Trade Readjustment Allowance (TRA) benefits (worth eleven to twenty-two thousand dollars). The Company went along with this in many instances, because the government and the pension plan were footing a large part of the liability that was owed to these workers. I didn't care where the money came from, as long as these workers got what they were due.

After weeks of haggling and resistance, the Company caved and settled most of the grievances. There were five cases McCluskey refused to settle. He tried to force me to withdraw them. In addition to two massive severance cases and another contracting out case by Chuck Brantner out of the power and fuel department, there were two other big cases involving hundreds of employees and millions of dollars.

The "Big Shop"—Pride of the Valley

The Valley Machine Shop in the Homestead mill was the pride of the Steel Valley. It serviced machinery not only from Homestead but from other U.S. Steel facilities throughout the area. Part of the Central Maintenance Division, it employed more than four hundred workers at its peak. Its superintendent Steve Simko (who was also mayor of Homestead) was the most notorious "commandant" in the mill. He was featured numerous times in the *1397 Rank and File* newspaper.

Management started contracting out machine shop work job by job in 1983. They shut the entire shop down on August 31, 1984. On April 22, 1984, Valley Machine Shop grievance representative Sam Spence initiated a contracting out grievance; O'Toole followed with a chairperson's grievance against the contracting out on behalf of the entire Valley Machine Shop. The grievance was scheduled to be heard in arbitration on March 1, 1985.[2] At the last minute, the Company backed off, agreed that there had been illegal contracting out, and said they wanted to settle the case. When O'Toole met with the Company LCA, management claimed the illegal contracting out affected only 20 to 30 employees. The union claimed at least 150 to 200 employees were owed back pay. When no agreement could be reached, it was reappealed to arbitration on October 22, 1985. By then, I had taken over as grievance chair. A compliance hearing was scheduled for March 13, 1986, but then cancelled because of the breakdown in contract negotiations with the Company.

The Inter-Plant Job Opportunities Grievance

Another major case involved the transfer of dozens of laid-off Homestead workers to the Pittsburg Works in Antioch, California, under the Inter-Plant Job Opportunities provision in the contract.[3] In a nutshell, this provision allowed employees who had been laid off for more than sixty days to file a written request to be transferred to another facility. Provided these employees had the necessary qualifications, the Company had to place them at the requested facility before they hired someone off the street. An application had to be filed for each individual facility or mill.[4]

As he was going through an ugly divorce and on permanent layoff from Homestead, my former 160" Maintenance Department assistant griever Rick Koza had transferred to the Pittsburg Works in Antioch before winning his back pay award in 1985. Because the Pittsburg Works was 2,500 miles away in California, up to that point, hardly anyone else at Homestead had transferred there. Rick and I maintained a close friendship after his move and stayed in touch. In late March 1986, Rick called me at the union hall and told me the Pittsburg Works had just hired more than hundred people off the streets. He asked me how many grievances I could get filed (to get people out there).

On April 1, 1986, U.S. Steel signed a joint venture with South Korea's Po Hang Iron and Steel at the Pittsburg Works. It was now called POSCO. Immediately after the joint venture was signed, POSCO unilaterally decided to ignore certain sections of the contract including the Inter-Plant Job Opportunities transfer provisions. Trying to get laid-off employees to sign grievances to transfer 2,500 miles away was no easy task. Many had houses half paid off and family roots here. I had to convince some of them that the Company would probably make a financial offer rather than disrupt their operations in Antioch. I also stressed that maybe filing this grievance would help those displaced employees get placed at a mill closer to home. As things developed after the lockout, this last point proved prophetic.

All of these grievances: the severance cases for those laid off prior to February 1, 1982, the Chuck Brantner contracting out case, the

Valley Machine Shop contracting out settlement, and the Inter-Plant Job Opportunities transfers to California had been appealed to arbitration before the lockout ensued in 1986. At the time of the shutdown settlement, we were awaiting a scheduled date from the arbitration board for all of these cases.

Before the bulk of the grievances were finally settled on June 5, 1987, McCluskey beat up on me mercilessly. He constantly threatened, "Mike, if you don't drop these five grievances, we will settle nothing with you." It got very hostile. Each of us threatened to kill the other on more than one occasion. When I refused to drop the grievances, he threatened me even further: "We [management] are going to tell the guys in the mill who are owed pensions, severance pay, and back pay that they aren't getting their money because of you." I said, "Go ahead," and walked out of our last meeting in early April. It would be two months before they finally called me back in to settle the grievances.

Meanwhile, I was sweating bullets at the dilapidated storefront union hall, getting forty to fifty calls a day from guys wanting to know why nothing was being settled and asking when they were going to get their money and pensions. It was another divide and conquer situation. Management wanted me to sign away the rights of hundreds, so hundreds of others could get what they were owed. I held my ground.

The months at the storefront union hall in 1987 were the most lethal during the entire shutdown period. Not a week went by that someone didn't die prematurely of a heart attack, stroke, cancer, or suicide—usually two or three people. By the time I left the union hall storefront in 1987, more than seventy workers *I knew personally* had died—all under the age of sixty. For dozens of these workers, I had to deal with their widows and families to ensure they received the benefits they were owed. I can't even count all the funeral homes I visited in the period from 1985 to 1990. The suicides were the hardest; some were beyond heart-wrenching. Some of these workers I got to know quite well at the end, even partying with them, including Rich Locher and Kevin Terrick.[5] When I attended Kevin's wake, his uncle, Rich Terrick, who was the chief magistrate for the Steel Valley and also the local Democratic Party's chief political honcho, told me: "You know, Kevin voted for you, against his own family!"[6]

Perhaps the saddest case was that of James Radekovic, a 160" shipping employee. James Radekovic entered the Homestead mill fresh out of high school and had been there for thirty-six years. At the age of fifty-four, after watching the eleven o'clock news on February 28, 1988, he got his shotgun out of the closet and shot his wife and two teenage sons in the head, then turned the gun on himself. What exactly made him snap to such a degree, we'll never know. His house in suburban Verona was paid off, he had Company medical insurance and a nice pension, and his sons were at college on scholarships. He was one of those few guys who would line up a half hour before his work shift began, waiting patiently at the Amity Street Gate to go to work. He was one of the most diligent of employees, minding his own business and doing his job. I used to facetiously thank him weekly for all the overtime he worked. I had filed an overtime grievance for his department. His overtime alone resulted in several laid-off workers being paid thousands of dollars. He never complained; he just did his job.

The following Monday, WTAE Channel 4 asked me to be at the storefront union hall for an interview. Reporter Sally Wiggin put a mic in my face and asked, "So what happened? Why do you think he did it?" After thinking about it for a few seconds, I said, "U.S. Steel took three and a half decades to assemble his whole world, then they dismantled his whole world just like that," snapping my fingers. "They pulled the floor out from underneath him and he came crashing down." I told Sally, "If I could pull this sidewalk out from underneath you right now, I don't think you'd be standing or alive either." With no history whatsoever of mental illness, there can be no other explanation. In my experience as griever, lawyer, journalist, shrink, family counselor, and organizer at Local 1397, the psychological damage wrought by the shutdown far exceeded the economic damage. The average citizen cannot begin to comprehend the betrayal these workers felt.

Finally, on June 5, 1987, management called me out of the blue and said that they were ready to finalize the local settlement. They said I didn't have to withdraw the unsettled grievances. Thinking I'd kick their ass in arbitration on the Valley Machine Shop, Inter-Plant Job Opportunities, and Chuck Brantner cases, I signed the final shutdown agreement so the rest could get their money, severance, and pensions.

By the second week of June, I still hadn't heard anything on any of the cases still awaiting a hearing date. I called the only friend I had down at the International's arbitration department, John Foley. After checking on the cases, he called me back and said, "You better go down to the arbitration board; I think the District might have dropped your cases."

Downtown at the offices of the board of arbitration in the Oliver Building on Smithfield Street, I was questioning the secretary about the status of my cases, when Chair Al Dybeck stuck his head out of his office and said, "Mike, come in and shut the door behind you." I said, "What's up, Al?" He calmly uttered in a drone voice, "Your union withdrew your grievances." "Who?" I asked. He said, "Your staffman George Myers and Lou Kelley, the assistant to the District director." He gave me copies of the signed agreements.[7]

Seething, I went back to the hot, steamy storefront union hall. By this time, Ron Weisen and I were back on good terms. He seemed more somber after returning from Russia with his son Bobby. Our local union secretary Cheryl Bacco, Ronnie, and I went up to the District office in North Versailles. We marched past the front door receptionist and up the stairs to Lou Kelley's office. There was no "good cop, bad cop" on this occasion. While Ronnie was threatening to beat him up, I was threatening to sue him for millions of dollars, while Cheryl took copious notes. Lou was looking at us real nervously, smoking a cigarette, flicking ashes every three seconds. He kept repeating, "You don't think I have the power to make that decision, do you?" pointing his thumb in the direction of Director Andrew "Lefty" Palm's office. When we left, I told him I was going to give his personal phone number to all the guys he screwed. He changed his number.

Next, I went downtown and had a meeting with Bernie Kleiman, general counsel for the International Union. I liked Bernie a lot. We had been on speaking terms since the beginning of the Dorothy Six campaign. I went over all cases, pleading with him to reinstate them. I reminded him he represented the *members* of the union not just the bureaucracy and its officers. The International gave me a decision a few days later. One of his legal assistants called me and said, "Okay, we'll appeal the Inter-Plant Job Opportunities case to arbitration in California, but we aren't hearing the others; they're done." "Well, I'm not," I shouted, hanging up the phone.

The Inter-Plant Job Opportunities case went through seven arbitration hearings, multiple meetings—some of which required me to fly to California on my own dime—a series of delays engineered by both the union and the Company, and more time than was fair to any of the grievants before it was settled in 1993. The highlight of the union's obstruction was when California District 39 staff representative Glenn Nielson intentionally sent me a letter with the wrong time for one of the arbitration hearings in California.[8] U.S. Steel had to know I wasn't giving up on this grievance. From the summer of 1987 through 1988, they placed twelve of the original nineteen grievants in jobs at local mills. Most at them ended up at the Edgar Thomson Works in Braddock; others went to Lorain in Ohio or the Clairton Coke Works or Irvin Works in West Mifflin. Three of those remaining took an early retirement before the settlement. To settle the case, the Company offered the remaining grievants either lump sum payments or jobs at the Irvin Works with most of their seniority time. They all took the job offer. The Inter-Plant Job Opportunities grievance took more than seven years to settle. It was over, finally.[9]

CHAPTER 34

THE VALLEY MACHINE SHOP LAWSUIT

I n the summer of 1987, before pushing the Inter-Plant Job Opportunities grievance forward, we had to tackle the decision of the International to drop the Valley Machine Shop case. Several years earlier, Ronnie had met Chip Yablonsky during an interunion court battle in the Chicago-Gary area. Chip was the son of Jock Yablonsky, the United Mine Worker (UMW) official who ran for president against Tony Boyle and was murdered, along with his wife and daughter, on December 31, 1969. Chip was the only pro-worker lawyer we knew of that had beaten the International in court. We brought him in for a meeting. We asked him to file a lawsuit for misrepresentation and gross negligence against the Company *and* the International Union for colluding to willfully violate these workers' rights. We spent two weeks contacting former machine shop employees.

We finally met on June 18, 1987, at the storefront union hall. Only eight out of four-hundred-some machine shop employees showed up. Each of the eight put up five hundred dollars. Chip took the case as a class action suit. I didn't hear from him for almost four years. Knowing he was pissed off at the low worker turnout, I figured he had let the case fade away and die. I was dead wrong.

After the shutdown of the Homestead mill, I had been offered numerous organizing jobs by other unions, including the Communications Workers of America and the Teamsters. All these job offers involved moving out of the area, which I was unwilling to do. In another effort to buy my silence, Lou Kelley called me in June 1987 and said, "There's a crane job waiting for you over at Edgar Thomson." When I asked him about the dozens of crane operators with more seniority then me who had Inter-Plant Job Opportunities applications on file, he said, "Don't worry about them; just get your ass over there." Needless to say, I turned down his offer. The last company on the planet I wanted to work for was U.S. Steel, especially leapfrogging illegally over others who were out on the street.

When the Franciscan friars in Lawrenceville shut down their in-house printshop in the summer of 1988, Father Rich Zelik, whom I worked with in the Tri-State Conference on Steel (TSCS), told me they had quite a bit of printing equipment they needed to get rid of. Father Rich knew my family in Kentucky had a small printing business. He and other TSCS friends talked me into starting an employee-owned printshop. The United Steelworkers of America (USWA) had also just closed their in-house printshop and was dumping the printing equipment. After negotiating with both the head of the Franciscan friars and the USWA, they gave me their equipment. In exchange for the USWA equipment, which was negotiated through Jim Smith, an assistant to the president of the International, Lynn Williams, whom I had befriended during the Dorothy Six campaign, I agreed to make the printshop a steelworker union shop, instead of joining the Allied Printers and Trades Council. With the help of the TSCS activists Melinda and Pierre Whalon and former USWA communications director Russ Gibbons, Steel Valley Printers opened for business on January 1, 1989. Several other displaced steelworkers, including fellow griever and friend Gregg Mowry, were employed at its inception and made co-owners. Though we nearly went under several times, the printshop was on its feet and making a profit five years later, employing as many as eight people.

One day in early June 1991, while hard at work at the printshop, I got a phone call from Chip Yablonsky. He was in town and wanted me to meet with him. We had dinner downtown at the William Penn Hotel. Chip explained that he had continued the lawsuit against the International Union and U.S. Steel. In the "discovery process," he had spent countless hours combing through U.S. Steel documents at their downtown headquarters, as well as taking depositions from both U.S. Steel and USWA officials. He said he needed my help. "I think I have the Company dead to rights," he said, "but that's not enough." He took me to his room, where he had about ten boxes spread against the walls around the room. He had ample evidence that U.S. Steel intentionally and illegally contracted out work from the Valley Machine Shop. He even had the script to a slideshow that a management "SWAT team" took mill by mill in 1983, showing their front-line foremen, superintendents, and labor contract administrators (LCAs) how to violate the contract while legally covering their asses.

There was enough information to prove that hundreds of machinists had been improperly displaced. Chip said, "Here's the problem, though. All the evidence is about the Company. The lawsuit is against the Company *and* the International Union. We have to convince the judge that the International Union was willfully negligent and willfully violated these employees' rights. No matter how much the Company was at fault, we couldn't win the lawsuit without also proving our case against the union. Chip continued, "I need your testimony, because you're the only one who was around at the end." I said "No problem, you got it."

"There are going to be repercussions," Chip said. Nodding, I said, "I know." I was a little nervous about it. I knew the printshop would probably get blackballed. We had been fighting for three years to get printing bids from the International and were on the verge of a breakthrough. A former Duquesne local union official who now worked for the International, Frank Romano, had slipped us a humongous printing order that kept us from going bankrupt and stopped the IRS from padlocking our doors. He also got us put on the vendor's list to be contacted for bidding on future work. All of that was about to go down the drain. On June 7, 1991, I was issued a subpoena to be deposed by both the Company and the International Union on June 18, the day before my forty-second birthday.

Rich Brean, the International Union lawyer handling the lawsuit at the time lived across the Mon River from Homestead in the Pittsburgh's Squirrel Hill section. He came to my house at 7:30 p.m., on June 14, the Friday night before the deposition hearing to be held on the following Tuesday. He asked me not to associate with Chip and to work with him on my deposition. I refused, telling him, "I took an oath, and I'll do whatever I have to do to represent these workers." Being a lawyer in the union ivory towers whose job was to defend the bureaucrats, Brean just didn't get it.

Subpoenaed by the Company and the union, I was deposed in front of a judge for over three hours, at least two of those by Brean and the union. My testimony was critical, because both Lou Kelley and George Myers had stated in their depositions that I had agreed to withdraw the Valley Machine Shop contracting out grievance. That, of course, was a total lie.

Even worse than the lies Lou Kelley and George Myers told was what Chip uncovered through the discovery process in District Director Andrew "Lefty" Palm's deposition. In early 1987, a close friend and personal lawyer of Palm's, Dave Lichtenstein, contacted him about buying the Valley Machine Shop. Lichtenstein represented and owned a company called Innovative Technologies Corporation. Apparently, when Palm contacted U.S. Steel about the possible sale, the company informed him that there would be no sale until the Valley Machine Shop contracting out grievance was dropped. Palm then ordered his assistant Lou Kelley to withdraw the case. During his deposition, Kelley testified that he informed USWA headquarters that he had withdrawn the grievance. He was led to believe this would enable the sale to Innovative Technologies Corporation. Wow! Hundreds of union employees sold down the river by a union official to help a friend in a business deal![1]

In December 1991, the lawsuit was settled in favor of the Valley Machine Shop employees for a whopping 1.9 million dollars. My guess is that the union and U.S. Steel split the bill. A total of 231 former machine shop employees were paid anywhere from one thousand to ten thousand dollars, depending on their seniority. The eight employees who filed the lawsuit and put up the money were offered either fifty-five thousand dollars each or an early retirement pension. All of them took the money, as I would have.

When we won the Valley Machine Shop lawsuit, Yablonsky sent an explanation letter and checks to the 239 former employees. Just imagine if you came home from work one day and there was a check in the mail for ten thousand dollars! With their checks, each Valley Machine Shop employee was sent a letter that explained why they were receiving the money, which also said:

> Equally important is the fact that the officers and representatives of Local 1397 would simply not let this case die. Ron Weisen, John O'Toole, and Mike Stout actively assisted us at every turn. Mike Stout in particular was subjected to a lengthy and difficult deposition that required enormous patience and guts. You'd

never know that Local 1397 was disbanded from the way these guys continued to fight USX and the International. Please take a moment to drop them a thank you card, note, or telephone call.

I was a bit disappointed to only get cards or thank you notes from 15 of 239 guys. Seven of those were from widows. I guess the rest just thought it was our job. The Valley Machine Shop contracting out grievance was filed in April 1984; it took over seven years to finally achieve justice!

What is doubly shameful about this whole episode is the way U.S. Steel played "Lefty" Palm for a chump to get him to withdraw the grievance and arbitration case. They had no intention of selling the Valley Machine Shop—to anyone! Like the rest of the Homestead Works, it was chopped up into pieces and sold for scrap. In a deal reached with the Park Corporation, the scrap dealer that dismantled the mill, most major pieces of equipment and machinery could only be sold to foreign entities from places like Iraq and India. According to Kelly Park from Park Corporation, nothing could be sold to anyone competing with U.S. Steel.

After this lawsuit was settled, the printshop was blackballed for a year or two. However, there were numerous personnel and department head changes at the International, resulting from mergers and retirements. We had numerous rank-and-file friends there, including my future wife. I was soon getting bids again, and that lasted for a few years. However, after the United Steelworkers (USW) merged with the Paper, Allied-Industrial, Chemical and Energy Workers International Union (PACE) in late 2004, and I started cranking out anti-war songs in response to the invasions of Afghanistan and Iraq, I never received another printing bid from the International.

CHAPTER 35

SAVING THE HISTORY OF LOCAL 1397

I n mid-June of 1987, I drove by the former Local 1397 union hall at 615 McClure Street on my way to the storefront up the hill. I noticed there was a gigantic dumpster parked in front of the hall. The kind used when gutting an entire building. A year earlier, I had seen the same type of dumpster in front of the Duquesne Local 1256 union hall and watched them empty out the entire hall. I saw them throw an important piece of history down the drain, gone forever. I was determined to make sure the same thing didn't happen at Homestead's local union hall. It seemed that the District and International leadership of the union at the time had no concept or appreciation of the importance of local union history. This history is important, especially for future generations of union organizers and activists.

As luck would have it, on Friday evening, June 18, 1987, the Mon Valley Unemployed Committee (MVUC) and State Representative Dave Levdansky were holding hearings on their campaign to get unemployment compensation (UC) extended. It really pissed me off. We couldn't have the union hall for helping our members who were trying to secure their benefits owed, but outsiders could use the hall. It was another slap in the face.

I called my good friend Barney Oursler, one of the MVUC organizers of the event and asked him how he got access to the hall. He told me that District 10 Director Andrew "Lefty" Palm had given him a key (after the lockout, Districts 15 and 20 were merged into District 10). Barney was to return the key the following Monday to the District office in North Versailles. I met with him two days later and asked him to give me the key, saying I would return it myself. While somewhat hesitant at first, Barney saw the determined look in my eyes. He told me to stop by the union hall when they were closing up Friday night.

I immediately got on the phone and called my old friend Dr. Irwin Marcus, a history professor up at Indiana University of Pennsylvania (IUP), which is about an hour and a half east of Homestead. Dr. Marcus had always been a big supporter of our rank-and-file movement at Homestead, featuring us numerous times at conferences at IUP. When I got him on the phone, I said, "Irwin, I have a historical jewel for you; get me at least three able bodies, a hundred empty cardboard boxes, and a twenty-four-foot Ryder truck and have them meet me in front of our union hall at six o'clock Saturday morning." He said, "No problem." Three workers from the Special Collections and University Archives at IUP were there waiting for me when I arrived with the union hall key at 6:00 a.m. on what was my thirty-eighth birthday. One of them, Eileen Lovejoy, barely weighed a hundred pounds. When I asked her to stand guard and watch the Ryder truck while we loaded it, she grabbed an empty box and said, "No way!" The anticipation, excitement, and enthusiasm in her and the other volunteers' eyes were like that in the eyes of a six-year-old getting their first big Christmas present.

In one hour and twenty minutes, we loaded up seventy-two 11" × 17" boxes. We cleaned out the grievance chair's office, Ron Weisen's office, and the secretary's front office. The item's preserved included written grievance records from third and fourth steps dating back to the 1950s, a complete history of every steelworker union arbitration award, dozens of labor history books, internal documents on the workings of our local union, intraunion disputes, and campaigns and elections, as well as all correspondence from the 1950s forward, workmen's compensation and Trade Readjustment Allowance (TRA) case files, a general history of the Homestead steel mill—all saved from the dump. In addition, I gave them most of my personal files, news clippings, correspondence, and internal documents on the various campaigns I had been involved in, such as the coalition with the Denominational Mission Strategy (DMS), the Tri-State Conference on Steel (TSCS), and the formation of the Steel Valley Authority (SVA). They also got the only complete set of the *1397 Rank and File* newspaper. It was a historical treasure indeed. All of it is now preserved intact, organized, categorized, and chronicled in the Special Collections and University

Archives Department on the third floor of the IUP library. Anyone doubting the accounts, grievances won, and events I've detailed in this book can go to the IUP library history archives and see for themselves.

While a few acquaintances said to me, "But, Mike, isn't that stealing?" My answer was: "Absolutely not"—unless you consider taking stuff from a trashcan stealing. When the Duquesne Works Local 1256 union hall was closed and put up for sale, everything inside was pitched in one of those big dumpsters. You don't have to be a detective to surmise what would have happened with the Local 1397 documents; especially in view of the adversarial relations between our local and the International during the last decade. I'm pretty sure they wanted to bury the whole episode. No, by preserving it, I did labor and union history a service! The following Monday morning, June 21, 1987, I dropped off the key to the union District office receptionist at the front window and said, "This is from Barney." She smiled and said, "Why, thank you very much." I said, "No, thank you!"

CHAPTER 36

RUNNING FOR STATE REPRESENTATIVE–A POLITICAL NIGHTMARE

As the grievances and local union battles were winding down, in August 1987, I was approached by State Representative Mike Dawida to run for his seat in the Pennsylvania legislature. He was running for the Senate seat against incumbent Jim Romanelli.

During the grievances and the shutdown battles, I saw the important role the state government played. It was critical in the fight to extend unemployment compensation (UC) and other benefits for displaced workers, as I detailed in an earlier chapter. It could play a pivotal role in gaining support and financing to save plants and at least a portion of our manufacturing industrial base in the Valley. Seeing the corrupt corporate influence on the whole political process—by *both* parties—I strongly advocated that workers and their communities should have their own political voices at the local and state level.

After being approached by Dawida, I ran the proposition by a number of Homestead workers that lived in the legislative district. Homestead steelworkers, including Jay Weinberg, Ronnie Pristas, Walt Lippay, and Rich Majorsky, not only thought it was a good idea, they volunteered to help coordinate my campaign. Whoever won the primary was a shoo-in for the legislative seat, as the overwhelming majority of voters, especially the super-voters (those who voted in every election) were registered Democrats and voted on strict party lines. To be eligible to run in the primary election, I reregistered, shifting from being an independent to the Democratic Party.

Hundreds of dislocated mill workers had high hopes they would finally have one of their own in Harrisburg, a voice for the working people. I ended up losing by only fifty-five votes, against eight other opponents. Another Homestead steelworker and our local union legislative chair at the end, Ed Wuenschell, came in third, only 420 votes behind me. Together, two steelworkers crushed the opposition. Looking back, thirty years later, I can safely say that this personal venture into politics was one of the worst experiences of my life. The local Democratic Party, which had been in power since the mid-1930s, was riddled with patronage, nepotism, and corruption. While there were obviously some local party people and politicians who honestly wanted to do good and fight for the people, like Betty Esper in Homestead, Ronnie Watkins in Munhall, and Ruth Mehalik in West Homestead, others talked to and treated you like a prostitute.

When I door knocked the legislative district, especially in the city wards, most voters seemed to only care about one issue, whether it was guns, abortion, or blacks moving into their neighborhood. The slander and character assassination were the worst. The idea of a young dislocated steelworker running on a progressive, socialist-sounding program was thirty years ahead of its time and way too much for the older and more conservative constituency to handle. I was labeled a communist, socialist, radical unionist, gay for supporting same-sex marriage, a Denominational Mission Strategy (DMS) church invader, and an outsider. The smut flyers put out were beyond disgusting; one claimed I was a "gun-toting, snake oil peddler who had abandoned his family."[1] The chair of the Munhall Democratic Party at the time, a retired district steelworker union official named John Maher told a Democratic Party committee gathering that I was a liar and didn't really fight and win the grievance cases I claimed to have fought and won, even though I had just handed out written proof, arbitration case numbers and all, and he hadn't been in the union since I started. He then ended the meeting before I could respond, leaving me shouting the truth to a departing, confused crowd. It was an early version of the "fake news" bully pulpit lying popularized by Trump three decades later. Trying to even address all this bullshit merely fed the slander fire.

In Lincoln Place, the 31st Ward of Pittsburgh, a retired police sergeant sent a personal letter out to super-voters with a picture of Jesse Jackson and me together in front of the Homestead mill with a headline, "Do you want this nigger lover representing you in Harrisburg?" (In much of this same legislative district, exactly thirty years later, in 2018, a twenty-nine-year-old African American woman, Summer Lee, was elected to the Pennsylvania legislature by a two to one margin, crushing her six-term white male opponent, including beating him handily in Lincoln Place—running on much the same program as I did thirty years before. The point being that the political climate in the Valley and elsewhere has radically changed!)

The lesson of this political experience, as it relates to the closing of the Homestead mill and our local union's fight for democracy, is that in this period—the late 1980s—even if I would have gotten elected, any voices in the state legislature calling for economic justice, support for unions, or other progressive causes were in the process of being suffocated, snuffed out. Every progressive representative in support of worker and poor people's causes, from Allen Kukovich and Jim Ferlo in the state senate to a host in the legislature, was forced to retire or gerrymandered out of office over the next decade. Looking back on the corruption, gerrymandering, and lobbyist invasion that descended on Harrisburg in subsequent years, I'm glad I lost. I'm sure I wouldn't have lasted more than a term or two, at most. All in all, it would have been a futile gesture, a waste of time and energy. The psychological warfare would have been even worse than in the mill. I can see the headlines on the front page of the *Post-Gazette* a few months later, had I won: "I Smoked Marijuana with State Legislator in the Mill!"

CHAPTER 37

THE WAR IS OVER, ONE LAST FIGHT

Long after the District closed our storefront in 1987, closure was needed for a number of outstanding issues. For example, in early 1993, I was notified by one of our local union secretaries, Cheryl Bacco (now McGartland), that she was denied severance pay from the union when it was officially closed. When Local 1397 declared bankruptcy in late 1986 and was placed under trusteeship by the International, all officers and employees were asked to submit to the bankruptcy court any back monies owed. The secretaries submitted a claim for severance pay. The secretaries' contract with the local specifically stated they would receive the same amount of severance pay (eight weeks at their pay scale) as if they had worked in the mill. Ronnie and I filed charges on their behalf, not only for Cheryl but also for the other two secretaries, Darlene McIntosh (by then Darlene Deffenbaugh) and Linda Lapko. While Linda had been let go after several years when the layoffs picked up steam in 1981, Darlene stayed on until late 1984, and Cheryl worked until December 18, 1986, when gun-toting George Myers fired her.

Cheryl and Darlene became close personal friends of mine. While I was grievance representative and grievance chair, a bunch of us always went out to lunch together. They were both good workers who were loyal to the union. When disputes arose between Ronnie and me, especially during the Denominational Mission Strategy (DMS) period, they never took sides. We always remained good friends. This had to have been especially hard for Cheryl, who was Ronnie's personal secretary, confidante, friend, and ardent defender. When Darlene refused to spy

Cheryl McGartland, Moureen Trout, and Darlene Deffenbaugh.

and report on my whereabouts and to whom I talked on the phone, she was let go. While she was probably going to get laid off eventually due to the drastic drop in dues-paying members, the timing was all too obvious. I will never forget the solidarity I received from these sisters.

Winning their severance pay, though small change compared to some of the other grievances I fought and won, was especially sweet. Instead of sending a union staff representative, the International hired an outside attorney, John Smart, from Grogan Graffam and Lucchino, one of the biggest local labor law firms used by the United Steelworkers of America (USWA) at the time. We kicked their tush, and the gals got their severance pay, once again proving that justice was more powerful than a law degree.[1]

While there remained some lingering hostility with the International, especially their legal department, over grievances being dropped and issues like the secretary severance pay, by 1993, my relationship overall with the International Union had improved, especially with the lower-level workers downtown. I was once again getting printing bids, thanks to a number of the secretaries who worked in different departments and were responsible for sending out bids. In 1996, one of the lowest paid and hardest working woman and my wife to be Stephanie also worked downtown. I made a lot of friends during the Dorothy Six and Electric Furnace campaigns. As I later discovered, there was a sizable group of fairly militant workers at the International who were waging their own internal fights over grievances being dropped. A number of International workers had always been sympathetic to Local 1397, some even paying their dues to our local. Treating everyone at the International as one monolithic "enemy," as some leftist fringe groups had been doing, was clearly off the wall and just plain wrong. To reiterate one of my firmest principles: the bureaucracy and structure are not the union, the members are! When it came to the bureaucracy, especially the legal department, I never hesitated to take them on to defend union members' rights, particularly members whom I had taken an oath to represent and defend. One of the many good things my dad taught me was that your word, especially when sworn, was as sacred and important as any written contract. During my tenure as a local union official at Homestead, some bureaucrats in the union didn't seem to understand that.

CHAPTER 38

CONCLUSION

There have always been two general trends of thought among trade unionists when it comes to what a union should look like and how it should function. One trend, the business union model, says our only choice is to work within a collective bargaining system with a written contract and the framework of whatever legal system exists. Local strikes, and certainly wildcats, are out of the question—and illegal—while the contract is in effect. A hierarchical structure usually exists where locals must answer to district, regional, and national officers. Most, if not all, contracts contain "Management Rights" clauses giving workers no say on investment decisions, company policies, or anything other than wages, benefits, and working conditions.

Another trend espoused by the Industrial Workers of the World (IWW) and likeminded radicals is labeled simply as "solidarity unionism." Utilized a century ago, back in the heyday of the IWW in the early twentieth century, it was resuscitated and given new life with the 1978 publication of Staughton Lynd's *Labor Law for the Rank and Filer*, reissued and updated with Starbucks organizer Daniel Gross in 2008.[1] In contrast to business unionism, this type of unionism opts for concerted joint action where workers decide together to take direct action on the shop floor, including slowdowns, strikes, and other illegal joint activity. With this style of unionism, there is no formal structure, bureaucracy, or "elected" officials. It also asserts that workers have a fundamental right to take part in the Company's major decisions—a concept that was espoused by the Amalgamated Association of Iron and Steelworkers at Homestead back in 1892. With 90 percent of the current U.S. workforce without a union and the legal system so tilted in favor of Company owners and management, "solidarity unionism" has become increasingly popular, as witnessed by recent strikes at companies like Uber, Lyft, and Amazon, and by teachers in numerous states. As Daniel Gross put it in a recent interview, a key advantage of the solidarity model in some of the recent successes by nonunionized workers is that there is no "need to win a majority of workers, typically in a secret ballot election," and "if the company hangs on through the election, union organizers usually pack up and leave. . . . [S]olidarity unions can challenge employers for years without an election."[2]

In my experience at the Homestead Works, as well as numerous other plants—especially those where the United Electrical, Radio and Machine Workers Union (UE) exists, you can do both. Today, UE is regarded as one of the most democratic and politically progressive national unions in the United States. Its philosophy and principle of militant, politically independent democratic unionism is summed up in its longstanding slogan: "The members run this union." UE's commitment to internal democratic accountability includes a provision in its constitution that no officer or staffer shall be paid a salary higher than the highest wage earned by rank-and-file members, and that pay raises for the national officers and staff must be ratified by a membership vote of the locals. Now representing thirty-five thousand workers in a variety of industries, the UE continues actively organizing private and public sector workers, and its democratic structure and practices have attracted several small independent unions to affiliate. It's a union that identifies itself as internationalist, building alliances with unions in other countries and refusing to blame the problems facing U.S. workers on the specter of "foreigners." For example, in the fight against NAFTA in the early 1990s, rather than adopt jingoist anti-Mexican rhetoric, the UE reached out to a like-minded labor organization in Mexico, the Frente Autentico del Trabajo (Authentic Labor Front; FAT), and established an ongoing alliance and working partnership, with the two organizations cooperating on organizing the unorganized and other fights for workers' rights on both sides of the border. Another aspect of UE's internationalism and its political independence has been its role in the peace movement. The UE was the first U.S. union to oppose the Vietnam War and has been outspoken in its opposition to the U.S. government's military interventions, support for regime change coups, and alliances with oppressive corporate-friendly anti-worker governments.

My point is: *you have to play the cards you're dealt.* You can use the system and contract in place to defend and empower the members, while also showing the limitations of the system and the need for more direct action, more powerful laws, and a more equitable system that ensures workers' rights, safety, and dignity on the job. Workers' rights, especially having a safe workplace, should be considered human rights. Faced with the overwhelming power of corporations and companies, collective concerted action by workers should be protected by law. Regardless of the legal system in place, the *right to strike*, even at the local plant level, should *always* be in the union's arsenal. More working people went on strike in 2018–2019 than had done so in decades. Teachers strikes in nearly a dozen states have not only resulted in major economic gains, they have empowered working people with a spirit and sense of solidarity, knocking down the walls of race, religion, nationality, and gender divisions that have kept us down for more than a century. A 2019 strike by the Chicago Teachers Union for smaller classroom sizes and other benefits for students extended the strike objectives beyond the standard issues of wages, benefits, and working conditions.

During my short time in the mill, I saw with my own eyes a hundred different ways workers opposed unsafe working conditions and unjust management treatment on the shop floor, with or without a grievance procedure. Individual or small group work stoppages were constant. Doing every job "the right way," was another weapon used in the mill, especially by crane operators and maintenance personnel. This means performing every task according to the rules and letter of the contract, with doing work safely having the cumulative effect of slowing production. Absenteeism was a common way of wildcatting when faced with an unjust schedule or forced overtime.

Without worker cooperation on the shop floor, performing most jobs—especially in dangerous settings like a steel mill—would be impossible to accomplish productively and would result in serious injury or death. Without worker solidarity in the union, management will simply use their legal and financial resources to trample us one by one. The tension between community and selfishness is magnified many times in a heavy industry setting. Workers looking out for each other—i.e., solidarity—is a prerequisite for survival. That's what a union is supposed to be all about.

There are many people in the general population, including some in the union, who think the activists and militants at Local 1397 caused the shutdown of the great Homestead steel mill. They don't know about or fail to understand the fundamentally flawed policies of the steel industry owners from the end of World War II to the incremental dismantlement of our basic steel industry at the end of the twentieth century. For a half century, these shortsighted, profit-hungry owners refused to modernize their mills, opting for investment in steel industries overseas or disinvesting into other ventures. They also didn't understand what a union is supposed to be about: "an injury to one is an injury to all." I took this concept to heart. I was not about to sell out *some* of the workers I represented so *others* could get ahead.

Anyone who thinks that unions are outmoded, unnecessary, and a relic of the past is completely ignorant of how corporations behaved in the past and still do. When I was working in the mill in the 1970s and 1980s, companies like U.S. Steel were ruthless, vindictive, money-hungry behemoths that did not hesitate to trample on workers' rights and lives in pursuit of the almighty dollar. They broke their word, including written and signed contracts, almost daily. They went out of their way to screw a dedicated workforce out of the benefits they were legally owed. This included many of their own frontline foremen. Failure to oppose these illegalities, this criminal behavior, and these indignities would have been a heinous dereliction of duty—both as a union representative and as a human being.

In the political world, without a strong union that has an independent voice, companies and corporations will always use their superior financial wherewithal and legal shenanigans to bend the laws and system in their favor. Without their own political voice, workers and unions will always get sold down the river by the current two-party system with its army of paid corporate lobbyists and the rampant corruption that has infested both the Democratic and Republican Parties at the top.

This was a major lesson of the 1397 Rank and File Caucus experience at Homestead during our efforts at the end to save our jobs, some portions of our mills, and revitalize our manufacturing base. Even when we had the support of honest, hardworking Democratic Party officials at the local, county, and state levels, the top party officials and their big money backers sabotaged and crushed our efforts. Organized labor and working people need their own independent political voice. They need to stop the bloodletting and stop throwing money at politicians who just end up stabbing them in the back.

All one has to do is review the past eighty years of political reality: whether we had a Democratic or Republican administration, from the Wagner Act through the firing of the air traffic controllers in 1981 to agreements like NAFTA,[3] workers got screwed and unions were given the shaft. Even in this day and age, many union leaders advocate the same garbage as Lloyd McBride did decades ago: that the only policy for unions is crawling into bed with the very politicians and corporations that are hell-bent on destroying them or selling them out.

Most union people are well aware of the anti-worker, antiunion bias of the Republican Party, whose hatred of unions is front and center. The far-right, fundamentalist, big-money cabal that has taken over the Republican Party is hell-bent on dismantling unions and workers' rights, and they make no bones about it. On the other hand, the upper echelons of the Democratic Party pretend to be labor's friend, promising poor and working people the world, especially at convention time, where they flaunt their diversity and sympathy. Once the election circus is over, the corporate party bosses take control, leaving their base and all of us in the lurch time and time again.

To this day, I have many good friends who are still activists and members of the Democratic Party; they still think the party can be changed from within. Of course, I will continue to work with these folks, especially at the grassroots level, whether around the issues of workers' rights, discrimination, the environment, or health care, because their hearts are in the right place, and their feet are in the struggles. The new wave of "Democratic socialists" recently elected, mostly young women, are the kind of "democrats" who know how to keep one foot in the party and one foot out, maintaining their independence. But as far as the party hierarchy is concerned, both recent history and my own experience tells me they have just become additional representatives of the billionaire class, the filthy rich 1% who are deregulating, privatizing, and dismantling our social safety net and destroying this planet.

Their betrayal of working people, especially steelworkers, has been consistent. It was Democratic Party liberal Jimmy Carter who reneged on the federal loan to the Youngstown coalition in early 1980, sinking the heroic effort of workers and townspeople to save their mills. While there are a number of reasons Carter lost his reelection bid, including the secret deal between George H.W. Bush, who would become vice president when Ronald Reagan won the election in 1980, and Iran to hold American hostages until after the election, the sellout of the Youngstown effort buried Carter's chances for reelection in steel producing areas, as workers in Youngstown, Homestead, and elsewhere voted in droves for the more antiworker Ronald Reagan. I witnessed it firsthand, as numerous Local 1397 union "militants" publicly bragged about voting for Reagan at the union hall on election day.

Fifteen years later, it was a Democrat, Bill Clinton, who pushed through NAFTA, destroyed the welfare system, and passed the 1994 Omnibus Crime Bill that saw the prison population explode from seven hundred thousand to over two million. It was Clinton who passed the draconian "three strikes and you're out" drug laws and increased the length of prison sentences, militarized the police, and deregulated the Federal Communications Commission (FCC), so a handful of corporations could control what most Americans listen to on the radio and watch on TV. And it was the neoliberal Clinton and his corporate Democrats that struck down the sixty-year-old Glass-Steagall Act, allowing the banks and Wall Street to deregulate and run rampant with derivative bundling and the other big money-making schemes that resulted in the 2008 meltdown. It was Barack Obama who continued George W. Bush's fall 2008 bailout of the big Wall Street banks and firms when he became president in 2009, leaving homeowners and working people in the lurch. Obama justice officials both shielded and feted these criminals, while simultaneously prosecuting and imprisoning powerless Americans for far more trivial transgressions. The revolting and inexcusable 306-billion-dollar bailout of Citigroup was the first major act of his presidency. According to reporter Edward Xavier in an April 3, 2009, article, at a gathering of Wall Street's elite bankers and CEOs at the White House, on March 27, 2009, the newly elected president told these titans of finance: "My administration is the only thing between you and the pitchforks." The fresh details about the meeting—some never before revealed—come from an account provided to Politico by one of the participants.[4] A second source who attended the meeting confirmed the details, and two other sources familiar with the meeting offered additional information.

When Obama had a majority in both houses in 2009–2010, nothing was done to push through the Employee Free Choice Act, a bill that would have made it much easier for workers to organize unions and raise their standard of living, and a major bill advancing environmental justice passed in the House and died in the Senate, with Obama sitting quietly on the sidelines. In fact, the worse tragedy of the past half century is the fact that the corporate wing that controls the Democratic Party has betrayed the very principles that made it such a dominant political force during the Roosevelt years and the post–World War II period, turning its back on an electorate that is fully aware it has been abandoned by the party elite. The fact is that even when they had the power and numbers in Congress and the Senate, they never stood up and fought for legislation that advanced the common good for the common people. Instead, they opted to chase after the big corporate donors. Most of their defeats have been essentially capitulations, self-inflicted wounds.

Since the recession in 2008, The Federal Reserve has handed over an estimated $29 trillion of fabricated money to America's biggest banks. *$29 trillion!* Both the Republican Party *and* the Democrat Party happily went along with this giant Ponzi scheme!

Just think what could have been done with that money had it been used to help the rest of us and our country. Kevin Zeese and Margaret Flowers (on the website Popular Resistance, https://popularresistance.org/) calculate that we could have provided free college tuition to every student, financed a Medicare for all health care system, repaired our crumbling infrastructure and built a viable mass transit system in every major city, transitioned to clean, renewable energy, forgiven student debt, raised wages, bailed out underwater homeowners, formed public banks to invest at low interest rates in our communities, provided a guaranteed minimum income for everyone, and organized a massive jobs program for the unemployed and underemployed.[5] Sixteen million children would not go to bed hungry. The mentally ill and the homeless—an estimated 553,742 Americans, many of whom are veterans—would not be left on the streets or locked away in our prisons. Instead, twenty-nine trillion dollars in fabricated money was handed to Goldman Sachs and other financial gangsters who are about to make most of it evaporate and plunge us into a depression that will rival that of the global crash of 1929.

A careful scrutiny of both Republican Party and Democratic Party administrations shows an equal number of former Goldman Sachs executives. These Wall Street gangsters select the candidates for both parties and promote an agenda that has resulted in the greatest disparity of wealth the world has ever seen. It's time for the good hardworking people at the base of both parties to break away from the corporate whores at the top—and that includes honest Republicans who are concerned with conservation and protecting our land, air, and water. It's no wonder a hundred million or more eligible adults don't vote every election cycle or refused to vote for the Democratic candidate in 2016. On top of the myriad of social issues that divide us, such as guns, abortion, gay rights, etc., a lot of working people don't see either party as doing anything about their economic well-being. For millions of working and poor people, there is no "lesser of two evils"—only evil, period!

On the issue of coalitions: with their ranks and political influence steadily shrinking, unions will not survive, much less grow, without actively coalescing with other segments of society that are being crushed by this same unjust, exploitative system. And with the continuous havoc and destruction wrought by climate change, *a coalition of organized labor and the environmental movement should be the top priority.*

Many would be surprised to learn that a major industrial labor union, the United Auto Workers (UAW), played a prominent role in the emergence of the modern-day environmental movement. In fact, Earth Day, with over a billion participants at its founding on April 22, 1970, would have never happened without the participation of the UAW. According to Earth Day's first national coordinator Denis Hayes, "The UAW was by far the largest contributor to the first Earth Day, and its support went beyond the merely financial. It printed and mailed all our materials at its expense—even those critical of pollution-belching cars. According to Joe Uehlein, UAW organizers turned out workers in every city where the union had a presence. Joe Uehlein is the son of former USW legislative director Jules Uehlein. He is a longtime labor organizer, worker, and activist, a friend and fellow labor musician. He also has been a strong voice in the environmental movement. As he stated so eloquently in the April 22, 2010, Grist newsletter:

> When it comes to the environment, organized labor has two
> hearts beating within a single breast. On the one hand, the

millions of union members are people and citizens like everybody else, threatened by air and water pollution, dependent on fossil fuels, and threatened by the devastating consequences of climate change. On the other hand, unions are responsible for protecting the jobs of their members, and efforts to protect the environment sometimes may threaten workers' jobs. First as a working-class kid and then as a labor official, I've been dealing with the two sides of this question my whole life.

Uehlein added:

UAW president Walter Reuther, who wrote that first check supporting the first Earth Day, spelled out what that should mean for organized labor:

> The labor movement is about that problem we face tomorrow morning. Damn right! But to make that the sole purpose of the labor movement is to miss the main target. I mean, what good is a dollar an hour more in wages if your neighborhood is burning down? What good is another week's vacation if the lake you used to go to is polluted and you can't swim in it and the kids can't play in it? What good is another $100 in pension if the world goes up in atomic smoke?[6]

Instead of sitting down as equals and finding common ground with environmental activists, some union officials—especially those in the industrial and construction sectors—have at best been suspicious of environmentalists, and in many instances have outright shunned the environmental movement. I've personally heard union officials on a number of occasions call environmentalists "quacks" and "tree huggers." Union members and environmentalists need each other. Without a true coalition based on mutual respect and common objectives—living-wage jobs, clean air, clean water, clean food, and a safe environment, neither will survive—literally.

When I raised this issue with a number of USW officials in 2018, their response was: "Of course, that's why we have the BlueGreen Alliance." Founded in 2006 by the United Steelworkers (USW) and Sierra Club, the BlueGreen Alliance boasts fourteen of the nation's largest labor unions and most influential environmental organizations. According to a press release issued at a press conference held at the USW International's headquarters: "It's now more important than ever that we work to find solutions to climate change that also create good jobs and economic opportunities for working people in this country," said USW International President Leo W. Gerard, a cofounder of the BlueGreen Alliance. "We need solutions that rebuild, repair, and modernize our infrastructure systems and invest in manufacturing the cutting-edge technologies of the future, including clean energy and energy efficiency, and we're proud to have LCV join our ranks to help us in this fight."[7]

The premise of the BlueGreen Alliance created by the USW International Union officials acknowledges the environmental crisis and was an important step forward for the USW more than a decade ago, with much of its rhetoric around upgrading our infrastructure overlapping with that of other environmental organizations. The staff of the BlueGreen Alliance work for and answer to the USW International's top officers, who fund it and call all the major shots. That's not a coalition, and in fact the BlueGreen Alliance has ceased to function of late. Given that an entire generation and hundreds of organizations have sprung up since the USW International formed the BlueGreen Alliance in 2006, the USW and other unions need to sit down with a broad range of other environmental activists and leaders. This is especially true concerning the Sunrise and Climate Extinction movements embraced by a younger generation of activists, who will be living through the worst aspects of the climate chaos to come. Representing workers in both the fossil fuel and renewable energy sectors (steelworkers represent oil, chemical, and wind turbine workers), the USW is uniquely positioned to take the lead in sitting down with environmentalists and in ensuring that organized labor and workers have a voice at the table, that there is a just transition that protects worker pensions, families, and communities, and that any new jobs are unionized and pay a living wage. The USW has hired a number of very bright, progressive, and energetic organizers of late. They should reach out to the UE and other unions that are on board with a just transition to a renewable energy–based economy. And they can and should do this with mutual respect and a shared decision-making process. The long-established "my way or the highway"

Steel Labor

THE VOICE OF THE UNITED STEELWORKERS OF AMERICA

Vol. XXXVIII   Second class postage paid at Indianapolis, Indiana   July, 1973   PRINTED IN U.S.A.   No. 7

CLEAN AIR AND JOBS

STEELWORKERS SAY NO! TO ENVIRONMENTAL BLACKMAIL

CLOSED

SEE PAGES 8-9

Credit: Fred Wright.

approach of some top union officials will no longer suffice and will only continue to drive unions to the edge of irrelevance in the eyes of the public.

Four decades ago, when steel companies threatened to shut plants down because of orders and decrees by the Environmental Protection Agency (EPA) to install water and air pollution control technology, the USWA International stood with workers *and* the environment. The International needs to come full circle and do the same today.

What good are decent paying jobs if the air and water quality continue to worsen and the cancer rates (especially among young people) go through the roof? If health care costs continue to soar and pharmaceuticals become cost prohibitive? If the planet literally becomes uninhabitable? Union members breathe the same air, drink the same water, and eat the same food as everyone else. They have a vested interest in keeping it clean and healthy. If unions do not abandon their "circle the wagons" approach, focusing solely on jobs for their own members, they will be crushed and suffocated and will wither on the vine, rapidly going extinct. If they are to survive, unions must sit down and talk with the environmental movement and attempt to find common ground. This needs to happen now, at every level—local, regional, and especially state.

At the same time, environmentalists should stop grouping unions and union workers with the polluters and their whores in government. In 2019, a number of unions—the Association of Flight Attendants (AFA), the United Electrical, Radio and Machine Workers Union (UE), the Service Employees International Union (SEIU), a host of state federations, and others have come out strongly in favor of a Green New Deal, forming coalitions with environmentalists across the country. With extreme weather and the resulting turbulence and chaos grounding more and more flights and making air travel ever more dangerous, Sara Nelson, head of the fifty-thousand-strong AFA, explained that for her industry "it's not the solutions to climate change that kill jobs. Climate change itself is the job killer."[8]

At their August 2019 convention in Pittsburgh, the UE became the first national industrial union to endorse the Green New Deal concept, in a major resolution that read:

> Millions of workers could be employed strengthening our infrastructure, rebuilding our rail and transit systems, converting to renewable energy sources, protecting against the effects of rising temperatures, and in many other areas. . . . Like the transformation of our manufacturing infrastructure and economy that took place during World War II, a just and successful transition . . . will require massive infusion of federal and state resources, coordination between government, industry and labor, and democratic participation of workers through widespread unionization.[9]

Most union leaders, including the AFL-CIO head honchos, know we have a climate crisis and something needs to get done about it. To quote AFL-CIO leader Rich Trumka at the 2018 Global Climate Action summit:

> I learned something about science in the [coal] mine. When the boss told us to ignore the deadly hazards of the job . . . that

sagging timber over our heads . . . that Black Lung cough . . . science told us the truth. And today, again, science tells us the truth: climate change threatens our workers, our jobs and our economy.

He then asked one question: "Does your plan for fighting climate change ask more from sick, retired coal miners than it does for you and your family? If it does, then you need to think again."[10] On this point, he is correct.

Environmentalists at every level need to fight to make sure *every worker*—whether a coal miner, a construction worker, or an industrial worker—who loses his or her job to a reduction in fossil fuel use is directly retrained and placed at a job of equal pay with equal benefits. Environmental activists should be on the front lines with retired coal miners protecting their pensions and disability funds. Not to do so is to condemn these industrial workers to wallow in a slow, grinding existence of uncertainty, poverty, sickness, and early death. Jobs in the renewable energy sector are growing at a rapid pace, leaving jobs in the fossil fuel sector in the lurch. Environmental activists should fight for these jobs and demand that they are unionized, with a living wage and decent benefits. These jobs should not only be guaranteed to current union members but to those sectors of the workforce—women, minorities, and the poor—who have routinely been excluded, left at the bottom of the minimum wage dung heap. Any Green New Deal should ensure the principles elaborated here. To not do so will result in the abandonment of an entire class of workers, pushing them economically further toward the bottom and politically into the camp of the hundred million who don't vote and don't participate in any way, shape, or form in our political system—or, even worse, into the camp of shysters, bringing us more Donald Trumps in the future, because, as one iron ore worker said during the 2016 presidential campaign: "False hope is better than no hope."

The same is true for the issue of universal health care. There is a sizable portion of the U.S. population, in fact an overwhelming majority, who support single-payer Medicare for all. With a flat tax rate similar to the ones we already pay for social security and Medicare, soaring premiums, copays, and deductibles would become a thing of the past and save families thousands of dollars annually. Pitting "employment-based" health insurance against Medicare for all creates another false dichotomy. The majority of workers today are transient, constantly moving to new jobs in new locations. While many national, as well as local, labor unions have endorsed and support universal affordable health care, the union movement as a whole should be at the forefront of this effort, coalescing with health care activists across the country. Soaring health care costs are front and center in every labor contract negotiation, as management and corporations attempt to pass this mounting cost on to their workers. How will our health care system measure up to the rest of the world, if every other country on the planet subsidizes their workers' health care? A number of single-payer Medicare for all bills have been introduced in various states. Senator Bernie Sanders has introduced such bills in Congress. Not one penny should go to any politician who does not support these bills. Of course, none of this will happen without a strong grassroots coalition and a political revolution, as Senator Sanders has reiterated over and over.

There is commonality in all movements out there—be it Black Lives Matter, the #MeToo women's movement, health care, immigration rights, worker rights, the environmental movement, or the movements against the many unjust wars our government is waging. Everyone needs a decent job, reasonable benefits, a democratic voice, a healthy environment, equal treatment, dignity, and a peaceful life. Until organized labor joins in a sustained coalition with these movements as one voice, as well as with *our* elected representatives, we will remain isolated, picked off one by one. Imagine the political clout we would have if we were united around one platform and only backed or ran candidates who supported that platform! That is exactly what the right wing of the Republican Party has done so successfully. Our system has become totally corrupt, infested with corporate money and lobbyists. Both political parties at the top have been bought. It's past time for a new system and an independent political movement.

I advocate class struggle, because the ruling class of 1% billionaires who own and control the means of production and the technology has been waging war on workers and the poor since day one. This is what they did to us at Homestead, and it continues to this day. Workers continue to be exploited, abandoned, and treated like a serf class by the powers that be. Outside of technology and greater displacement not much has changed in the past century. The disparity in wealth has only continued to get worse—much, much worse. The claims of "historically low unemployment" and massive job creation ring hollow in most workers' ears when they examine the overwhelming percentage of low-paying retail and food industry jobs being created, or when they consider that millions of workers have to work two or three jobs to make what they used to earn working one. And that's not even counting the millions working off the books and under the table!

The Lessons of Homestead

As for the 1397 Rank and File Caucus union experiment and our inability to stop the eventual shutdown of the mill, I'm sure there are workers, including even some of its most active members, who thought the rank-and-file insurgency was ultimately a failure. Some probably think that if it wasn't for the militants and Ron Weisen, parts of the plant would still be operating today. From a narrow, self-serving point of view, maybe a few departments and several hundred workers would still be working—that is, if we had caved in and sacrificed the rest of the thousands of workers and given up the fight for the benefits and back pay they were owed. But then maybe Edgar Thomson would have never reopened. It would have been a wash and slaughter either way. In the Mon Valley alone, over twenty-seven thousand U.S. Steel employees lost their jobs between 1979 and 1986. The Company relentlessly poured capital into facilities overseas and downsized their steel operations at home, while divesting into other more profitable businesses like oil and real estate. No number of concessions would have changed this reality. It would have taken a nationwide workers' revolution, a general strike, and a federally funded industrial policy to reverse this globalization process.

For a short period, the rank-and-file movement at Homestead was an experiment in democracy like nothing I've seen or read about anywhere else. The takeover and restructuring of the grievance procedure by a few high school graduates who put it at the service of thousands of members was unparalleled anywhere in the union. The *1397 Rank and File* newspaper was the ultimate expression of truth, democracy, and free speech. Every member had a voice, if he or she chose to use it. Art, culture, union politics, muckraking journalism, and a free press became a powerful weapon in the hands of ordinary workers. The fact that it only lasted eight years is beside the point; it should serve as a template for future generations of workers, union- ized or not. Bureaucracies and structures are not the union, or any organization, for that matter. The *members* are the union. The union is only as powerful as the sum of all its workers speaking with one voice.

Pertaining to my working and political life, nothing felt more fulfilling and satisfying than the time I spent as organizer, griever, and journalist at Local 1397. The solidarity I felt, especially during the 1978–1982 period, is probably only matched by that of soldiers together in a foxhole in the heat of a bloody war. The fact that we were up against insurmountable odds didn't dampen my spirits one iota. Put in a work scenario and union situation where your lives literally depended on each other, the spirit of oneness and solidarity (i.e., love) was like superglue. Many of the workers I met and befriended were truly the salt of the earth. These brothers and sisters would give you the shirts off their backs. Their dedication and hard work on behalf of the union should be recognized and remembered by history. Rank- and-file activists like Ronnie Pristas, Kathy Kozachenko, Moureen Trout, Betty Esper, Paul Mervis, John Pressley and Carolyn Grinage Pressley, Carol Belluci, Lynn Morton, Mary Hirko, Kenny Bergert, Rick Koza, Kay Bolton, Ralph Budd, Bob Collins, Warren Rudolph, John Burkhardt, Gary Kasper, Denny Eskin, Doug Coggin, Joe Diaz, Mike Wargo, Cal Schuchman, Jimmy Thorhauer, Artie Leibowitz, Joe Nestico, Jay Weinberg, Jerry Laychak, Chuck McCann, Chuck Deardorf, Chuck Brantner, Bill Hanchey, Jimmy Kraus, and Ron Volpe—all friends long after the mill shut down—at one time or another all stuck their necks out for their fellow workers.

While leaders like Ron Weisen and his activities were well docu- mented in newspapers and books, many of the local union officers that made up the Rank and File Caucus remained true to the rank-and-file mission and the membership to the end. My experience was only one piece of this fascinating puzzle of history. I'm sure each of these activ- ists and workers had his or her own story to tell. For the most part, they did their jobs selflessly, always in the background and out of the lime- light. Their union positions never went to their heads, but remained in their hearts. This list included Frank Domagala , John Pressley, John O'Toole, Gregg Mowry, John and Darlene Deffenbaugh, Eddie Piskor, Paul Tague, Bill Evans, Bill Moutz, George Hunter, Ron Lee, Ed Hamlin,

Ed Salaj, Tom Jugan, Jim Kooser, Sam Spence, Jack Bair, Davie Horgan, Terry Bernh, Tommy Farren, Ron Funk, Don McKinney, Cheryl (Bacco) McGartland, John Ingersoll, Frankie Boyle, Brian "Red" Durkin, John Sinchak, and the host of other assistance grievance representatives whose names I've forgotten, and the women mentioned earlier who made up the women's, unemployed, and food bank committees. Nobody fought harder for veterans than Vietnam veteran Joe Nestico. Their contributions need to be given their rightful place in Homestead history.

Michele McMills, c. 1980.

In particular, there's not enough space for the accolades and due that should be given to Michele McMills. A young woman in a rough and tumble steel man's world, she was the spark that lit the prairie fire, the genius and the brains, the strategist and tactician without whom the rank-and-file movement would have never happened. It was her heart and lungs that exhaled the breath of democracy into the local union with her raucous and irreverent rank-and-file newspaper— the greatest expression of true democracy I've ever witnessed or read about. While her leadership and activism only lasted a short five years, in my book she is up there with Fannie Sellins, Mother Jones, and the other brave women memorialized in labor history.

Most of these workers and union officers, even at the height of tensions between Ronnie and me, never took sides but stayed true to the union. One of these guys, Frank Domagala, exemplified the type of activist and friend that comes along once in a lifetime. Frank was Ronnie's main lieutenant in the local. He stood with Ronnie every day, from the very beginning through all the Denominational Mission Strategy (DMS) church stuff and beyond the mill closing. At different stages of the internal squabbling, Frank must have heard despicable things about me, especially from the DMS when Ronnie and I had our falling out. Yet he never took sides. He stayed both Ronnie's friend *and* my friend thirty years after the mill shutdown. When Frank Domagala died, succumbing to cancer in 2013, I wrote and recorded the following song to commemorate him and all those like him:

Frankie Domagala

Frankie was a leader of the rank and file, down at the Homestead mill.
With a heart of gold, a spirit bold, he rolled that stainless steel.
Voice for the ones who could not speak, champ for the underdog;
Fighter, drinker, working-class thinker, trying to right what's wrong.
A union soldier in a holy war to save our manufacturing base;
Back in the years when good jobs were here, heroes had their place.
He believed in a democratic union, for the members he took a stand,
Against the powers that be, in solidarity with the working woman
   and man.

With Ronnie, and Johnny, Tommy, Michele, Jack, Dave, the rest of
   the gang,
Turned our local around, upside down; the bells of freedom rang.
Though ego and power stole the hour, showers of shutdowns rained,
Frankie still shined, on the front lines, fightin' all the way to the end.
When the movement split, some tried to force me to quit, Frankie
   refused to take sides.
At every bend, he stayed my friend; this memory will never die.
Just like we were true blood brothers we had each other's backs.
Three decades later, our friendship greater, this bond did never crack.

One day the paper came, I saw Frankie's name, buried on the obit
   page.
Another cancer victim, the big "C" kicked him at way too young an
   age.
In the funeral den, with his family and friends, I told them about the
   days;
In the labor wars, on the shop floors, his love and his passion raged.
Among the ranks, taking on the big banks, Frankie Domagala stood;
Up against the clowns who tore the mills down, giving it all he could.
He believed in democracy and justice; courage ran through his veins.
Like the others who fought, that history forgot, I'll make sure they
   remember his name.

Frankie was a leader of the rank and file, down at the Homestead mill.
He had a heart of gold, a hero's soul, a spirit that will never cease.
He had a heart of gold, a hero's soul, may his body rest in peace.

After sending the song to his family, I received a phone call from his widow Bonnie, who told me that every year on the anniversary of his death, she will drive to his gravesite, play the CD on her car stereo, cranking it as loud as she can for Frank to hear.

The Aftermath

Much study, analysis, writing, and storytelling has been done through the decades concerning the great Homestead Strike of 1892, a momentous event that shaped labor history and union struggles for years to come. Outside of William Serrin's book, *Homestead—Glory and Tragedy of an American Steel Town*,[11] next to nothing has been written about the end of the Homestead mill, in particular the rank-and-file movement for democracy in the late 1970s and 1980s and what it represented—its radical use of the legal system/grievance procedure to both involve and defend workers' rights; its inside-outside strategies and efforts to address the bigger problems confronting the entire steel industry and our country; its openness to the wider movement for social and economic justice; its radical newspaper that encouraged and allowed maximum participation by ordinary workers down to the lowest job class. For me, *1892 and 1982 are part of a whole*, two points on the same pole of resistance and spirit of solidarity that sprung up, thrived, and was eventually suffocated at the great Homestead steel mill. While the union candle was temporarily snuffed in 1892, for more than forty years, it never died. Just take a good look around at the new activists and leaders that have sprung up, whether in the steel industry or elsewhere. Leaders like Rosemary Bezy, vice president of Local 1557 at the U.S. Steel Clairton Works, or Sara Nelson, president of the Association of Flight Attendants-CWA. Like flowers at springtime, they continue to sprout, grow, and beautify life in a dirty, dangerous, hardworking setting. The only way the union flame could be permanently extinguished at Homestead was by pulling the floor out from underneath us, shutting down the whole thing, and erasing our important historical contributions. My hope and prayer are that millennial workers and union activists will hear about this early history and continue the fight for justice, equality, and democracy.

In the summer of 1992, in an angry dither when every Homestead steelworker was excluded by the International Union during the hundredth anniversary of the historic Homestead Strike of 1892, I penned another song that summed up the last decade, my experience at Homestead, and its historical importance for the labor, cultural, and social justice movements that blossomed in the late 1960s through the 1980s:

When the Heyday Was Here

In the twilight of a moment, in a neon time gone,
When fire sparks were stars, smoke and dust were the dawn;
When the streets were clogged with people and the jobs were plenty.
Reckless and abandoned, we were standin' brave and tall,
Mesmerized by the lies that said we'd never fall,
And that our plates and expectations would never be empty.

Outside the iron walls of the pewter citadel,
Marching through the halls, our hearts and ranks would swell,
As we sang about ideas we thought would always be spoken.
Standing like a trump card in a game as real as life;
Running with the vanguard who thought they'd never die,
And that the spirit and the oneness of our circle could never be broken.

And the tribes came together back then,
When the bottom rose up to the brim,
And the way forward was so crystal clear. . .

They can never take back what we had,
All the struggles, the good and the bad,
All the troubles, the happy, the sad—
When the heyday was here.

You talk about gangs, we really had one.
We flew every color there was under the sun.
When one of us was messed with, the others were right by their side.
Our voices and our visions cracked the silence of deceit.

Our pens broke traditions so the powerless could speak,
Unholy truths and views that for so long had to run away and hide.

And though time shattered our dream,
And the pendulum did certainly swing,
Back to before the red skies appeared. . .

They can never take back what we gave,
Or cover up the roads that we paved,
Or bury the history we made—
When the heyday was here.

We were feeling our oats, rocking their boats,
Shaking the foundations unheard.
And after every battle, we'd party and laugh,
Drinkin' and smokin' at the bash.
Our comradery was more than just words.

You know some say it was a waste of time, that we barely made a dent;
That we lost the wars when they closed the doors; we were so naive
      and innocent;
That the wheels of age had simply turned the page once again.
But as I stare out at the ashes of the ruins of the past,
Back through the clashes before the die was cast,
When democracy from below, was more than just a means to an end.
And though power eluded our reach, when the floor was pulled way
      underneath.
Our pictures might be buried for years. . .

They can never retract what we meant.
They can never hide the places we went,
Or smother the message we sent—
When the heyday was here.

At the Service Employees International Union (SEIU) Convention
in April 2000, my rock band, The Human Union, opened for Earth
Wind and Fire at the since torn down Civic Arena, in the Hill District
end of downtown Pittsburgh. After our performance, in between

acts, then USW president George Becker gave a hellfire and brimstone speech railing against globalization and the recent bankruptcy of Bethlehem, National, LTV, and other major steelworks, resulting in the loss of tens of thousands of jobs. As my wife Stephanie and I relaxed five or six rows up in seats adjacent to the stage, Becker and then USW Communications Department director Marco Trbovich walked by. Spotting us in the stands, Becker yelled at us, waving his speech notes: "You guys at 1397 were right; we should have been fighting these bastards all along!"

Four years later, in September 2004, I lay in a recovery bed at Mercy Hospital in Pittsburgh, anesthetized from yet another of my many kidney stone attacks and operations over the years. A hospital orderly came over to my bed. He stared at me with a shit-eating grin on his face. My mind was in an anesthetic drug fog. I knew the face but couldn't remember his name. It was Bill Matthews, a former scarfer who worked in the slab yard. He had lost his job in 1984. As I faded into unconsciousness, I heard him whisper, "Hey, Mike, we sure could use a 1397 *Rank and File* newspaper around here."

AFTERWORD

by Staughton Lynd

This book should be read by activists in workplace situations all over the United States, not just as a stirring story but as a manual in response to the question: What is to be done?

In the late 1970s, at about the same time that Mike Stout moved from New York City to the Pittsburgh area and went to work at U.S. Steel's Homestead Works, my wife Alice and I moved from Chicago to Youngstown, Ohio. Shortly before Christmas 1979, U.S. Steel announced the closing of all its Youngstown facilities. I became lead counsel on behalf of sixty-five individual steelworkers, six local unions, a coalition of local churches, a Pittsburgh-based organization called the Tri-State Conference on Steel (TSCS), and our Republican congressman, in a lawsuit seeking to take the U.S. Steel complex into "worker-community ownership." After a spirited legal battle, we failed.

In this remarkable account of the tragedy at Homestead, Mike describes a parallel process. Whereas the corporation closed all its Youngstown area facilities simultaneously, in Homestead, U.S. Steel shut down one division at a time throughout the first half of the 1980s. Fundamentally, though, the following generalizations appear to apply to both places.

1. The main obstacle to worker or worker-community ownership and operation was the huge amount of capital required.

During World War II, Allied bombers destroyed German and Japanese steel mills. After the war, steel companies in those countries built new mills with electric or basic oxygen furnaces (BOF). U.S. Steel, however, continued to use its obsolete open-hearth furnaces in both Youngstown and Homestead up until their closings. The corporation's strategy of seeking to invest in new areas that were more profitable than steel climaxed in November 1981, when the Company used a painfully accumulated war chest of 6.3 billion dollars in cash and credit not to modernize its steel mills but to buy the Marathon Oil Company.

For us in Youngstown, or Mike and his colleagues in Homestead, to have purchased any of the mills without modernizing them would have meant having to shut them down again in short order, because competitors could make steel more cheaply. U.S. Steel's Youngstown operation was not as large as the Homestead Works, but we estimated that acquisition of the land, buildings, and machinery would cost about twenty million dollars, while the cost of a technologically up-to-date "hot end" (furnaces and caster) would be about two hundred million dollars. Only the federal government could have provided funding on that scale and, as Mike indicates, the Carter administration decided against it.

2. The Homestead struggle demonstrated that imaginative and aggressive use of contract language can result in substantial monetary compensation for workers who are displaced.
After his uncontested election to the positions of zone grievanceman and grievance chairman for Local 1397, Mike Stout managed to win hundreds of thousands of dollars for local union members who were put out of work, as well as hundreds of early retirement pensions, worth millions of dollars. He did so by combining two tools. First, Section 2-B of the Basic Steel Contract provided that local practices and agreements, even oral agreements, could be enforced. Second, and this is unlikely to exist in most workplaces, the national union agreed to let Mike and fellow griever John O'Toole decide whether to take a grievance to arbitration and, if the answer was yes, to present the grievance at the hearing with workers from the affected section of the mill in attendance.

Mike writes that "the key to winning cases was the employees, the members themselves." What this means will differ in specific situations, but certain practices can be generally recommended. "A grievant should have the opportunity to be present at every 'step' at which his or her grievance is discussed." "Don't work overtime while people in your department are laid off." One area that calls for creativity is

Aerial view of Homestead.

obtaining documents to suggest or back up witness testimony. In our Youngstown case, the court ordered U.S. Steel to continue operations until the court ordered otherwise. The corporation's high-priced lawyer declared that U.S. Steel did not have the raw materials on hand in Youngstown to comply. Somehow, by the next morning, I was able to put in the hands of the judge a document showing that substantial amounts of the necessary materials were readily available on site. "Where did you get that?" opposing counsel demanded angrily. I turned to the worker at my side who, with sober demeanor and a straight face, answered, "It fell off a truck."

We have all had frustrating disappointments with the courts and the National Labor Relations Board (NLRB). But let's not forget Section 7 of the Labor Management Relations Act (the new name for the old National Labor Relations Act) that protects concerted action for mutual aid or protection.

3. The spirit of solidarity so abundantly displayed in Local 1397's struggle is what the rank-and-file labor movement—as well as the broader movement to change the larger society—is all about.
Over and over Mike comes back to this in a variety of ways.

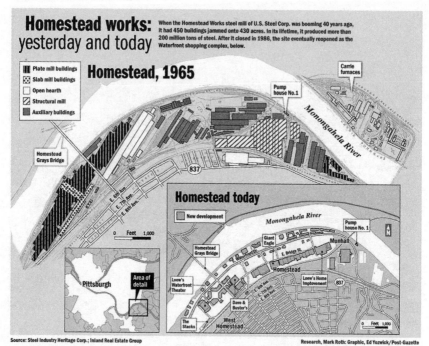

Homestead works: yesterday and today

When the Homestead Works steel mill of U.S. Steel Corp. was booming 40 years ago, it had 450 buildings jammed onto 430 acres. In its lifetime, it produced more than 200 million tons of steel. After it closed in 1986, the site eventually reopened as the Waterfront shopping complex, below.

Homestead, 1965

- Plate mill buildings
- Slab mill buildings
- Open hearth
- Structural mill
- Auxiliary buildings

Carrie furnaces

Pump house No.1

Monongahela River

Homestead Grays Bridge

837

0 Feet 1,000

Homestead today

New development

Monongahela River

Pump house No. 1

Homestead Grays Bridge

Giant Eagle

Munhall

E. Bridge St.

Homestead

Pittsburgh

Area of detail

Loew's Waterfront Theater

Loew's Home Improvement

837

Dave & Buster's

The Stacks

West Homestead

0 Feet 1,000

Source: Steel Industry Heritage Corp.; Inland Real Estate Group

Research, Mark Roth; Graphic, Ed Yozwick/Post-Gazette

Homestead yesterday and today. © *Pittsburgh Post-Gazette*, 2019, all rights reserved. Reprinted with permission.

The activists who took over Local 1397 wanted to "set an example for other unions." Obnoxious as was the conduct of many supervisors, and notwithstanding the merciless character of the illustrations in the *1397 Rank and File* newspaper displayed throughout this book, the attitude nurtured by Mike and his friends was to hate the war but not the warriors. The United Steelworkers of America (USWA), top down from its inception and initially staffed by men like Philip Murray, imported from the United Mine Workers (UMW), was to be resisted when it sought to meddle with actions or internal affairs of its local unions but not unnecessarily caricatured.

For Mike, as for myself, certain individuals whom we came to know in the context of their union activity offer the best way to explain what we mean by "solidarity." In Youngstown, there was Ed Mann. Grievance committeeman for many years, then three times elected as president of Local 1462 at LTV's Brier Hill Works, Ed was at the opposite extreme from candidates for union office who show up only at election time and who, once elected to an office that takes them out of the mill, do everything they can to avoid going back inside.

One of Ed's finest hours came on January 28, 1980, when he got up in front of a hall crowded with members of the U.S. Steel local in Youngstown. Those present had been listening for a couple of hours to politicians who had nothing concrete to suggest. Ed referred to the U.S. Steel administration building at the foot of the hill, saying, "Now, I'm going down that hill and I'm going into that building." An occupation of the Company's Youngstown headquarters followed.

On another occasion Ed came to work and found that a well-regarded fellow worker who was only a few days from retirement had been crushed to death by a truck backing up without adequate warning signals. Ed got up on a bench in the washroom and asked whether those present intended to go to work. A several-day wildcat strike followed, resolved only when the Company agreed to a number of safety measures.

Reflecting on these experiences, Ed concluded that you cannot be an organizer who leaves town the day after the vote on union affiliation, win or lose. You have to accompany your fellow workers; you have to be present. "Who knows what is going to make the workers say, 'This is enough'? But the point is—somebody has got to be there."

Mike Stout, a singer/songwriter and an activist, caught the spirit of Ed's remarks in some lines from a song that he wrote about the same time he was completing this book.

> I don't want to teach or preach to you;
> Lecture, conjecture, give a speech to you.
> I only want to reach out, stand next to you—
> Won't you let me accompany you?

ACKNOWLEDGMENTS

I owe a debt of gratitude to many people for their assistance in telling this story and writing this book. First and foremost are the dozens of rank-and-file activists and friends at Homestead's Local 1397. Not only was their dedication to democratic unionism a major source of inspiration, but without their friendship and assistance I would have never been able to accomplish what little I did. Many of these workers have long passed away, succumbing to cancer, heart disease, or other ailments. It is certain that working in the mill in such a stressful environment contributed to their deaths. Others, I have simply lost touch with through the passage of time. Special thanks start with Ron Weisen, John O'Toole, and Michele McMills. Without their courage and foresight, I would have never been a grievance representative or been involved with the newspaper. For those like Ronnie and Michele, who have passed on, my deepest sympathy and heartfelt gratitude goes out to their families.

So many coworkers I befriended in the mill helped to organize the Rank and File Caucus, grievances, the food bank, and other activities that they are almost too numerous to list. Most, I have already mentioned in my concluding chapter. Among the Local 1397 officers, several are worth singling out: Tom Jugan was one of the hardest workers I ever met and Dave Horgan and Ron Funk the most diligent. Jim Kooser, Joe Nestico, Paul Mervis, and Frank Domagala stood by me at several critical junctures when I was being physically threatened. John Deffenbaugh, Gregg Mowry, and Tom Farren selflessly stood with me through some very tough and tense situations, especially fighting grievances during the final days of the shutdown without pay. Mark Kenezovich, Paul Michele, Twiggy, George Tallon, Eric Greb, John Ingersoll, Jack Bair, Elmer DelleDonne, John Sincak, Don McKinney, Joe Stanton, Ron Mamula, Ray Gerst Jr., and so many others put their heart and soul into breathing democracy into our local union.

Thanks to the many grievance representatives, their assistants, and fellow workers who waged a valiant uphill battle on behalf of their constituents and coworkers, including Billy Barron, Warren Rudolph, John Burkhardt, Ralph Budd, Bob Collins, Rick Koza, George Hunter, Ron Lee, O.B. Horn, Denny Esken, Gary Kasper, Sam Spence, Terry Bernh, Bill Evans, Bill Moutz, Eddie Piskor, Frankie Boyle, and Red Durkin—and, of course, our two secretaries Cheryl Bacco McGartland and Darlene McIntosh Deffenbaugh, two of the hardest working and most devoted union women I ever met.

My gratitude to the dozens of workers who helped get the unemployed committee, food bank, and benefit concerts off the ground, as well as taking numerous bus trips to Harrisburg and Washington, DC, to extend unemployment compensation (UC) and secure the Trade Readjustment Allowance (TRA): Lynn Morton, Ronnie Pristas, Mike, Mari, and Candy Wargo, Kena Diggins, Jay Weinberg, Jerry Laychak, Artie Leibowitz, Steve Minnaji, Moureen Trout, Sue Harakal, Barb Weibelt, Kathy Kozachenko, Carolyn Grinage Pressley, Jim Thorhauer, Cal Schuchman, Paul Mervis, O.J. Simpson, Dale Wharton, and the countless others whose names I cannot remember. I've always had a near photographic memory for numbers, times, and dates. Having represented and worked with thousands of workers, remembering names and faces has not been one of my strong suits.

A special thank you to the many steelworkers and friends who went above and beyond helping with my ill-fated run for the state legislature: Ronnie Pristas, Jay Weinberg, Rich Majorsky, Ed Salaj, Walt Lippay, Eddie Piskor, Tom McKight, Apples McIntosh, Ed Lutheran, Ralph Budd, LTV Steel's Bill Sulanowski and John Gross, Jim and Martha Kraus, Ken Regal, Kenny Bergert, Judy Ruszkowski, Karen Krop, Rege Moskiewski, Homestead mayor and good friend Betty Esper.

There are a number of folks outside the mill to whom I owe a special debt of gratitude. My good friend Charlie McCollester was a longtime supporter of the Homestead rank and file and co-initiator and co-organizer of the reconstituted Pittsburgh-based Tri-State

Conference on Steel (TSCS), which waged a valiant fight to save and revitalize some of our manufacturing base. The early oral history interviews with me that he directed grad students to conduct when he was a professor at the Indiana University of Pittsburgh were a big help in jarring my memory and helping me to recount these events. Without his prodding and constant encouragement, this book would never have gotten off the ground.

Staughton and Alice Lynd's valiant efforts during the Youngstown shutdown fight were a major source of inspiration. As with Charlie, without their friendship, support, and encouragement, this book would never have happened. Their belief in the rank-and-file workers, democracy, and the struggle for a more just and peaceful world have always been my spiritual guidance. There wasn't too much I said, did, or thought these past forty years that didn't get bounced off them. They taught me how to be a long-distance runner in the race for a better life.

My good friends Barney Oursler, Paul Lodico, and John Stember worked with me to get UC extensions and TRA for hundreds of our members. These benefits were the difference between floating or sinking when the mill closed, and workers were making a difficult transition to another life.

My gratitude to the hardworking crew and friends in the TSCS— Father Gary Dorsey, Father Rich Zelik, Judy Ruszkowski, Anne Marie Draham, Jim Benn, Jim Dolson, Bob Erickson, Pierre and Melinda Whalon, Carrie Leana, Nora Johnson, Russ Gibbons, Billy Eakin, and many others—who waged a valiant fight to save our mills and some semblance of our manufacturing base. Their dreams were my dreams.

My appreciation to Brett Reigh, Indiana University of Pittsburgh graduate from the class of 1997. His master's thesis, "The Rank and File Movement at the Homestead Steelworks—USWA Local 1397 from 1977 to 1986," with all the research he put into it, is an excellent outline and guide to certain critical campaigns and junctures of the rank-and-file movement and history. He also conducted numerous oral history interviews with John Ingersoll, Michele McMills, Greg Klink, and Ed Salaj that provide unique written reminiscences about their experiences at Homestead.

The labor history and historical archives crew at Indiana University of Pennsylvania (IUP)—Irwin Marcus, Jim Dougherty, Anne Marie

Draham, and Rick Peduzzi—researched and assembled the best political history of the town of Homestead and the union movement and workers' struggle at the Homestead mill from after 1892 through the 1970s that I've run across anywhere. Their research document, as well as film footage, is safely stored at IUP's Special Collections and University Archives.

The Library crew at IUP, including Phil Zorich, Eileen Lovejoy, and Larry Kroh, had the courage and audacity to assist me in rescuing and preserving the Local 1397 papers and documents. Special thanks to the current library curator Harrison Wick, who oversaw the organizing, cataloging, and preservation of these valuable documents.

The incredible book *Homestead: Glory and Tragedy of an American Steel Town* by the late Bill Serrin (died February 15, 2018) is a historical gem. It is the best, most concise, and most readable history of the Homestead mill and town, as well as of the steel industry and the steelworkers' union. It is the only book with any account of the last decade of the mill and local union's existence. Bill spent five years away from home, living in a dingy one-room apartment above Buffington's Tavern on 8th Avenue, conducting interviews, doing research, and watching events unfold. Though, sadly, out of print, his book should be required reading for every history class at Steel Valley High School.

Charles Showalter at TUE Printing provided the space to work, scan photos, and copy drafts. Kallie Sheets assisted in conducting and transcribing oral history interviews. A special thanks to her sister Brittany Sheets for her design expertise and hard work putting the pieces together.

Former *Labor Notes* coeditor Martha Gruelle provided her valuable editing skills to help make this important piece of history come alive.

Environmental activists Patricia DeMarco, Joe Uehlein, and Matt Mehalik offered their insight and suggestions on the need for a labor-environmental coalition and what its platform should be.

Thanks to all of those who reviewed my book and added valuable historical insight about the events that unfolded in the Steel Valley during that tumultuous period, especially good friends Barney Oursler, John Stember, John Pressley, the UE's Al Hart, and Steffi Domike. Special thanks go to Munhall resident, former Clairton worker, and Steel Valley High School teacher Mark Fallon for his invaluable help in locating old photos in his archival treasure.

I owe a debt of gratitude to all my friends in the Battle of Homestead Foundation, too numerous to mention (you know who you are), for standing up for the preservation of our history.

To my son Mike, and my stepkids Richie, Shannon, and Kerry—it was your time that was sacrificed while I was off fighting these battles. Like a soldier in the heat of battle, I felt I had to do my duty, that I was put in the mill and the local union at that time for a reason. Thank you for your love and understanding.

Most important of all, the biggest thanks go to my wife Stephanie. These memoirs would not have been readable without her down to earth, working-class editing skills. Her patience, encouragement, and sacrifices have been my strength and impetus. Her love is the boat that gets me across the river every day.

NOTES

INTRODUCTION

1 Studs Terkel, *Working* (New York: Pantheon Books, 1974).

2 Louis Uchitelle, *The Disposable American: Layoffs and Their Consequences* (New York: Alfred A. Knopf, 2006).

PREFACE

1 The Industrial Workers of the World (IWW), or Wobblies, is an international labor union founded in 1905 in Chicago, Illinois. They believe that there should be "one big union," crossing craft and guild lines and including every worker down to the lowest paid. Defining their style and program as "radical unionism," they are anti-capitalist, believe that workers and bosses have nothing in common, and are advocates of shop floor work stoppages. I was a proud member of the IWW on several occasions during my working life. I'm a firm believer that if unions are to survive in the future, there needs to be "one big union."

2 MIT Sloan Institute for Work and Employment Research, MIT Sloan School of Management, September 2, 2018.

3 The Thomas Merton Center is a Pittsburgh-based nonprofit grassroots organization cofounded in 1972 by Molly Rush and Larry Kessler. Formed at the height of the Vietnam War and named after the Trappist monk Thomas Merton, its mission is to educate and raise awareness around the issues of war, poverty, workers' rights, racial and gender discrimination, and environmental protection. Still in existence a half century later, it has become a center of activity for numerous causes and organizations fighting for social and economic justice.

4 William Serrin, *Homestead: The Glory and Tragedy of an American Steel Town* (New York: Vintage Books, 1993).

5 Elizabeth Kolbert, *The Sixth Extinction: An Unnatural History* (New York: Henry Holt and Company, 2014); backed by scientific facts and analysis, Kolbert asserts that current human activity, especially its reliance and continued pursuance of fossil fuel extraction, will bring about the extinction of life on earth as we know it—including human life, and that this has happened on five previous occasions in the five-billion-year history of planet earth.

6 From its inception in 1937 until April 14, 2005, the Union was known as the United Steelworkers of America (USWA). On that day, the USWA merged with the "Paper,

Allied-Industrial, Chemical and Energy Workers" (PACE) to form the largest industrial union in North America, the United Steel, Paper and Forestry, Rubber, Manufacturing, Energy Allied-Industrial and Service Workers International Union (USW). With more than 850 thousand active members in over eight thousand bargaining units in the United States, Canada, and the Caribbean, "America" (which usually refers to the USA) was dropped from both its name and acronym.

CHAPTER 1

1   Richard Boyer and Herbert Morals, *Labor's Untold Story* (New York: Cameron Associates, 1955).
2   Philip S. Foner, *History of the Labor Movement in the United States*, vols. 1–10 (New York: International Publishers, 1947–1994).
3   William Serrin, *Homestead: The Glory and Tragedy of an American Steel Town* (New York: Vintage Books, 1993), 64–65.
4   Ibid., 86.

CHAPTER 2

1   The "pumphouse" is a building at the east end of the mill that housed the steam room. It sits on the site where the Pinkertons landed in 1892 and the great battle took place. Through the concerted efforts of former workers, union retirees, and several college professors who formed the Battle of Homestead Foundation, the building was bought by the Steel Industry Heritage Task Force (today called Rivers of Steel) and has been preserved and is used for lectures, film presentations, and other educational activities.

CHAPTER 3

1   William Serrin, *Homestead: The Glory and Tragedy of an American Steel Town* (New York: Vintage Books, 1993), 63.
2   Brett Reigh, "The Rank and File Movement at the Homestead Steelworks USWA Local 1397 from 1977–1986" (master's thesis, Indiana University of Pennsylvania, 1997), 1.
3   Charles McCollester, *The Point of Pittsburgh: Struggle and Production at the Forks of the Ohio* (Homestead, PA: Battle of Homestead Foundation, 2008), 138.
4   Serrin, *Homestead*, 86.
5   McCollester, *The Point of Pittsburgh*, 139.
6   Ibid., 146.
7   The *Paris Commune* was a short-lived workers' uprising in France in 1871, during which radical workers took control of the capital and set up a revolutionary socialist government that lasted two months, March 28–May 28, before being crushed by the French Army.

CHAPTER 4

1   "Ron Weisen interview," *1397 Rank and File*, September 1980. The *Working Men's Declaration of Independence* was written in 1829 by George H. Evans (1805–1856), this document appeared in New York City weekly the *Working Man's Advocate* and the Philadelphia union newspaper the *Mechanic's Free Press*. Evans helped found the Working Men's Party in New York City in 1829. He also published several labor newspapers, including the aforementioned *Working Man's Advocate*.
2   U.S. Steel, United Steelworkers of America (USWA), Basic Labor Agreement, March 1, 1983, page 10: "the term 'local working conditions' as used herein means

specific practices or customs, which reflect detailed application of the subject matter within the scope of wages, hours of work, or other conditions of employment and includes local agreements, written or oral, on such matters."

3   United Steelworkers of America Local Union 1397, Manuscript group 62, Indiana University of Pennsylvania, Special Collections and University Archives, Series B and C, Boxes 1–7.

CHAPTER 5

1   OH5, the last open-hearth furnaces at Homestead, had been built by the U.S. government during World War II. The open-hearth process was developed at the turn of the twentieth century. It took the pig iron produced at the blast furnaces and turned it into steel ingots, which were then rolled into slabs at the 45″ Slab Mill or blooms and billets at the Structural Mill.

2   Yippies were members of the Youth International Party, which was initiated by songwriter and activist Phil Ochs, along with radical activists Abbie Hoffman, Jerry Rubin, Paul Krassner, Stu Albert, Judy Gumbo, and others in the summer of 1968. It was an attempt to get "hippies" and young people politically active against the Vietnam War and its chief proponents in the government, including both the Democratic and Republican Parties.

3   Malcom X, with Alex Haley, *The Autobiography of Malcolm X* (New York: Random House Publishing Group, 1964).

4   For more on the Panther 21, see Sekou Odinga, Dhoruba Bin Wahad, and Jamal Joseph, *Look for Me in the Whirlwind: From the Panther 21 to the 21st Century*, ed. Matt Meyer (Oakland: PM Press, 2017).

5   "COINTELPRO" was short for Counter Intelligence Program, a covert operation initiated by FBI czar J. Edgar Hoover in the 1950s and 1960s. Initially it targeted the Communist Party USA and the Socialist Workers Party, then black activists and organizations, and later anti-war organizations, using infiltrators, undercover informants, and provocateurs. Often these provocateurs encouraged and engaged in violence and any number of illegal activities to disrupt, discredit, and neutralize these organizations and their movements. The secret program was brought to light during the (Senator Frank) Church Committee hearings in 1974–1975. See Ward Churchill and Jim VanderWall, *Agents of Repression: The FBI's Secret Wars Against the Black Panther Party and the American Indian Movement* (Boston: South End Press, 1990).

CHAPTER 6

1   "Mini-mills" began sprouting up all over the United States in the 1960s and 1970s. They were usually built in rural areas, especially down south, where jobs were scarce and unions nonexistent. They were much more cost-efficient than traditional integrated steel mills, as they were equipped with electric arc furnaces that used scrap steel and completely bypassed the blast furnace and open-hearth or basic oxygen furnace stages of production.

2   William Serrin, *Homestead: The Glory and Tragedy of an American Steel Town* (New York: Vintage Books, 1993), 323–24.

3   A more detailed explanation of the five-step grievance procedure can be found in both the 1980 and 1983 Basic Labor Contract, Section 6, 24–35.

4   Brett Reigh, "The Rank and File Movement at the Homestead Steelworks USWA Local 1397 from 1977–1986" (master's thesis, Indiana University of Pennsylvania, 1997), 3.

CHAPTER 7

1 William Serrin, *Homestead: The Glory and Tragedy of an American Steel Town* (New York: Vintage Books, 1993), 339.

2 John Ingersoll oral history interview with Brett Reigh, December 6, 1996.

3 "Lost time" is the term used when a union official takes time off from his mill job to work on behalf of the union. The union would pay the hourly rate of the worker's job class in the mill.

4 Michele McMills oral history interview with Brett Reigh, December 12, 1996.

5 "Special Convention Report", *1397 Rank and File*, Collection 62, IUP Library Special Collections, Indiana, Pennsylvania, Series J, Box 3, 1.

6 Edward Sadlowski died June 14, 2018, at the age of seventy-nine. Born September 10, 1938, he was a third-generation steelworker who dropped out of high school, and after a two-year stint in the army, at eighteen, he became an apprentice machinist in 1956. He rose through the ranks of the union from Local 65 president at the U.S. Steel South Works in Chicago at twenty-six to District 31 director of the Chicago-Gary area in 1973. A radical from his earliest days, he opposed the Vietnam War and Richard Daley, Chicago czar and mayor in the 1960s and 1970s, and carried with him throughout his union career the fiery rhetoric of his early heroes John L. Lewis and the UAW's Walter Reuther. Though he was defeated in is 1977 bid for USWA International president, his campaign shook the bureaucrats to their core, resulting in a resolution being passed outlawing any "outside" contributions for any union election.

7 "Special Convention Report", *1397 Rank and File*, Collection 62, IUP Library Special Collections, Indiana, Pennsylvania, Series J, Box 3, 1.

8 "Special Election Issue," *1397 Rank and File*, IUP Special Collections 62, Series J, Box 3.

9 "An Election Prediction," George Tallon, *1397 Rank and File*, April 1979, 1. Collection 62, IUP Library Special Collections, Indiana, Pennsylvania, Series J, Box 1.

10 Ed Salaj oral history interview with Brett Reigh, December 18, 1996.

11 "Special Election Issue," *1397 Rank and File*, IUP Special Collections 62, Series J, Box 3.

12 John Ingersoll oral history interview with Brett Reigh, December 6, 1996.

13 George Tallon article, *1397 Rank and File*, August 1978 Collection 62, IUP Library Special Collections, Indiana, Pennsylvania, Series J, Box 3.

14 "Special Election Issue," *1397 Rank and File*, IUP Special Collections 62, Series J, Box 3.

15 "Incentive pay" was salary on top of the regular job class rate of pay spelled out in the labor contract. Usually, a management "time study" person would define what the average rate of production or amount of steel produced was per hour or day, for each operation in the mill. If the crew exceeded that average, say at 125 percent, they were paid a bonus at 125 percent of their regular pay. For maintenance employees, it theoretically was the exact opposite: the quicker they did their jobs and the less mill "down time" there was, the higher their incentive pay.

16 "Incentive Rip-off—Eyewitness Report," *1397 Rank and File*, September 1977, 1, IUP Archives, Series J, Box 3.

17 "Central Maintenance Rips Off U.S. Steel for $385,000," *1397 Rank and File*, December 1977, IUP Archives, Series J, Box 3.

18 Ibid.

CHAPTER 8

1   Tom Jugan, "Ask Andy," *1397 Rank and File*, April 1978, IUP Special Collections 62
     Archives, Series J, Box 3.

2   John Ingersoll oral history interview with Brett Reigh, December 6, 1996.

CHAPTER 9

1   "Red-baiting" is a tactic used to discredit radicals, dissidents, or any other oppo-
     nent of the status quo by labeling them "communists." While there obviously
     were a few professed communists and socialists in the opposition ranks, the
     vast majority of workers smeared with this broad red-baiting brush were merely
     rank-and-file militants demanding democracy and a more representative fighting
     union.

2   Mike Stout, "Rank and File Opens Headquarters, Find a 'Temporary' New Home,"
     1397 Rank and File, 1, IUP Archives, Series J, Box 3.

3   Staughton Lynd, *Labor Law for the Rank and Filer: Building Solidarity While Staying
     Clear of the Law* (Oakland: PM Press, 2008 [1978]).

4   A thorough history and analysis of the Revolutionary Union (RU) and their
     attempted merger with other organizations in the 1973–1975 period, as well
     as their infiltration at the highest levels by the FBI, is best detailed in Aaron J.
     Leonard and Conor A. Gallagher, *Heavy Radicals: The FBI's Secret War on America's
     Maoists* (Alesford, UK: Zero Books, 2014).

5   George Tallon, "An Election Prediction," *1397 Rank and File*, April 1979, 1, IUP
     Archives, Series J, Box 3.

CHAPTER 10

1   The United States District Court for the Northern District of Alabama Southern
     Division: CONSENT DECREE 1, IUP Archives, Series G, Box 1.

2   Basic Labor Agreement between United States Steel Corporation and the United
     Steelworkers of America, Section M, Interplant Job Opportunities, 112–21, IUP
     Archives, Series K, Box 6.

3   Ellie Wymard, "Them Too—Women Who Toiled in Steel Mills Faced Their Own
     Harassers," *Pittsburgh Post-Gazette*, June 3, 2018, accessed December 9, 2019,
     https://www.post-gazette.com/opinion/Op-Ed/2018/06/03/The-Next-Page-
     Them-too-women-who-toiled-in-steel-mills-faced-their-own-harassers/stories/
     201806030013.

4   Ibid.

5   Randy Strohman, dir., *Women of Steel* (Pittsburgh: Mon Valley Media, 1984).

6   Ibid.

7   Michele McMills, "What is a Sentinal?" *Sentinel*, June 14, 1979, IUP Archives, Series
     J, Box 3.

8   Letter on file, IUP Archives, Series J, Box 3. Also reprinted in *1397 Rank and File*
     newspaper, December 1980, 16.

9   William Serrin, *Homestead: The Glory and Tragedy of an American Steel Town* (New
     York: Vintage Books, 1993), 358.

CHAPTER 11

1   Bobby Stevenson, "The Rank and File Candidates," *1397 Rank and File*, April 9, 1979,
     IUP Archives, Series J, Box 3.

2   "President's Message," *1397 Rank and File*, December 1979. IUP Archives, Series J,
     Box 3.

3   The phrase, "mill hunky" arose with the thousands of Slavic and Hungarian immi-
      grants who fled the Austro-Hungarian Empire to America en masse at the turn of
      the twentieth century, seeking opportunity and a better life. By the time I arrived
      in the late 1970s, it was used as a derogatory term and ethnic slur by management
      to describe any worker in the mill they considered less intelligent than themselves.
      The term was satirized and made popular as a "badge of honor" by former Edgar
      Thomson steelworker Larry Evans, with his raucous publication *The Mill Hunk
      Herald*, a regional magazine published from 1979 to 1989. It was a takeoff from
      the *1397 Rank and File* newspaper, replete with cartoons, poetry, songs, contro-
      versy, and humor. Larry died in a tragic car accident on November 15, 2014, at age
      sixty-seven.

CHAPTER 12

1   Holly Knaus and Nadav Savio, "USX: A Heart of Steel," *Multinational Monitor* 12,
      no. 4 (April 1991), accessed January 8, 2020, https://www.multinationalmonitor.
      org/hyper/issues/1991/04/knaus.html.
2   Staughton Lynd was the lead attorney for the valiant Youngstown community
      effort to save their mills. He was the lead lawyer for the Mahoning Valley coali-
      tion that took U.S. Steel to court in an attempt to stop the closing of the Ohio-
      McDonald Works, including deposing David Roderick at a hearing on March 17,
      1980. He was a staunch advocate for the voice of the rank and file and advocated
      the Industrial Workers of the World (IWW) motto: "An injury to one is an injury
      all." He was also instrumental in the formation of the Tri-State Conference on
      Steel (TSCS).
3   *Youngstown Vindicator*, January 27, 1980.
4   In the conflict between the U.S. and Iran in the aftermath of the Iranian Revolution,
      a group or Iranian students held fifty-two U.S. diplomats hostage in the U.S.
      embassy in Tehran for 444 days, from November 4, 1979 to January 20, 1981.

CHAPTER 13

1   The Trade Readjustment Allowance, known as TRA benefits, was negotiated in
      the 1974 Labor Agreement, when the right to strike was taken away. According to
      this provision, if workers at a particular mill or facility filed a petition with the
      federal government and could prove they lost their jobs as a direct result of foreign
      imports, they received an additional year of unemployment compensation (UC)
      benefits, as well as up to two years of paid schooling. UC benefits were extended
      for people who had lost their jobs by no fault of their own.
2   "Company, Government, International Union Gang Up on Unemployed
      Steelworkers," *1397 Rank and File*, December 1980, 14–15, IUP Archives, Series J,
      Box 3.

CHAPTER 15

1   John Ingersoll oral history interview with Brett Reigh, December 6, 1996.
2   A BOF is a "basic oxygen furnace."
3   *1397 Rank and File* Newspaper, December 1980, IUP Archives, Series J, Box 3.

CHAPTER 16

1   "Super-seniority" was a provision of the Basic Labor Agreement between the
      Company and union, covered under Section 13-I, 106–7. It allowed elected griev-
      ance representatives and the top five officers of the local to stay on the job no

matter how much seniority they had, as long as there was somebody else still working under their jurisdiction.

2   John O'Toole oral history interview with the author, October 2017.

3   Any employee discharged or fired by the Company would have their case expedited to the third step of the grievance procedure within five days under section 8-B of the Basic Labor Contract, 43–44.

4   Arbitration No. USS-17951, IUP Historical Archives, Special Collections MG 62, Series D, Box 10.

CHAPTER 17

1   William Serrin, *Homestead: The Glory and Tragedy of an American Steel Town* (New York: Vintage Books, 1993), 331.

2   Roderick letter to Allegheny County commissioners, *U.S. EPA Environmental News*, May 22, 1979.

3   Greg Klink and Ron Weisen press release concerning Homestead layoffs, Collection 62, IUP Special Collections, Indiana, Pennsylvania.

CHAPTER 18

1   Staughton Lynd, *The Fight Against Shutdowns—Youngstown's Steel Mill Closings* (San Pedro: Singlejack Books, 1982), 123–25.

2   Dave Marsh, *Born to Run: The Bruce Springsteen Story* (Garden City, NY: Dolphin Books, 1979).

CHAPTER 19

1   Job Protection Team document, April 1982, IUP Historical Archives, Special Collections MG 62, Series J, Box 2.

2   Brett Reigh, "The Rank and File Movement at the Homestead Steelworks USWA Local 1397 from 1977–1986" (master's thesis, Indiana University of Pennsylvania, 1997).

3   Gregg Mowry oral history interview with Brett Reigh, December 1996.

4   *1397 Rank and File, September 1982*, IUP Archives, Collection 62, Series J, Box 3.

5   Larry Adelman, Larry Daressa, and Bruce Schmeichen, dir., *The Business of America* (San Francisco: California Newsreel, 1984), accessed December 11, 2019, https://archive.org/details/thebusinessofamerica.

CHAPTER 20

1   Labor Notes is a pro-union media project established in 1979 and still active today, accessed December 18, 2019, labornotes.org.

CHAPTER 21

1   *Pittsburgh Post-Gazette*, December 26, 1982, IUP Special Collections, Indiana, Pennsylvania.

2   *Wall Street Journal*, February 13, 1985, IUP Special Collections, Indiana, Pennsylvania.

3   Ray Rogers was founder and director of New York City–based Corporate Campaigns, Inc. (CCI), which championed labor, human rights, and environmental causes. When Ray was hired to take up a labor dispute, he would take on the entire corporation, its policies, and its officers with a media blitz of internal dirt, along with direct actions, education, boycotts, etc. His unorthodox tactics resulted in a successful campaign to organize a union at J.P. Stevens in North

Carolina in 1980, which was the basis for the movie *Norma Rae*; Martin Ritt, *Norma Rae* (Los Angeles: 20th Century Fox, 1979).

4 Dale A. Hathaway, *Can Workers Have a Voice? The Politics of Deindustrialization in Pittsburgh* (University Park: Pennsylvania State University Press, 1993), 59.

5 Ibid., 53.

6 Ibid., 58.

7 McBride letter, Collection 62, IUP Special Collections, Indiana, Pennsylvania, Series I, Box 6.

8 Long after the Mesta Machine battle was over, the Borough of West Homestead signed on and joined the Steel Valley Authority, with Mayor Dindak's full support.

9 Network flyer, July 1983: Collection 62, IUP Special Collections, Indiana, Pennsylvania, Series I, Box 6.

10 *1397 Rank and File*, March 1984, IUP Special Collections Archives, Series J, Box 3.

11 Network flyer passed out at an August 1985 Local 1397 union meeting, Collection 62, IUP Special Collections, Indiana, Pennsylvania. Series I, Box 2.

12 *New York Times*, April 7, 1988, A25, quoted in Hathaway, *Can Workers Have a Voice?*

CHAPTER 22

1 Grievance No. 82–119, Collection 62, IUP Special Collections, Indiana, Pennsylvania, Series C, Box 9.

2 USS-8002, Collection 62, IUP Special Collections, Indiana, PA, Series D, Box 4.

3 Clarence Darrow was a famous American lawyer and member of the American Civil Liberties Union (ACLU) who fought numerous cases on behalf of workers and the downtrodden. His most famous case, the "Scopes Trial," was about a teacher in Dayton, Tennessee, teaching evolution in public schools. With his adversary, three-time presidential candidate William Jennings Bryan, the case garnered maximum publicity nationwide and opened the door to modern science being taught.

4 Arbitration No. USS-18587, Collection 62, IUP Special Collections, Indiana, Pennsylvania, Series C, Box 9, Series D, Box 10.

5 While Dick Natili was one of my major opponents in the mill, with confrontations often turning extremely hostile, in 2014, he brought his wife by my printshop and introduced her to me, saying, "I want you to meet the best union man I ever went up against; he really cared for his people." Before parting, I gave him a big hug, tears in both our eyes.

6 "Sub-pay" was a provision negotiated under the 1963 Labor Contract, which supplemented a laid-off worker's unemployment compensation (UC), bringing the total up to two-thirds of what they were making when working.

CHAPTER 23

1 Weekly statistic sheet samples, 1983–1986, Collection 62, IUP Special Collections, Indiana, Pennsylvania, Series K, Box 17–18.

2 USS-20871, Collection 62, IUP Special Collections, Indiana, Pennsylvania, Series D, Box 11.

3 Arbitration no. USS-21603, Collection 62, IUP Special Collections, Indiana, Pennsylvania, Series D, Box 12.

4 U.S. Steel labor contract administrator John McCluskey deposition, Collection 62, IUP Special Collections, Indiana, Pennsylvania, Series G, Box 1. The estimate of an average of 250 thousand dollars was based on an employee over a nineteen- or twenty-year period collecting roughly the equivalent of an unemployment check,

plus medical benefits until they turned sixty-five and became eligible for Social Security and a regular pension.

CHAPTER 24

1   "Message from Your President," *1397 Rank and File*, March 1984, 1.

2   Ron Weisen press release, December 6, 1983, Collection 62, IUP Special Collections, Indiana, Pennsylvania.

3   Daniel Helpingstine, "Supporters of Weisen Forming Caucus," *Hammond Times*, February 18, 1984.

4   USWA Rank and File Caucus Agenda flyer, IUP Special Collections, Indiana, Pennsylvania.

5   Ibid.

CHAPTER 25

1   Larry Adelman, Larry Daressa, and Bruce Schmeichen, dir., *The Business of America* (San Francisco: California Newsreel, 1984), accessed December 11, 2019, https://archive.org/details/thebusinessofamerica.

CHAPTER 26

1   "Boss" was the moniker given to Springsteen from his earliest concert days, because of his ability and endurance to perform shows for up to four hours, sometimes without a break.

CHAPTER 27

1   The Stern Foundation was started by philanthropist Irving Stern, in Chicago, in 1957, and was noted for providing grants and donations to progressive groups and causes, including Edward Sadlowski's campaign when he ran for the USWA presidency in 1976–1977. Our contact there was David Hunter out of New York City, who had heard of our Dorothy Six campaign and orchestrated the first major foundation funding of the Tri-State Conference on Steel effort.

2   Betty Esper was the most senior woman working at the Homestead steel mill. When she lost her job in November 1985, with the closing of the 160" mill, she had thirty-two years of service. In 1980, she was elected to Homestead borough council, and, in 1992, she was elected mayor, a position she still holds as of this writing. Since the early days of the plant shutdown struggle, through my run for state representative, she was a major supporter, ally to the steelworkers and her hometown, and personal friend.

3   Molly Rush was one of the founders of the Thomas Merton Center in 1972. A mother of six, she was arrested in 1980, along with seven others, for trespassing on a nuclear military base. Once there, they poured blood on and smashed the nose cone of a nuclear trident missile, while reading the biblical passage about "turning swords into ploughshares." Molly was also on the board of and very active in the Tri-State Conference on Steel efforts in the mid-1980s.

4   Martin Davidson, *Eddie and the Cruisers* (Los Angeles: Embassy Pictures, 1983).

5   James Rankin, "Benefit Concert Hit with 'Act-Friendly' Crowd," *McKeesport Daily News*, November 23, 1985.

6   Staughton Lynd and Alice Lynd, *The New Rank and File* (Ithaca, NY: ILR Press/Cornell University Press, 2000), 132–33.

CHAPTER 28

1   In September 1990, a federal district court judge in Birmingham, Alabama, found USWA District 36 director Thermon Phillips and assistant director E.B. Rich guilty of conspiring with the corporation to obtain lucrative pensions for themselves in exchange for negotiating a concessions contract in December 1983. Both were sent to jail.

CHAPTER 30

1   John Ingersoll oral history interview with Brett Reigh, December 6, 1996.

2   Bob Dylan and Jacques Levy, "Hurricane," *Desire* (New York: Columbia Records, 1976).

CHAPTER 32

1   The North American Free Trade Agreement (NAFTA) took effect January 1, 1994, creating a trade zone the encompassed the United States, Mexico, and Canada. As a result of this agreement, signed by then president Bill Clinton, more than two million manufacturing jobs were lost in the United States and more than two million Mexicans driven off their land and into poverty, resulting in a mass migration to the U.S. in search of work.

CHAPTER 33

1   See "Check et al. lawsuit," Collection 62, IUP Special Collections, Indiana, Pennsylvania, Series G, Box 1.

2   See "Valley Machine Shop lawsuit," Collection 62, IUP Special Collections, Indiana, Pennsylvania, Series G, Box 1.

3   For a complete documentation of this grievance, including all four arbitration hearings, as well as court transcripts, see "IJOP arbitration proceedings," Collection 62, IUP Special Collections, Indiana, Pennsylvania, Series G, Box 1.

4   For a detailed description of the Inter-Plant Job Opportunities provision in the contract, see "Agreement between United States Steel Corporation and the United Steelworkers of America," Section 13-M, 112–21.

5   Rich Locher's last days and suicide are recounted in William Serrin, *Homestead: The Glory and Tragedy of an American Steel Town* (New York: Vintage Books, 1993), 369–71, 398. After becoming grievance chair, I got to know Rich quite well, as he became one of the most militant and outspoken workers opposing the Company and the lack of government support for displaced steelworkers.

6   In the May 1988 Democratic Primary, at the urging of dozens of workers I ran for state representative for the 36th District, which included the Mon Valley and parts of south Pittsburgh. My eight opponents included Mike Terrick, brother of magistrate and Rich and Kevin Terrick's uncle. I lost by fifty-five votes to Chris McNally, son of a Pittsburgh fire chief.

7   Letter signed by Lou Kelley, union staff representative and assistant to the District director, IUP Archives, Collection 62, Series G, Box 1.

8   "IJOP Abitration Proceedings," Collection 62, IUP Special Collections, Indiana, Pennsylvania, Series G, Box 1.

9   Ibid.

CHAPTER 34

1   Andrew "Lefty" Palm deposition, Collection 62, IUP Special Collections, Indiana, Pennsylvania, Series G, Box 1.

CHAPTER 36

1   "Mike Stout—A Voter's Guide to the Real Story," Collection 62, IUP Special Collections, Indiana, Pennsylvania, Series L, Box 1.

CHAPTER 37

1   "Secretaries Law Suit, Severance Pay," Collection 62, IUP Special Collections, Indiana, Pennsylvania, Series G, Box 1.

CHAPTER 38

1   Staughton Lynd, *Labor Law for the Rank and Filer: Building Solidarity While Staying Clear of the Law* (Oakland: PM Press, 2008 [1978]).
2   Noam Scheiber, "United Workers without a Union," *New York Times*, October 19, 2019.
3   The Wagner Act of 1935, also known as the National Labor Relations Act, was enacted to protect workers from interference by industry in their involvement with unions. It also restricted the ways that employers could meddle with and react to labor practices in the private sector, including collective bargaining, labor unions, and striking.
4   Eamon Javers, "Inside Obama's Bank CEOs Meeting," *Huffpost*, April 5, 2009, accessed January 6, 2020, https://www.politico.com/story/2009/04/inside-obamas-bank-ceos-meeting-020871.
5   Kevin Zeese and Margaret Flowers, "Tenth Anniversary of Financial Collapse, Preparing for the Next Crash," *Popular Resistance Newsletter*, September 2, 2018, accessed January 6, 2019, https://www.unz.com/article/tenth-anniversary-of-financial-collapse-preparing-for-the-next-crash/.
6   Joe Uehlein, "Labor and Environmentalists Have Been Teaming Up Since the First Earth Day," Grist, April 22, 2010, accessed January 10, 2020, https://grist.org/article/2010-04-21-labor-and-environmentalists-have-been-teaming-up-since-the-first/full/.
7   "League of Conservative Voters Joins BlueGreen Alliance," BlueGreen Alliance, October 11, 2018, accessed January 10, 2020, https://www.bluegreenalliance.org/the-latest/league-of-conservation-voters-joins-bluegreen-alliance/.
8   Aviva Chomsky, "Unions vs. Environmentalists or Unions and Environmentalists?—Jobs, the Environment, and a Planet in Crisis," Vancouver Ecosocialists, August 7, 2018, accessed January 6, 2020, http://ecosocialistsvancouver.org/article/unions-vs-environmentalists-or-unions-and-environmentalists-jobs-environment-and-planet.
9   "A Green New Deal for People and the Planet," UE, September 2019, accessed January 6, 2020, https://www.ueunion.org/ue-policy/a-green-new-deal-for-people-and-the-planet.
10 Richard L. Trumka, "Trumka: Fight Climate Change the Right Way," AFL-CIO, September 13, 2018, accessed January 6, 2019, https://aflcio.org/speeches/trumka-fight-climate-change-right-way.
11 William Serrin, *Homestead: The Glory and Tragedy of an American Steel Town* (New York: Vintage Books, 1993).

INDEX

Page numbers in *italic* refer to illustrations. "Passim" (literally "scattered") indicates intermittent discussion of a topic over a cluster of pages.

ABOUT THE AUTHORS

Mike Stout

Mike Stout has been an anti-war, union, and community organizer for more than fifty years. Mike was also the last Local 1397 union grievance chair at the U.S. Steel Homestead Works. He is currently president of the Allegheny chapter of the Izaak Walton League, the oldest environmental conservation organization in the United States, as well as being a singer/songwriter and recording artist. With 18 CDs and more than 150 songs written and recorded, Mike has used his music to inspire the movements for social and economic justice and to raise tens of thousands of dollars for a host of organizations and causes.

JoAnn Wypijewski

JoAnn Wypijewski is a writer and editor based in New York City. Her work has appeared in numerous magazines, including *CounterPunch*, where she writes a monthly column, "Diamonds and Rust." Her latest book, with Kevin Alexander Gray and Jeffrey St. Clair, is *Killing Trayvons: An Anthology of American Violence* (CounterPunch 2014).

Charlie McCollester

Active in the civil rights and anti-war movements of the 1960s, McCollester earned a doctorate in philosophy in 1968 based on research in Paris and Jerusalem ("Emmanuel Levinas and Modern Jewish Thought") at the Catholic University of Louvain, Belgium. After teaching college in East Chicago, Indiana, with extensive travel in Africa (across the Sahara, then crossing the width of the continent from

Dakar to Dar-es-Salaam), he and his wife Linda arrived in Pittsburgh in 1973 and were blessed with five children. After working in restaurants (elected union steward HERE Local 57) and construction, he became a machinist at the Union Switch and Signal, where he was elected chief steward UE Local 610 (1982–1986). Working with Mike Stout and others, he helped organize the Tri-State Conference on Steel (TSCS) and the Steel Valley Authority (SVA) to resist plant shutdowns and community abandonment. Hired at Indiana University of Pennsylvania (IUP) (1986–2009), he became professor of Industrial Labor Relations and director of the Pennsylvania Center for the Study of Labor Relations. Former president of the Pennsylvania Labor History Society, he was a founder of the Battle of Homestead Foundation and is the author of *The Point of Pittsburgh: Production and Struggle at the Forks of the Ohio* (Battle of Homestead Foundation 2008). To help defend our human right to clean water, air, and earth, he recently joined the Izzak Walton League of America.

Staughton Lynd

Staughton Lynd received a BA from Harvard, an MA and PhD from Columbia, and a JD from the University of Chicago. Lynd, also a historian, taught American history at Spelman College in Atlanta and is lifelong union and peace activist. He is the author of over a dozen books, including *Wobblies and Zapatistas: Conversations on Anarchism, Marxism, and Radical History*, with Andrej Grubačić (PM Press 2008).

ABOUT PM PRESS

PM Press is an independent, radical publisher of books and media to educate, entertain, and inspire. Founded in 2007 by a small group of people with decades of publishing, media, and organizing experience, PM Press amplifies the voices of radical authors, artists, and activists. Our aim is to deliver bold political ideas and vital stories to all walks of life and arm the dreamers to demand the impossible. We have sold millions of copies of our books, most often one at a time, face to face. We're old enough to know what we're doing and young enough to know what's at stake. Join us to create a better world.

PM Press
PO Box 23912
Oakland, CA 94623
www.pmpress.org

PM Press in Europe
europe@pmpress.org
www.pmpress.org.uk

FRIENDS OF PM PRESS

These are indisputably momentous times—the financial system is melting down globally and the Empire is stumbling. Now more than ever there is a vital need for radical ideas.

In the years since its founding—and on a mere shoestring—PM Press has risen to the formidable challenge of publishing and distributing knowledge and entertainment for the struggles ahead. With over 450 releases to date, we have published an impressive and stimulating array of literature, art, music, politics, and culture. Using every available medium, we've succeeded in connecting those hungry for ideas and information to those putting them into practice.

Friends of PM allows you to directly help impact, amplify, and revitalize the discourse and actions of radical writers, filmmakers, and artists. It provides us with a stable foundation from which we can build upon our early successes and provides a much-needed subsidy for the materials that can't necessarily pay their own way. You can help make that happen—and receive every new title automatically delivered to your door once a month—by joining as a Friend of PM Press. And, we'll throw in a free T-shirt when you sign up.

Here are your options:

- **$30 a month** Get all books and pamphlets plus 50% discount on all webstore purchases

- **$40 a month** Get all PM Press releases (including CDs and DVDs) plus 50% discount on all webstore purchases

- **$100 a month** Superstar—Everything plus PM merchandise, free downloads, and 50% discount on all webstore purchases

For those who can't afford $30 or more a month, we have **Sustainer Rates** at $15, $10 and $5. Sustainers get a free PM Press T-shirt and a 50% discount on all purchases from our website.

Your Visa or Mastercard will be billed once a month, until you tell us to stop. Or until our efforts succeed in bringing the revolution around. Or the financial meltdown of Capital makes plastic redundant. Whichever comes first.

Wobblies and Zapatistas: Conversations on Anarchism, Marxism and Radical History

Staughton Lynd and Andrej Grubačić

ISBN: 978-1-60486-041-2
$20.00   300 pages

Wobblies and Zapatistas offers the reader an encounter between two generations and two traditions. Andrej Grubačić is an anarchist from the Balkans. Staughton Lynd is a lifelong pacifist, influenced by Marxism. They meet in dialogue in an effort to bring together the anarchist and Marxist traditions, to discuss the writing of history by those who make it, and to remind us of the idea that "my country is the world." Encompassing a Left libertarian perspective and an emphatically activist standpoint, these conversations are meant to be read in the clubs and affinity groups of the new Movement.

The authors accompany us on a journey through modern revolutions, direct actions, anti-globalist counter summits, Freedom Schools, Zapatista cooperatives, Haymarket and Petrograd, Hanoi and Belgrade, 'intentional' communities, wildcat strikes, early Protestant communities, Native American democratic practices, the Workers' Solidarity Club of Youngstown, occupied factories, self-organized councils and soviets, the lives of forgotten revolutionaries, Quaker meetings, antiwar movements, and prison rebellions. Neglected and forgotten moments of interracial self-activity are brought to light. The book invites the attention of readers who believe that a better world, on the other side of capitalism and state bureaucracy, may indeed be possible.

"There's no doubt that we've lost much of our history. It's also very clear that those in power in this country like it that way. Here's a book that shows us why. It demonstrates not only that another world is possible, but that it already exists, has existed, and shows an endless potential to burst through the artificial walls and divisions that currently imprison us. An exquisite contribution to the literature of human freedom, and coming not a moment too soon."
—David Graeber, author of *Fragments of an Anarchist Anthropology* and *Direct Action: An Ethnography*

"I have been in regular contact with Andrej Grubačić for many years, and have been most impressed by his searching intelligence, broad knowledge, lucid judgment, and penetrating commentary on contemporary affairs and their historical roots. He is an original thinker and dedicated activist, who brings deep understanding and outstanding personal qualities to everything he does."
—Noam Chomsky

Labor Law for the Rank and Filer: Building Solidarity While Staying Clear of the Law (2nd Edition)

Staughton Lynd and Daniel Gross

ISBN: 978-1-60486-419-9
$12.00   120 pages

Have you ever felt your blood boil at work but lacked the tools to fight back and win? Or have you acted together with your co-workers, made progress, but wondered what to do next? If you are in a union, do you find that the union operates top-down just like the boss and ignores the will of its members?

Labor Law for the Rank and Filer: Building Solidarity While Staying Clear of the Law is a guerrilla legal handbook for workers in a precarious global economy. Blending cutting-edge legal strategies for winning justice at work with a theory of dramatic social change from below, Staughton Lynd and Daniel Gross deliver a practical guide for making work better while re-invigorating the labor movement.

Labor Law for the Rank and Filer demonstrates how a powerful model of organizing called "Solidarity Unionism" can help workers avoid the pitfalls of the legal system and utilize direct action to win. This new revised and expanded edition includes new cases governing fundamental labor rights as well as an added section on Practicing Solidarity Unionism. This new section includes chapters discussing the hard-hitting tactic of working to rule; organizing under the principle that no one is illegal; and building grassroots solidarity across borders to challenge neoliberalism, among several other new topics. Illustrative stories of workers' struggles make the legal principles come alive.

"*Workers' rights are under attack on every front. Bosses break the law every day. For 30 years* Labor Law for the Rank and Filer *has been arming workers with an introduction to their legal rights (and the limited means to enforce them) while reminding everyone that real power comes from workers' solidarity.*"
—Alexis Buss, former General Secretary-Treasurer of the IWW

"*As valuable to working persons as any hammer, drill, stapler, or copy machine,* Labor Law for the Rank and Filer *is a damn fine tool empowering workers who struggle to realize their basic dignity in the workplace while living through an era of unchecked corporate greed. Smart, tough, and optimistic, Staughton Lynd and Daniel Gross provide nuts and bolts information to realize on-the-job rights while showing us that another world is not only possible but inevitable.*"
—John Philo, Legal Director, Maurice and Jane Sugar Law Center for Economic and Social Justice

Strike! 50th Anniversary Edition

Jeremy Brecher with a Preface by Sara
Nelson and a Foreword by Kim Kelly

ISBN: 978-1-62963-800-3
$28.95   640 pages

Jeremy Brecher's *Strike!* narrates the dramatic story
of repeated, massive, and sometimes violent revolts
by ordinary working people in America. Involving
nationwide general strikes, the seizure of vast industrial
establishments, nonviolent direct action on a massive
scale, and armed battles with artillery and tanks, this exciting hidden history is told
from the point of view of the rank-and-file workers who lived it. Encompassing the
repeated repression of workers' rebellions by company-sponsored violence, local
police, state militias, and the U.S. Army and National Guard, it reveals a dimension
of American history rarely found in the usual high school or college history course.

Since its original publication in 1972, no book has done as much as *Strike!* to bring
U.S. labor history to a wide audience. Now this fiftieth anniversary edition brings
the story up to date with chapters covering the "mini-revolts of the 21st century,"
including Occupy Wall Street and the Fight for Fifteen. The new edition contains
over a hundred pages of new materials and concludes by examining a wide range
of current struggles, ranging from #BlackLivesMatter, to the great wave of teachers
strikes "for the soul of public education," to the global "Student Strike for Climate,"
that may be harbingers of mass strikes to come.

"Jeremy Brecher's Strike! *is a classic of American historical writing. This new edition,
bringing his account up to the present, comes amid rampant inequality and growing
popular resistance. No book could be more timely for those seeking the roots of our
current condition."*
—Eric Foner, Pulitzer Prize winner and DeWitt Clinton Professor of History at
Columbia University

*"Magnificent—a vivid, muscular labor history, just updated and rereleased by PM Press,
which should be at the side of anyone who wants to understand the deep structure of
force and counterforce in America."*
—JoAnn Wypijewski, author of *Killing Trayvons: An Anthology of American Violence*

*"An exciting history of American labor. Brings to life the flashpoints of labor history.
Scholarly, genuinely stirring."*
—New York Times

*"Splendid . . . clearly the best single-volume summary yet published of American general
strikes."*
—Washington Post

Solidarity Unionism: Rebuilding the Labor Movement from Below, Second Edition

Staughton Lynd with an Introduction by Immanuel Ness and illustrations by Mike Konopacki

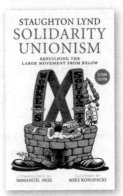

ISBN: 978-1-62963-096-0
$14.95   128 pages

Solidarity Unionism is critical reading for all who care about the future of labor. Drawing deeply on Staughton Lynd's experiences as a labor lawyer and activist in Youngstown, OH, and on his profound understanding of the history of the Congress of Industrial Organizations (CIO), *Solidarity Unionism* helps us begin to put not only movement but also vision back into the labor movement.

While many lament the decline of traditional unions, Lynd takes succor in the blossoming of rank-and-file worker organizations throughout the world that are countering rapacious capitalists and those comfortable labor leaders that think they know more about work and struggle than their own members. If we apply a new measure of workers' power that is deeply rooted in gatherings of workers and communities, the bleak and static perspective about the sorry state of labor today becomes bright and dynamic.

To secure the gains of solidarity unions, Staughton has proposed parallel bodies of workers who share the principles of rank-and-file solidarity and can coordinate the activities of local workers' assemblies. Detailed and inspiring examples include experiments in workers' self-organization across industries in steel-producing Youngstown, as well as horizontal networks of solidarity formed in a variety of U.S. cities and successful direct actions overseas.

This is a tradition that workers understand but labor leaders reject. After so many failures, it is time to frankly recognize that the century-old system of recognition of a single union as exclusive collective bargaining agent was fatally flawed from the beginning and doesn't work for most workers. If we are to live with dignity, we must collectively resist. This book is not a prescription but reveals the lived experience of working people continuously taking risks for the common good.

"*Solidarity Unionism* is an essential text for all rank-and-file workers as well as labor activists. Beautifully succinct, it outlines how CIO unions grew into an ineffectual model for rank-and-file empowerment, and provides examples of how alternative labor organizations have flourished in the wake of this. Lynd illustrates to a new generation of workers that we do have alternatives, and his call for a qualitatively different kind of labor organization gives us an ideological and strategic framework that we can apply in our day-to-day struggles on the shop floor."
—Diane Krauthamer, *Industrial Worker*

Socialist and Labor Songs: An International Revolutionary Songbook

Edited by Elizabeth Morgan with a Preface by Utah Phillips

ISBN: 978-1-60486-392-5
$14.95   96 pages

Seventy-seven songs—with words and sheet music—of solidarity, revolt, humor, and revolution. Compiled from several generations in America, and from around the world, they were originally written in English, Danish, French, German, Italian, Spanish, Russian, and Yiddish.

From IWW anthems such as "The Preacher and the Slave" to Lenin's favorite 1905 revolutionary anthem "Whirlwinds of Danger," many works by the world's greatest radical songwriters are anthologized herein: Edith Berkowitz, Bertolt Brecht, Ralph Chaplin, James Connolly, Havelock Ellis, Emily Fine, Arturo Giovannitti, Joe Hill, Langston Hughes, William Morris, James Oppenheim, Teresina Rowell, Anna Garlin Spencer, Maurice Sugar—and dozens more.

Old favorites and hidden gems, to once again energize and accompany picket lines, demonstrations, meetings, sit-ins, marches, and May Day parades.

"I've always known our political and social movements as singing movements, and have been continually astonished at the scope and variety of our people's music . . . These songs are like endangered species that have been restored to the present, to the land of the living. They stuck up for us long ago during dark and troubled times. Our times are dark and troubled, too, but our old songs are still here with us to see us through. Sing away!"
—Utah Phillips